Purchased

SURVEY OF LONDON
VOLUME XXXV

PARISHES DESCRIBED IN PREVIOUS VOLUMES
OF THE SURVEY OF LONDON

THE THEATRE ROYAL, DRURY LANE, 1791–4

Henry Holland, architect. *Destroyed by fire 1809*

From a watercolour drawing of 1795 by Edward Dayes in
the Henry E. Huntington Library and Art Gallery, California

SURVEY OF LONDON

GENERAL EDITOR: F. H. W. SHEPPARD

VOLUME XXXV

The Theatre Royal
Drury Lane
and The Royal Opera House
Covent Garden

THE ATHLONE PRESS
UNIVERSITY OF LONDON
Published for the Greater London Council

1970

Published by
THE ATHLONE PRESS
UNIVERSITY OF LONDON
at 2 Gower Street, London W C 1

Distributed by
Tiptree Book Services Ltd, Tiptree, Essex

Australia and New Zealand
Melbourne University Press

U.S.A.
Oxford University Press
New York

SBN 485 48235 5

Printed in Great Britain by
WILLIAM CLOWES AND SONS LTD
LONDON AND BECCLES

Preface

'THE PRETTIEST and most elegant theatre that London could ever boast', wrote a reporter in 1785 of the Theatre Royal, Drury Lane. But in this fascinating and scholarly work by Dr. Sheppard and his colleagues we go behind the scenes. From the opening night in 1663 of the first little playhouse, licensed by letters patent from Charles II, right up to the present day, we learn of the disputes and intrigues, the bankruptcies and successes.

The ubiquitous Pepys saw the smart theatre boxes dressed with bands of gilt leather, while he sat with his wife on the second night of the very first production, *The Humorous Lieutenant*. He also rather acidly commented, on a later visit, that rain and hail, as well as light and air, came into the auditorium.

The dreaded Plague closed the first theatre in 1665. It reopened, but we hear later of plays banned by the Lord Chamberlain, of endless arguments over the patents, of squabbles over money.

By 1743 the famous David Garrick was the rising star at Drury Lane. Thirty-two years later Robert Adam transformed the theatre, but in 1794 Henry Holland designed not only a brand new theatre but a surrounding complex of taverns, shops and coffee-houses. He shared some of the problems of our own times. A strike, of carpenters, which Sheridan settled by giving them a barrel of ale. When the theatre was finished the Prince of Wales's box gleamed in blue and silver, the King's box was furnished in crimson and gold; and Rudolph Cabanel, machinist, of Lambeth, had worked 'Nine clear and compleat days and nights . . .' to fix the stage machinery needed for *Macbeth*.

But after only fifteen years this splendid theatre was destroyed by fire. The present building by Benjamin Dean Wyatt—its original auditorium now completely reconstructed—followed in 1812, and Crabb Robinson 'went to Drury Lane to see the house, not the performance'. Perhaps he was right, since the opening night had been an extraordinary mixture. An address written by Byron, then *Hamlet*, followed by a musical farce—*The Devil to Pay*.

You will find all these intriguing touches in Dr. Sheppard's amazingly detailed survey, but although loath to leave Drury Lane, I was especially interested in the history of The Royal Opera House.

John Rich was the most successful theatre manager of the eighteenth century and it was he who opened the theatre at Covent Garden in 1732. Built by Edward Shepherd, its patrons later saw the first production of *She Stoops to Conquer*, and Sheridan's *The Rivals*. It was, alas, burnt down, and in 1809 Sir Robert Smirke built the second theatre. In the old accounts I noticed that he paid over £6,000 to a plasterer, Francis Bernasconi. I wonder how many English houses and public buildings would have been the plainer, and sadder, without the talents of Italian craftsmen.

By the 1820's Covent Garden was in low water. Charles Kemble complained that 'the late hours of dining take away all the upper classes from the theatre'.

In 1856 it was leased for six weeks, perhaps out of desperation, to a conjurer, J. H. Anderson, known as the 'Wizard of the North'. He already had the dubious distinction that two theatres had burnt down over his head. He organized a masked ball at Covent Garden, and during this party, unbelievably, added the third.

The following year E. M. Barry started to build the Royal Opera House which we know today. I have been there so often. To Galas—to hear Callas, unforgettable as Floria Tosca, to hear Christoff, magnificent as Boris Godunov, to performances where those dreaded slips fell from the programme to announce the tenor's illness, or to take my small daughter to see *The Sleeping Beauty*. I have so often gazed at the beautiful aquamarine ceiling; a piece of Fabergé made for a Giant. I am always impressed by the grandeur of the red velvet curtains and the symmetry of the mermaid-angels whose lights adorn tier upon tier of seats.

The Royal Opera House has neither the exquisite beauty of the Cuvilliés Theater in Munich, nor the charm of the opera house in Parma, but it has great drama and a feeling of occasion which is essentially British.

Dr. Sheppard tells me that this book could not have been written without the great kindness of the Trustees of the Bedford Settled Estates in allowing access to their archives, and to them the Greater London Council is enormously grateful. I, as chairman, and all the members of the Historic Buildings Board do want to thank Dr. Sheppard especially, and all those other wonderful people who have so generously given their time and ability to ensure that this record of two famous theatres will be available to scholars and historians of our own and future generations.

RAINE DARTMOUTH
Chairman, Historic Buildings Board
of the Greater London Council
March 1969

Thanks

THE CHAIRMAN and Members of the Historic Buildings Board are extremely grateful to all those kind people who have helped in the preparation of this volume, particularly the following:

Mr. Robert Eddison, the distinguished actor, who placed his splendid collection of theatrical material at the disposal of the Council's research staff, twenty-one of the illustrations in this volume being taken from drawings and prints in his collection, some of them hitherto unpublished.

The staff of the Trustees of the Bedford Settled Estates: Mr. J. M. Sword, General Manager; Mr. W. Corbett, Chief Accountant; Mr. L. A. Ayling, Steward to the London Estate; and Major T. L. Ingram, formerly the Trustees' archivist, all of whom gave their time and knowledge so freely in the study of the Trustees' records.

Mr. Raymond Mander and Mr. Joe Mitchenson, Mr. Richard Leacroft, the Hon. Kensington Davison of the Royal Opera House and Professor Edward A. Langhans of the University of Hawaii, who made suggestions and provided information.

The Directors of Coutts and Company; Mr. Cecil Farthing; Miss Valerie Gillam; Miss J. Godber; Mr. John Harris; Mr. J. Howgego; Mr. J. M. Keyworth; Lord Latymer; Mr. George Nash; Miss Veronica Stokes; Miss Dorothy Stroud; Miss Margaret Swarbrick; Mr. Robert E. Wark; Mr. R. McD. Winder.

The staff of Thomas Agnew and Sons Limited; All Souls College, Oxford; Berkshire County Record Office; the British Museum; Corporation of London, Guildhall Library; Dorset County Record Office; Enthoven Theatre Collection, Victoria and Albert Museum; Guildford Museum and Muniment Room; Hoare's Bank; Henry E. Huntington Library and Art Gallery, California; the London Museum; the National Monuments Record; the National Register of Archives; the Principal Probate Registry, Somerset House; the Public Record Office; the Royal Institute of British Architects; Second Covent Garden Property Company Limited; Westminster Public Library, Archives Department.

Contents

Plates *at end*

List of Plates

List of Figures in the Text

CHAPTER I

The Killigrew and Davenant Patents

ALONE among the theatres of London, the Theatre Royal, Drury Lane, and the Royal Opera House, Covent Garden, enjoy the distinction of deriving their rights to present theatrical entertainments not from licences issued by the Lord Chamberlain or the local authority, but by direct grant from the Crown. These rights are of great antiquity. They were conferred by Charles II by two letters patent granted on 25 April 1662 to Thomas Killigrew[1] and on 15 January 1662/3 to Sir William Davenant.[2] Drury Lane Theatre exercises its rights under Killigrew's patent, the original document being now in the possession of the present lessees, Theatre Royal Drury Lane Limited.[3] The rights of the Royal Opera House stem from Davenant's patent, but the original document is now lost.[4]

The two patents severally conferred upon Killigrew and Davenant the right to build a theatre in London or Westminster and to establish and manage a company of actors to perform in it; Killigrew's actors were to be styled the King's Company, and Davenant's were to be known as the Duke of York's. All other companies performing in London and Westminster were to be suppressed forthwith.

The grants to Killigrew and Davenant thus established in London a dual monopoly of theatrical rights which, although frequently evaded in varying degrees, nevertheless survived as a powerful element in the history of the metropolitan theatre until the passing of the Act for regulating theatres of 1843. This Act ended the monopoly, but did not otherwise affect the rights conferred by the patents, which (as has been mentioned above) continue to be exercised down to the present day.[5] During this long quasi-monopolistic period from 1662-3 to 1843 the two patents therefore became a valuable form of property which could be and indeed frequently was bought, sold, divided, shared or bequeathed like any other property. The purpose of this chapter is to trace, so far as possible, the extremely complex history of their ownership.

When Charles II returned to England in May 1660 the theatrical affairs of London were in some confusion. In March 1660 Sir William Davenant, the dramatist and poet laureate, who still had in his possession a patent for a playhouse granted by Charles I, had taken a lease of Lisle's Tennis Court in Portugal Street near Lincoln's Inn Fields, for conversion into a theatre.[6] He had then departed to France, presumably to persuade the King to restore and confirm his rights.[7]

Already in France with the King was Thomas Killigrew, playwright, one of the grooms of the bedchamber, and according to Pepys, 'a merry droll, but a gentleman of great esteem with the King',[8] who may well have already promised him some theatrical preferment.[9] At all events, on 9 July, less than six weeks after the Restoration, a royal warrant required the issue of a patent under the Great Seal authorizing Killigrew to establish a company of actors and build a theatre. The warrant recognized Davenant's rights under his patent from Charles I, but all other companies of actors were to be suppressed.[10] Davenant, however, appears not to have been satisfied with this indirect authority and ten days later he drafted a second warrant which was to authorize by a patent the establishment of a theatrical monopoly to be shared by Killigrew and himself.[11]

This proposal evoked the hostility of Sir Henry Herbert, the master of the revels, who on 4 August presented a petition to the King opposing it on the ground that it would be 'destructive' of the authority of his office.[12] The question was referred to the attorney general, Sir Jeffry Palmer, who reported that he thought 'the matter more proper for A tolleration; than A Grant under the greate Seale of England'.[13] The grant nevertheless passed the privy signet on 21 August 1660, but did not reach the final stage of a patent under the Great Seal. This was probably because Davenant had decided not to press the matter in face of the opposition of the master of the revels, for in September Palmer added a note to Herbert's petition, stating that he had 'foreborne to proceede further haveinge alsoe receaved an intimacion by Letter from Sir William Davenant that I was freed from further hearing in this matter'.[12]

The grant under the privy signet authorized Killigrew and Davenant to build or hire two playhouses in London and to maintain two companies to act in them. But although the grant stated that there were to be no other theatrical establishments rival companies nevertheless continued to act,[14] and Killigrew and Davenant were not immune from the hostile authority of the master of the revels. So on 25 April 1662 Killigrew at last obtained from the King a patent under the authority of the Great Seal. This contained two vital new clauses, the first of which authorized him to enjoy his rights 'peaceably and quietly without the impeachment or impediment of any person or persons whatsoever' (i.e., including the master of the revels); the second categorically required the suppression of all other playhouses in London except Davenant's.[1] On 15 January 1662/3 Davenant was granted a similar patent,[2] and the joint monopoly of the London theatre which persisted, in theory at least, until 1843 had been established.

In later years Killigrew's patent was used as the authority for Drury Lane Theatre and Davenant's for Covent Garden. But in the seventeenth century theatrical affairs were still extremely fluid and it was not until the opening of Covent Garden by John Rich under Davenant's patent in 1732 that a more stable pattern began to emerge. For the first seventy years of their existence, therefore, the history of the patents is extremely confused, a major factor in this confusion being an agreement of 1682 between the then owners of the two patents whereby they united their two acting companies and Killigrew's patent, which was thus made redundant, became dormant. It remained in this ambiguous and perplexing condition, even its continuing legal validity being sometimes open to doubt, until as late as 1813, when its purchase by the owners of Drury Lane Theatre was finally completed.

When he received his patent in April 1662 Thomas Killigrew and his actors, known as the King's Company, were at a theatre in Vere Street, near Clare Market, but he was already building a new theatre in Brydges Street—the forerunner of, and occupying part of the site of the present Drury Lane Theatre—and in May 1663 he and his company removed to this new home.[15]

Until the union of 1682 the Killigrew patent provided the authority to act at this theatre in Brydges Street, which by the 1690's had become known by its modern name, the Theatre Royal, Drury Lane. As a valuable article of property the patent soon formed part of the consideration in a number of legal transactions. After the destruction of the theatre by fire in January 1671/2 Killigrew in 1673 mortgaged all his interests in the property, including the patent, and three years later these mortgages had been assigned to trustees for Richard Kent.[16]

In February 1680/1 Kent and a number of his associates filed a bill in Chancery[17] complaining that Charles Killigrew, one of Thomas's younger sons and manager of the theatre since 1677, had denied them the profits which were due to them under these assignments. The case was settled on 14 December 1682, when the Court decreed that the Killigrews should be 'for ever debarred and foreclosed of all Equity of Redemption' of the property which had been assigned to Kent's trustees, and that Kent should hold and enjoy it.[18]

Three months after being thus deprived of all his theatrical interests Thomas Killigrew died, bequeathing the bulk of his estate to his eldest son, Henry,[19] who in May 1683 instituted proceedings in Chancery in an attempt to recover his father's patent and other theatrical interests from Kent's trustees. He challenged Kent's title to the property and accused him of having made a secret agreement to assign all his interests to Charles Killigrew—Henry's half-brother.[20]

In his reply Kent quoted the decree which established his title, and the agreement which he had indeed made to sell his interest to Charles Killigrew 'in consideration of £500 and a greater sum to be thereafter paid'.[18] A copy of this agreement exists, and is dated 15 August 1682,[21] four months before the Chancery decree which confirmed Kent's title. There is no record of any judgment in this suit, but it appears that the agreement between Kent and Charles Killigrew, whether secret or not, was upheld, for the latter was in possession of the patent when he died in 1724.[22]

Meanwhile since 1661 Sir William Davenant and his actors, known as the Duke's Company, were acting in the Duke's Theatre, Lincoln's Inn Fields, a conversion of Lisle's Tennis Court.[15] The company was still there when Sir William died in 1668, intestate. The estate was administered for a few years by his widow (his eldest son, Charles, being still a minor), and during this period a new Duke's Theatre was built at Dorset

Garden, fronting the Thames to the south of Fleet Street in the City. The company moved here in 1671, and prospered.[23]

By 1682 the King's Company at Drury Lane had declined to a very parlous condition, and on 4 May of that year Charles Killigrew entered into an agreement with Charles Davenant and his principal associates at Dorset Garden for the union of the two establishments. One clause of the agreement provided that the two patents were to be united.[24] In November 1682 the new amalgamated company opened at Drury Lane under the authority of Davenant's patent. Killigrew's was no longer needed and so became dormant, but the Killigrew family nevertheless retained possession of the actual document.[25]

From 1682 until 1695 there was only one company performing in London, sometimes at Dorset Garden but more usually at Drury Lane. On 30 August 1687 Charles Davenant sold his patent and theatrical interests for £2,400.[26] The purchaser was his brother, Alexander Davenant, but five-sixths of the money (£2,000) was supplied to him by Sir Thomas Skipwith,[27] a Lincolnshire baronet whose womanizing propensities had earned him an 'unenviable notoriety' at Court.[28] Less than two weeks later, on 12 September 1687, Skipwith agreed to lease the benefit of his five-sixths share to Alexander Davenant for seven years in return for certain ticket privileges and a weekly rent of £6. On 17 March 1689/90 Davenant sold his remaining one-sixth share for £400 to Christopher Rich, an attorney of inexhaustible guile who had previously been associated with Skipwith in building development in the area of Theobalds Road. On the following day Rich leased this share back to Davenant on terms similar to the arrangement already made with Skipwith, but at a weekly rent of £1 4s.[27]

These arrangements between Alexander Davenant on the one hand, and Skipwith and Rich on the other (subsequently confirmed by another deed in March 1691), had provided that at the end of the seven-year term Davenant was entitled to redeem his property on payment of £2,000 to Skipwith and £300 to Rich.[29] Davenant's management of theatrical affairs proved financially unsuccessful, however, and in October 1693 he fled to the Canary Islands to escape his creditors.[30] His weekly rents were a year in arrears, and in December 1693 Skipwith

and Rich foreclosed on the equity of redemption of Davenant's patent and other theatrical property.[31]

At this time, therefore, Skipwith evidently owned five-sixths of the Davenant patent and Rich one sixth. But in a Chancery suit of 1704 Rich claimed to have bought three-eighths of the patent, and Skipwith five-eighths.[31] Four years later, however, Skipwith claimed only three-fifths, 'ye Whole into five parts being divided'.[32] It is not known which of these various versions is correct, but in 1761 Christopher Rich's son, John, mentioned in his will that his father's share in the Davenant patent had only been one sixth.[33]

After Skipwith and Rich had asserted their rights at Drury Lane in 1693 the effective control of the theatre passed to Rich.[34] His treatment of the players soon provoked them to rebellion, and under the leadership of the veteran Thomas Betterton they obtained from the Lord Chamberlain a licence to act (not a patent)[35] and removed to the old theatre at Lincoln's Inn Fields, where they opened on 30 April 1695.[36] The single-company monopoly which had existed since 1682 had been broken, and the grant of this licence also marked the first important breach of the monopoly rights claimed by the owners of the patents.

Both companies were soon in a state of considerable disarray, but until 1707 there was no change in the ownership of either of the patents, Skipwith and Rich being in possession of Davenant's, which was used at Drury Lane and occasionally at Dorset Garden, and Charles Killigrew still retaining his family's now dormant patent. The theatre at Lincoln's Inn Fields was, however, smaller than Drury Lane, and in 1705 the company was therefore glad to remove to the larger new theatre in the Haymarket—the Queen's Theatre, recently erected to the designs of (Sir) John Vanbrugh, the architect and playwright, who with William Congreve was granted a licence in December 1704.[37]

Meanwhile at Drury Lane Sir Thomas Skipwith, far from profiting from his interest there, found himself obliged to pay out 'considerable sumes of money under pretence of carrying the businesse of the said Playhouse on'. He was apprehensive of being 'drawn in and subjected to Great Debts and demands on that account',[32] and on 6 October 1707 he therefore assigned his share in the patent to Colonel Henry Brett of Sandywell Park, Gloucester, M.P., for a nominal sum.[38] When some financial improvement had ensued

Skipwith tried to recover his lost interests, and in February 1708/9 he filed a complaint against Brett alleging that he had intended the assignment of October 1707 to be only in trust and not absolute. Relying on Brett's integrity he had signed the document (which had been drawn up by Brett's attorney) before reading it through. In reply Brett claimed that the deed was an absolute assignment and that it had been intended to be so.[32] The case was not pursued because Brett withdrew from the management, being conscious, according to Colley Cibber, 'that as the World knew he had paid no Consideration for it, his keeping it might be misconstrued, or not favourably spoken of'.[39] The share in the patent evidently remained in Brett's possession until 8 August 1711 when he conveyed it to Sir George Bridges Skipwith,[40] the son of Sir Thomas, who was now dead.[28]

By this time Christopher Rich had fallen foul of the Lord Chamberlain. Several orders had been issued by which Rich had been 'Silenc'd from acting',[41] but whether these orders also temporarily suspended the authority of the Davenant patent is not clear. From November 1709,[42] however, Drury Lane was acting under the authority of successive licences granted by the Lord Chamberlain,[43] a practice which continued there until the early nineteenth century.* Rich, meanwhile, far from accepting defeat, acquired the lease of the now vacant theatre at Lincoln's Inn Fields and started rebuilding.[49] But he died on 4 November 1714,[50] six weeks before the new playhouse at Lincoln's Inn Fields was opened (by his son John Rich) under the authority of the Davenant patent.[51] By his will his one-sixth interest in the patent was divided unequally between his two sons: John Rich inherited three-quarters (i.e., one eighth of the whole), and Christopher Moyser Rich one quarter (i.e., one twenty-fourth of the whole).[52]

From 1714 until his death in 1761 John Rich proved to be one of the most successful and long-lived London theatre managers in the whole of the eighteenth century. In 1731-2 he was able to build a large new theatre in Covent Garden, to which he removed in the latter year, still acting under the Davenant patent, of which he himself only owned a very small part. The principal shareholder in the patent, Sir George Bridges Skipwith, with five-sixths, took no part in the management, and in August 1752 he assigned his share by deed of gift to Sir Francis Skipwith and the latter's son Francis William Skipwith, members of a collateral branch of the family.[53] Between 1752 and 1760 this share passed to another of Sir Francis's sons, (Sir) Thomas Skipwith, who by 1767 had sold it to John Rich's heirs.[54]

In 1759 John Rich had unsuccessfully attempted to buy his brother Christopher Moyser Rich's one twenty-fourth share of the patent.[55] John Rich died two years later and bequeathed to his brother an annuity of £200 or a capital sum of £4,000 on condition that Christopher Moyser Rich should within two months assign his share to John Rich's executors.[33] Christopher Moyser accepted these terms and on 2 January 1762 he executed the necessary deed.[53]

John Rich had already bought the whole of the dormant Killigrew patent, which after Charles Killigrew's death in December 1724[55] had been inherited by his son, also Charles.[56] At that time the value of the patent must have seemed extremely small, for when Charles Killigrew junior sold it along with other obsolete theatrical interests to Rupert Clarke of Kensington, gentleman, on 17 September 1729, the price was only £63.[57] On 9 June 1733 Rich and his trustee, Richard Wolfe, bought the patent from Clarke, and in January 1741/2 it was conveyed into Rich's sole possession.[58] How much Rich paid for it is not known but on the day of its purchase from Clarke, Wolfe and Rich mortgaged it for £400.[59]

THE KILLIGREW PATENT 1767–1813: THE DAVENANT PATENT 1767–1793

Thus by the latter part of the 1760's John Rich's heirs owned the whole of both patents,

* Between 1709 and 1714 the authority to act at Drury Lane was provided by the licences granted to William Collier, M.P., and some of the actors.[44] When the last of these licences terminated automatically on the death of Queen Anne in August 1714 the actor-managers dropped the Tory Collier and invited a Whig, (Sir) Richard Steele, to join them and use his influence at Court to obtain a new licence.[45] Steele immediately procured a licence dated 18 October 1714,[46] which was superseded on 19 January 1714/15 by a patent granted to Steele alone for a term expiring three years after his death.[47] Steele shared his patent with the actor-managers Cibber, Wilks and Booth and when it expired in 1732 they obtained a new but similar patent for twenty-one years from the Lord Chamberlain, the first of a series of five granted to Drury Lane, the last of which expired in 1837.[48]

Killigrew's being still dormant and Davenant's being the authority for Covent Garden Theatre. This straightforward situation did not last long, however, for in July 1767 John Rich's widow and four daughters sold their entire interest in both the lease and contents of Covent Garden Theatre and the freehold of the two patents for £60,000. The purchasers were Thomas Harris, John Rutherford, George Colman and William Powell, each of whom thus possessed one quarter share of the whole property.[60] Neither Harris, described as of Holborn, esquire, nor Rutherford, described as of Newman Street, esquire, appears to have had any previous theatrical experience, but Colman was an established dramatist and Powell was a successful actor at Drury Lane. This division of ownership produced a series of extremely complex transactions in which, until 1793, shares in the leasehold of Covent Garden Theatre and the freehold of both the Killigrew and Davenant patents were always bought and sold as one property. Ultimately Harris acquired the two quarter shares which had originally belonged to Rutherford and Colman, and one fifteenth of Powell's quarter, thus bringing his holding up to $\frac{46}{60}$ of the whole.

These transactions began in July 1767 when all four partners mortgaged their respective shares.[61] In September 1768 Rutherford sold two-thirds of his quarter (i.e., one sixth of the whole) to Henry Dagge of the Inner Temple, esquire, and the remaining one third (i.e., one twelfth of the whole) to James Leake of the Strand, esquire, for £18,500.[62] On 1 July 1774 Leake bought Colman's quarter share for £20,000,[63] but five days later he sold his one third of Rutherford's quarter (i.e., one twelfth of the whole) to Harris.[64] By 1784 Harris had bought the quarter which Leake had acquired from Colman[65] and in the following year he signed articles of agreement for the purchase of Dagge's one sixth.[66]* Harris's interest had thus risen to three-quarters of the whole—$\frac{1}{4}+\frac{1}{12}+\frac{1}{4}+\frac{1}{6}$.

But this calculation excludes the descent of William Powell's quarter share, in which Harris had also acquired a small interest. Powell had died suddenly in 1769 at the early age of thirty-four, and his widow, Elizabeth, had subsequently married John Abraham Fisher, the violinist.[68] In September 1778 the Fishers leased the use of their quarter share to Harris and Richard Brinsley

Sheridan for twenty-one years at a rental of £1,600 per annum.[53] In 1780, however, Fisher conditionally assigned the equity of redemption in one fifteenth of the quarter (i.e., one sixtieth of the whole) to Robert Kilbye Cox (or Cocks), esquire.[69] This mortgage was evidently not redeemed, for in 1781 Cox assigned his rights in this one-sixtieth share to Harris,[70] whose share in the whole property thus amounted in 1785 (after the other purchases described above) to $\frac{46}{60}$ ($\frac{3}{4}+\frac{1}{60}$), plus a twenty-one-year leasehold interest in the remaining $\frac{14}{60}$. The freehold of the $\frac{14}{60}$ descended in undivided moieties to Powell's two daughters, Ann (who married as her second husband John Martindale,[71] proprietor of White's in St. James's Street), and Elizabeth Mary, who married George White, esquire, a clerk at the House of Commons.[72]

Ever since 1777 Sheridan and Harris, as the principal proprietors of Drury Lane and Covent Garden respectively, had been planning to build a new theatre which they intended to manage jointly under the authority of the Killigrew patent.[73] By this means their theatrical monopoly would have been preserved, and by the establishment of a new theatre the public criticism of the monopoly would, they hoped, have been abated. For the proprietors of Drury Lane (who possessed neither the Killigrew nor the Davenant patent, and who had for many years acted under the more precarious authority of a series of twenty-one-year patents), the danger of the long unused or dormant Killigrew patent being sold away from Covent Garden and revived as the basis for a new theatre in competition with Drury Lane would have been averted.

By 1784 Harris had acquired the lease of a piece of ground near Hyde Park Corner for the proposed new theatre, but two years later the scheme had been altered to the establishment of a new opera house there—probably because the quality of the opera then being presented at the King's Theatre in the Haymarket was very poor.[74] In 1789, however, the King's Theatre was destroyed by fire, and the Pantheon in Oxford Street was granted a four-year licence for the presentation of opera. By 1791 the King's Theatre had been rebuilt, although it now had no licence, and large debts had accumulated at the Pantheon.[75] To settle these intricate difficulties Sheridan, in

---

* This latter acquisition appears not to have been legally completed until 1800–1, probably because Harris had not paid the full purchase money.[67]

October 1791, put forward an 'Outline for a General Opera Arrangement',[76] most of which was subsequently implemented. Several provisions were concerned with the patents. The King's Theatre was to have a monopoly in the presentation of opera. The proposed new opera house near Hyde Park Corner would therefore be abandoned, and the King's Theatre was to compensate Harris with an annuity of £250 redeemable for £5,000 for giving up the right to use the dormant Killigrew patent (of which he was the principal proprietor) for opera. Lastly, the dormant patent was to be 'annexed inseparably' to Drury Lane Theatre.

In order to implement this last proposal Sheridan, as the principal proprietor of Drury Lane Theatre, began in the autumn of 1791 to negotiate with Harris for the purchase of the dormant Killigrew patent.[77] Sheridan was then about to rebuild Drury Lane Theatre, where the last performance in the old theatre had taken place on 4 June 1791, and was intending to raise the necessary capital sum by three hundred subscriptions of £500 each.[78] Immediate possession of the dormant patent and the permanent authority to act which it conferred was therefore essential for his plans, for no one would subscribe to the costly rebuilding of a theatre which only possessed a patent limited to twenty-one-years' duration. Harris, however, 'readily consented to dispose of' the Killigrew patent for £15,000,[79] and everything was proceeding smoothly when George White (who through his wife owned the reversionary freehold in $\frac{7}{15}$ of Powell's one quarter share of Covent Garden Theatre and of both the patents, i.e. $\frac{7}{60}$ of the whole), objected to the sale. After a stormy meeting with Harris 'both parties separated with mutual displeasure' and in March 1792 White filed a bill of complaint against Harris. The Drury Lane subscribers at once refused to pay their subscriptions, and in July it was reported in the newspapers that 'all the proceedings towards erecting the new Theatre are of course stopped'.[80]

Despite this set-back Sheridan proceeded with the purchase of the patent. By the end of May 1792 he had agreed terms with Harris in the confident expectation that White ('a very good-for-nothing Fellow') must 'in common sense soon come in' to the sale.[81] And so it quickly proved, for in June Charles James Fox, acting as an intermediary between Sheridan and White,

arranged that the proprietors of Drury Lane (Sheridan and his father-in-law, Thomas Linley) should pay £5,000 for the freehold reversion of the $\frac{14}{60}$ of the Killigrew patent controlled by White (in right of his wife, $\frac{7}{60}$) and by Powell's other daughter, Ann (the other $\frac{7}{60}$).[82] In 1793 the trustees of Drury Lane bought Harris's interest ($\frac{46}{60}$) for £11,667 (the purchase being for the ultimate use of the proprietors, Sheridan and Linley), but Sheridan's contract for the purchase of the remaining $\frac{14}{60}$ was not completed, perhaps because by the terms of the 'General Opera Arrangement' the purchase money was intended to be charged on the King's Theatre in the Haymarket, which was already so deeply in debt that its proprietor was either unable or unwilling to pay.[83]

At the end of 1793, therefore, the ownership of the two patents was as follows: Harris held $\frac{46}{60}$ of the freehold of the Davenant patent under which Covent Garden acted, and also (in conjunction with Sheridan) the remainder of the twenty-one-year leasehold interest created in 1778 in the other $\frac{14}{60}$, of which White and his sister-in-law held the reversionary freehold. The Killigrew patent was owned, as to $\frac{46}{60}$, by the trustees of Drury Lane for the use of the proprietors, while the other $\frac{14}{60}$ were held in the same way as Davenant's.

By 1801 Sheridan had acquired the interests of the heirs of his former partner Thomas Linley (who had died in 1795), and therefore claimed to own *inter alia* the whole $\frac{46}{60}$ of the Killigrew patent, subject to large financial encumbrances administered by the trustees of Drury Lane. In 1802 Sheridan sold (*inter alia*) one quarter of his interest in the Killigrew patent to Joseph Richardson, who had assisted him for some years in the management of the theatre, and in 1806 he conveyed another quarter to his son, Thomas Sheridan.[84]

Meanwhile Drury Lane, not being in full possession of the Killigrew patent, continued to act under its twenty-one-year patent, which after the destruction of that theatre by fire in 1809, was extended to 1837. This grant[85] was made in 1812 to trustees for the newly formed Theatre Royal Drury Lane Company of Proprietors which, by an Act of 1810, had been authorized to raise a capital sum of £300,000 for the rebuilding of the theatre and the purchase of the outstanding shares in the Killigrew patent.[86] By October

1813 the new company had bought the entire theatrical interests of the two Sheridans and of Richardson's heirs (including their share of the Killigrew patent);[87] and after further negotiation the company at last also bought the outstanding $\frac{14}{60}$ share of the Killigrew patent from George White and his sister-in-law (now Ann Martindale) in December 1813 for £9,561 19s. 8d. The Killigrew patent—the original document itself— was at last lodged in the strong-room of Drury Lane Theatre, and a few days later George White died.[88]*

Since 1813 the Killigrew patent has remained annexed to Drury Lane Theatre, and although it has changed hands more than once its ownership has never again been sub-divided.

LATER HISTORY OF THE KILLIGREW PATENT FROM 1813

In July 1812 the ground landlord, the sixth Duke of Bedford, had granted an eighty-two-year lease of Drury Lane Theatre to the Company of Proprietors. A condition of this lease required that the Killigrew patent and any other patent which the company might acquire should 'be continued and go along with the said new Theatre' throughout the whole term granted.[90] The patent therefore remained in the possession of the company until 1894. By this time, however, its value had been greatly diminished by the Act of 1843 for regulating theatres, which, by requiring the Lord Chamberlain to licence theatres in London, had finally put an end to the monopoly conferred in 1662–3 by the Davenant and Killigrew patents. In April 1894, when the renewal of the lease to Sir Augustus Harris, manager of the theatre since 1879, was being considered, the Lord Chamberlain informed the eleventh Duke of Bedford that he was strongly of opinion that Drury Lane should in future be subject to annual licence like all other places of amusement in London[91] (except Covent Garden). The authority under which the theatre performed was, however, no concern of the Duke, and in negotiating

the agreement with Sir Augustus for a lease, 'all reference to the question of the Patent' was 'carefully avoided and it has been left to Sir Augustus either to purchase the existing Patent or to place himself under the Lord Chamberlain's Licence whichever he finds most advantageous'.[92]

After the death of Sir Augustus Harris in 1896 his executors surrendered his seven-year interest in the theatre to the Duke.[93] Harris had bought the patent from the old Company of Proprietors, and after his death his stage manager, Arthur Collins, who was acquiring an interest in the lease (see page 28), bought the patent. In May 1897 Collins contracted to sell all his interest in the theatre, including the patent, to the newly formed Theatre Royal Drury Lane Limited, which still owns both the lease and the patent.[94] In 1964 the patent was included among the company's assets at the nominal figure of one hundred pounds.[3]

LATER HISTORY OF THE DAVENANT PATENT FROM 1793

It will be recalled that at the end of 1793 Thomas Harris owned $\frac{46}{60}$ of the freehold of the Davenant patent, under which Covent Garden acted, and also (in conjunction with Sheridan) the remainder of the twenty-one-year leasehold interest created in 1778 in the other $\frac{14}{60}$. The freehold of these $\frac{14}{60}$ belonged to the descendants of William Powell—his daughter Ann (later Ann Martindale) and his son-in-law, George White. In 1803 Harris took John Philip Kemble, who had been for many years the leading actor at Drury Lane, into partnership and sold him a one-sixth share of the theatre and the Davenant patent for £22,000.[95] Three years later he granted a moiety of $\frac{1}{60}$ of the patent to George White and the other moiety to White's sister-in-law, now Ann Martindale,[96] thus increasing their share to one eighth each. By these transactions he reduced his own share to seven-twelfths $(\frac{46}{60} - \frac{1}{6} - \frac{1}{60} = \frac{7}{12})$, and at about the same time he gave one twelfth of his remaining holding to his son, Henry Harris.[97]

* It may be noted here that between December 1813 and the summer of 1837 Drury Lane Theatre possessed two separate concurrent patents—Killigrew's and the twenty-one-year patent mentioned above. The Lord Chamberlain appears to have been unaware of the purchase of the former in 1813, and after the expiry of the latter in 1837 he questioned the theatre's right to re-open. Alfred Bunn, who was then the manager, relates that 'The harpies of the Lord Chamberlain's office, with noses as sensitive for a fee as a ferret's for a rat, despatched a missive to Drury Lane Theatre to inquire by what authority I had presumed to announce its reopening'. Bunn replied that he did so under Killigrew's patent, 'and producing a tin box entrusted to me for the occasion', he 'displayed before the wondering eyes of the disappointed official the document itself, bearing the signature of "Howard", with the appendage of his lordship's ponderous seal of power'.[89]

building shareholders in the Theatre Royal, Drury Lane, were Thomas Killigrew and Sir Robert Howard (nine each), Lacy (four) and Burt, Cartwright, Clunn, Hart, Mohun, Shatterell and Wintershall (two each).[4]

On 28 January 1661/2 the two trustees, Hewett and Clayton, assigned the lease to the building shareholders. On the same day the latter entered into articles of agreement with a company of thirteen actors who undertook to perform in the new theatre at a rent of £3 10s. for each acting night. This rent was to be divided among the building shareholders in amounts proportionate to the number of shares held by each subscriber to the building fund. Thus, for instance, Killigrew, whose nine shares amounted to a quarter of the total subscription, would receive 17s. 6d. per night (£3 10s. ÷ 4 = 17s. 6d.).[5]

This, with constant permutations in matters of detail, was the complicated mechanism by which Drury Lane Theatre was managed (or mismanaged) until the middle of the eighteenth century. Three closely interdependent but fundamentally separate elements were involved. Firstly there was the owner (or owners) of the royal patent, originally granted to Thomas Killigrew in 1662 (see pages 1–2), or of the Lord Chamberlain's licence, or (in the first half of the eighteenth century) of the royal patents granted for a limited number of years, upon one or other of which depended the authority to act. Secondly there were the building shareholders, who had subscribed the original capital for the erection of the theatre and who charged a nightly rent to successive companies of actors for the use of their property; the building shareholders owned the ground lease, which was renewed to them by successive Dukes of Bedford, and their shares, always thirty-six in total number, were a form of property which they could bequeath or sell in the open market. Thirdly, there were successive groups of actors, who used the theatre either by agreement with or sub-lease from the building shareholders, to whom they paid a nightly rent. They retained whatever profits remained (if any) after payment of the nightly rent and all other expenses.

At first these three elements were extremely closely connected. Killigrew, for instance, owned both the patent and a quarter of the building shares, while eight other building shareholders, with a total of eighteen shares, were also actors in the company of thirteen actors who agreed to perform in the theatre. But with the passage of time, and the frequent transfer of building shares, either by sale or inheritance, the number of building shareholders who were also actors declined, and their connexion with the theatre consisted simply of drawing a rent from its users. This situation continued until 1753, when the fourth Duke of Bedford refused to renew the building shareholders' ground lease, and granted it instead to James Lacy and David Garrick, the manager and principal actor respectively at Drury Lane. The demise of the building shareholders marked the end of the triangular structure of management of the theatre, and as Lacy and Garrick had also, since 1747, owned the twenty-one-year patent under which Drury Lane then acted, an entirely new system of administration emerged in the second half of the eighteenth century.

The building of the first Theatre Royal on the site between Brydges Street and Drury Lane must have begun in the spring of 1662, for on 31 March 1662 Thomas Rugge referred in his diary to 'a very large playhouse the foundation of it laid in this month, in the back side of Bridges Street in Covent Garden'.[6] In February 1662/3 Pepys was there—'I walked up and down, and looked upon the outside of the new theatre, now a-building in Covent Garden, which will be very fine'—and although he was not present on the opening night, 7 May 1663, for the performance of Beaumont and Fletcher's *The Humorous Lieutenant*, he was there with his wife on the following day and recorded his impressions in some detail (see page 40).[7]

The cost of the playhouse was £2,400, which the building shareholders raised by a payment of £66 13s. 4d. for each of the thirty-six shares. They also had to pay their proportion of the Earl of Bedford's ground rent (about 27s. 9d. for each share), and in return they received about two shillings per share for each night of acting. The initial success of the venture can be judged from the fact that in November 1663 Walter Clunn, one of the actors who was also a building shareholder, was able to sell his two shares to Thomas Johnson, barber, for £215 each.[8]

But this prosperity was short-lived, for on 5 June 1665 the Lord Chamberlain closed the playhouse indefinitely on account of the plague.[9] Pepys has recorded that this period of enforced idleness was used to enlarge the stage,[10] but within a few years of the re-opening in the autumn of 1666 a more serious set-back occurred. On 25 January 1671/2 the theatre caught fire between seven and eight o'clock in the evening and was almost completely destroyed.[11] Many of the adjoining houses were also burnt and others were blown up to prevent the spread of the fire.[12] In all about sixty houses were destroyed, and the total damage was estimated at £20,000.[13]

As owners of the ground lease the building shareholders now had to raise fresh capital to rebuild the theatre, which, they estimated, would cost 'neere Two Thousand pounds more then it did when it was first built'.[14] This evidently proved difficult, for the Earl of Bedford did not grant them an extension of their existing lease, of which some thirty years remained unexpired, and they appealed to the King, apparently without success, for both a subsidy and for payment of arrears already due to them for performances at Court.[15] By 17 December 1673, however, the building of the new theatre had advanced far enough for the company of actors (of which Thomas Killigrew was now a member) to sign articles of agreement with those building shareholders who were not actors. The actors agreed to perform only in the new theatre, and if the building costs did not exceed £2,400 (the cost of the first theatre), to pay the building shareholders the old rent of £3 10s. for each night of acting; but if the building costs exceeded that amount, then to pay proportionately more.[16] Various estimates of the final cost have been made, ranging from £3,500 to £4,400.[17] Whatever the actual figure may have been it was certainly substantially more than £2,400, for the nightly rent subsequently charged was not £3 10s. but £5 14s., which would give a cost of £3,908. One of the building shareholders, Thomas Johnson, the barber who had bought Walter Clunn's two shares at a very high price in November 1663, was unable or unwilling to pay his full share of the capital. He subscribed his $\frac{2}{36}$ of £2,400 (i.e., £66 13s. 4d. for each share) but the excess required—about £50 for each share—was by agreement paid by Thomas Shepey, who in return received for each share a nightly rent of $\frac{1}{36}$ of £2 4s.—the difference between the £5 14s. paid

by the actors and the £3 10s. to which Johnson was entitled. 8*

The new theatre, the design of which has been attributed to Wren (see page 42), opened on 26 March 1674 with a performance of Fletcher's *The Beggar's Bush*.[18] Although much altered and enlarged, particularly during Garrick's long reign in the middle years of the eighteenth century, the building survived until the complete rebuilding undertaken in 1791–4. This extraordinary longevity, unequalled by any other seventeenth- or eighteenth-century London theatre, was not foreshadowed by the early history of the new play-house. Almost immediately there were dissensions between Thomas Killigrew and the actors, some of whom threatened to quit and demanded compensation under the terms of their contract, 'whereby the said Company was like to breake up and be dissolved for want of their principal Actors and for that the profitts did not come in sufficient to make the said payments'.[19] There were dissensions, too, between Thomas Killigrew and his son Charles, whom the Lord Chamberlain in February 1676/7 appointed to be 'Master of the Company' of actors. No improvement ensued, however. The political uncertainties of the years of the Popish Plot (1678–81) occasioned the banning of several plays, and there were frequent interventions in the affairs of the theatre by the Lord Chamberlain. At last in April 1682 Drury Lane closed and negotiations began for a union with Charles Davenant's flourishing establishment at the rival theatre at Dorset Garden.[20]

By articles of union dated 4 May 1682 between Charles Killigrew on the one hand and Charles Davenant and his principal associates at Dorset Garden on the other, Killigrew agreed to dissolve the Drury Lane company of actors forthwith and to join and unite the patent which had been granted to his father with that of Davenant (see page 3). The latter was to pay Killigrew a rent of £3 for each acting night at either Drury Lane or Dorset Garden, and Killigrew was also to have three of the twenty shares in the profits of the united company of actors now to be established. This company was to be under the joint direction of Killigrew and Davenant.[21]

Killigrew's share in the three constituent forms of property embodied in the theatre did not,

---

* This transaction incidentally provides the facts for another calculation of the actual cost of the theatre. Johnson subscribed £66 13s. 4d. for each of his shares, to which Shepey added another £50, bringing the total capital subscribed for each share up to £116 13s. 4d. With thirty-six shares this would give a total cost of £4,200.

of course, entitle him to make such an agreement. His title to the patent was being challenged in Chancery (see page 2), he only owned a quarter of the Drury Lane building shares and his holding in the company of actors there was even smaller. It was intended that the headquarters of the new united company should be at Drury Lane, and the successful implementation of the agreement would therefore depend on Killigrew's ability to persuade the other owners of building shares to grant Davenant and his associates a sub-lease of the building, at a much reduced nightly rent. By June 1682 he had won over shareholders owning twenty-one of the thirty-six shares,[22] but at the time of the re-opening of Drury Lane on 16 November 1682 no lease to the actors had actually been signed, and it was not until the following summer that he obtained the consent of all the building shareholders. On 7 June 1683 they subleased the theatre to Charles Davenant and his associates for a term expiring in November 1701— almost the whole of the remainder of their interest under their ground lease from the fifth Earl of Bedford, due to expire at Christmas 1702. The nightly rent was to be £3,[23] instead of £5 14s. as hitherto.

The events whereby Charles Davenant sold his theatrical interests to his brother, Alexander Davenant, after whose bankruptcy they passed in 1693 to Sir Thomas Skipwith and Christopher Rich, have been described on page 3. Skipwith now owned five-sixths of the sub-lease granted by the building shareholders in 1683, and due to expire in November 1701, but he had no wish to concern himself actively in theatrical affairs, and so effective control of Drury Lane therefore passed to his partner. Rich was a lawyer whose family connexion with the London stage was to extend over almost three-quarters of a century. He was said to be 'as sly a Tyrant as ever was at the Head of a Theatre',[24] and his treatment of the actors caused a number of them, led by Thomas Betterton, to remove to the old theatre at Lisle's Tennis Court, where they opened in April 1695 under the authority of a licence from the Lord Chamberlain. Shortly afterwards the building shareholders, fearful, perhaps, that Rich might attempt to forestall them,

obtained a renewal of their ground lease from the first Duke of Bedford (formerly the fifth Earl). This was granted on 29 June 1695,* and subject to payment of a fine of £200 was to extend from Christmas 1702 to Christmas 1716; the rent was to continue at £50 per annum. By this time only two of the lessees or building shareholders were actively connected with the theatre— Charles Killigrew and the actor Edward Kynaston; a third was the widow of the actor John Lacy, but the remaining thirteen were probably investors concerned only with the regular payment of their share of the nightly rent.[25]

Meanwhile Rich remained in charge at the theatre despite the precariousness of his position— he owned only a small part of the Davenant patent and neither he nor his sleeping partner, Sir Thomas Skipwith, owned any of the building shares. His principal asset was the sub-lease granted in 1683, but when this expired in November 1701 he somehow 'kept ye possession of ye said Theatre by force against ye Wills and Inclinacions as also against ye interest of ye said Builders, for several yeares after'.[26] Rich was able to do this because of disputes amongst the building shareholders, both as to the actual ownership of the shares and as to what should be done with the theatre. Some of them wished to grant a sub-lease to Betterton, still at Lisle's Tennis Court, but Rich was able to prevent others from signing the lease, and so he remained in possession.[27]

This unhappy situation, marked by endless disputes and intrigues, and from 1705 much complicated by the opening of Vanbrugh's new theatre in the Haymarket, continued for nearly eight years. From March 1706/7 the increasingly exasperated Lord Chamberlain issued a series of orders to Rich, who appears to have ignored them,[28] and at last on 6 June 1709 the Lord Chamberlain forbad all performances at Drury Lane until further notice.[29] The theatre remained closed for five months, but in November 1709 the Lord Chamberlain granted a licence to act at Drury Lane to William Collier,[30] 'a lawyer of an enterprizing Head and a jovial Heart', and Tory M.P. for Truro.[31] On 22 November Collier went to the theatre 'with a Corporal and divers Soldiers armed with swords

---

* The lessees, with their probable interest in the thirty-six building shares given in brackets, were as follows: Richard Bentley ($\frac{2}{5}$); George Bradbury (1); William Clayton (4); Henry Heiles ($\frac{3}{5}$); Charles Killigrew (9); Edward Kynaston (1); Margaret Lacy (4); Henry Mordaunt (1); Penelope Morley ($4\frac{1}{2}$); Thomas Napier (1); Mary Scrope (2); Thomas Shepey ($3\frac{3}{10}$); James Stone (1); Thomas Stringer (1); Richard Symes (1); Edward Watty (1).

and Musquett[s and] in a riotous and violent manner broke open the Doors of the sd Theatre and turned out Mr Rich's servants . . ., declareing that he took possession of the sd Theatre for himselfe'.[32] The theatre re-opened on the following day,[33] and a year later, on 15 November 1710, the building shareholders granted Collier a three-year sub-lease at a rent of £3 12s. per acting night, and with a covenant to grant him an extension of nine years after they had obtained an extension of their own ground lease from the second Duke of Bedford.[34] On 16 March 1710/11 the Duke, for a fine of 230 guineas, extended the building shareholders' term from Christmas 1716 to Christmas 1737,[35]* and subsequently they extended Collier's sub-lease, though for what term is not clear.[36] For the remainder of the reign of Queen Anne Drury Lane was managed by Collier in association with the actors Robert Wilks, Colley Cibber, Thomas Doggett and (from 1713) Barton Booth, to whom the Lord Chamberlain granted a succession of licences.[37]

With the death of Queen Anne in August 1714 the current licence become void, and in the ensuing political revolution the Tory Collier became a liability to the theatre. The actor-managers Wilks, Cibber, Doggett and Booth therefore sought the support of the Whig, (Sir) Richard Steele, through whose influence at Court they and Steele were granted a joint licence by the Lord Chamberlain on 18 October 1714.[38] They were soon involved in difficulties with Collier, however, who still held the sub-lease, but as he had now been deprived of the licence he appears to have assigned his leasehold interest to the actor-managers.[39] The theatre had in fact re-opened on 21 September 1714, before the new licence had actually been granted.[40]

But the theatre now had to face formidable new competition. Some time after his forcible ejection from Drury Lane in 1709 Christopher Rich had acquired the playhouse at Lisle's Tennis Court and rebuilt it. He had died on 4 November 1714 but the new theatre (now usually referred to as the Lincoln's Inn Fields theatre) had opened some six weeks later under the authority of the Davenant patent. The profits at Drury Lane

at once declined considerably,[41] and in order to strengthen his own position and that of his colleagues at Drury Lane, and to free themselves in some degree from the licensing authority of the Lord Chamberlain, Steele petitioned for a royal patent. This was granted to Steele alone on 19 January 1714/15, but unlike the earlier patents to Killigrew and Davenant, the term of the grant to Steele was limited to his lifetime plus three years.[42] Steele at once assigned equal shares in the patent to his colleagues, the actor-managers.[43]

The theatre was managed under these arrangements for some time, Doggett retiring after a year or two.[44] But there was constant tension with the Duke of Newcastle, who was then Lord Chamberlain, the extent of whose authority over a patent theatre was extremely obscure, and the mounting friction was exacerbated by political differences between Steele and the Duke.[45] In December 1719 the Lord Chamberlain summarily dismissed Cibber from the management for disobedience, and on 23 January 1719/20 he revoked the licence granted in October 1714. After three days, in which the theatre remained closed, he issued a new licence to Cibber, Wilks and Booth,[46] but from which Steele was excluded, and although the latter still held the life patent of 1715 its validity was for the moment so doubtful as to render it temporarily useless. Steele's suspension lasted until May 1721, when with the help of his political ally Sir Robert Walpole, who had become First Lord of the Treasury in the previous month,[47] he was restored by Newcastle's order to his share in the profits of the theatre.[48] But he took little further active part in the affairs of Drury Lane, and after his death in 1729 Cibber, Wilks and Booth purchased all his rights from his heiress for £1,200.[49]

During the four years which followed the death of Steele important changes were made in the management of Drury Lane. The increasing competition of new unauthorized theatres in the suburbs of London, and from John Rich's new theatre at Covent Garden, first opened in December 1732, made possession of a patent more valuable than ever. Steele's patent, still in the limbo of legal uncertainty, expired in 1732. But

---

* The lessees, with their probable interest (where known) in the thirty-six building shares given in brackets, were as follows: John Charwood (?); Rupert Clarke (1); Charles Killigrew (9); Margaret Lacy (4); Sir John Mordaunt (1); Robert Moreton (1); George Morley (4½); Mary Napier (1); Christopher Rich (2); Grace Shepey (?); Francis Stanhope (1); Elizabeth Stone (1); Nicholas Strawbridge (⅝); Richard Symes (1). One of the two trustees, Thomas Kynaston, appears to have had an interest in four shares. The other trustee, John Sherman, appears also to have had an interest.

with the Duke of Newcastle no longer at the Lord Chamberlain's office Wilks, Cibber and Booth were able on 3 July 1732 to obtain the grant of a new royal patent, limited to a term of twenty-one years.[50] This triumvirate had been extremely successful for many years, but now all three members were near the end of their careers. On 13 July 1732 Booth sold half of his share in the new twenty-one-year patent (i.e., one sixth of the whole) for £2,500 to John Highmore, a wealthy young gentleman with theatrical propensities, who in the following March also purchased Colley Cibber's one-third share for three thousand guineas.[51] Meanwhile Wilks had died and his widow, Mary Wilks, was represented by John Ellys, a painter. Booth died on 10 May 1733,[52] and in September of the same year his widow sold her remaining share for £1,350 to Henry Giffard,[53] manager of the new theatre at Goodman's Fields. So within fifteen months of the grant of the twenty-one-year patent to the three experienced actor-managers, the ownership of five-sixths of the patent had passed to men with no experience of theatrical affairs.

Meanwhile the building shareholders, none of whom (at least after the death of Barton Booth) had any share in the twenty-one-year patent, had surrendered the ground lease which the second Duke of Bedford had granted to them in March 1710/11. On 21 March 1731/2 the third Duke, in consideration of a fine of a thousand guineas, granted them a new twenty-one-year ground lease which would expire at Christmas 1753.[54*] The building shareholders were now able to grant a new sub-lease, the old one having expired at Christmas 1732, and in May 1733 Colley Cibber's son, Theophilus Cibber, persuaded a majority of them, representing $29\frac{3}{8}$ of the 36 shares, to grant to him and nine associates (of whom eight were actors) a fifteen-year sub-lease at a rent of £4 4s. per acting night.[53]

With the three constituent elements of patent owners, building shareholders and actor-sub-lessees thus completely divorced from one another (for none of the actors were either patentees or building shareholders), there now ensued a disastrous struggle for control of the theatre. The new owners of the twenty-one-year patent were in occupation, not having vacated the building after the expiry of the old sub-lease at Christmas 1732, and when on 26 May 1733 the new sub-lessees—Theophilus Cibber and his company of actors—attempted to gain possession, the patentees locked the doors against them.[52] Litigation in Chancery at once ensued,[53] but in the meantime Cibber and his associates removed to the Little Theatre in the Haymarket, where they opened without a licence on 26 September 1733.[55] In November Highmore, as principal owner of the twenty-one-year patent, attempted unsuccessfully to suppress Cibber by bringing a test case under a Vagrancy Act against one of the actors at the Haymarket, and in the same month the Lord Chief Justice ruled against Highmore and his co-patentees in an action for possession of Drury Lane.[56]

On 24 January 1733/4 Highmore accepted defeat and sold his share of the twenty-one-year patent (one half of the whole) for £2,250 to Charles Fleetwood of St. Clement Danes, esquire, who on the same day also bought Mary Wilks's one third for £1,500. But although Fleetwood now owned five-sixths of the patent (Giffard still owning the remaining one sixth), Cibber and his actors were in possession of the theatre. A meeting was therefore held at the Rummer tavern in Henrietta Street to discuss the situation, and on 12 March 1733/4 the actors agreed to perform at Drury Lane (where they had already triumphantly opened on 8 March) and to hold their fifteen-year sub-lease in trust for Fleetwood, provided that he could procure the consent of those building shareholders who had not yet executed the sub-lease.[56]

Fleetwood remained in control at Drury Lane for nearly eleven years, with Charles Macklin, the actor, as stage manager for much of this period. By 1743, however, he was in financial difficulties, salaries were in arrears, and there was a short-lived secession of the principal actors, led by David Garrick, now the rising star at Drury Lane. Towards the end of 1744 there was a riot in the theatre after the prices of admission had been raised, and a short while later Fleetwood sold

---

* The lessees, with their interests in the thirty-six building shares in brackets, were as follows: Captain John Aldred (1); Barton Booth (2); Rupert Clarke (3); Samuel Hill (1); Thomas Jackson (4½); Charles Killigrew (9); John Lewis (1); John Mordaunt (1); Robert Moreton (1); William Palmer (⅝); Grace Shepey (1¼); Mary Strawbridge (⅝); Richard Symes (1); George Turville (1); George Turner (2); John Wallis (1); the two trustees, Thomas Kynaston and Francis Stanhope, had the benefit of four shares and one share respectively.

all his interest in the remainder of both the twenty-one-year patent and the sub-lease to James Lacy,[57] John Rich's assistant manager at Covent Garden.[58] The purchase price was £6,750, but the property was also subject to a mortgage of £5,000,[59] and Fleetwood was to receive an annuity of £500 during the remaining term of the patent.[60] In making the purchase Lacy was acting in conjunction with Richard Green and Norton Amber, bankers, of the Strand, who provided the capital and were to receive two-thirds of the profits of the property.[61]

In December 1745 Green and Amber became bankrupt.[62] After prolonged negotiations Lacy and Garrick, by an agreement dated 9 April 1747, established the partnership under which Drury Lane was successfully managed until Lacy's death in 1774. The contract provided, firstly, that Lacy should by the end of the next month procure a new twenty-one-year patent for Garrick and himself, the term to commence from the expiry of the existing patent in 1753. Lacy was also to procure a release of all of Green and Amber's creditors' claims on the property. Subject to these two conditions it was agreed that he and Garrick should enter into equal partnership in the profits to be derived from the patent, sub-lease and theatrical equipment, and that they should be jointly responsible for paying off the existing debts up to a maximum of £12,000. Any charges over and above this sum were to be Lacy's sole responsibility. Both partners were to be entitled to take £500 per annum out of the receipts of the business 'for their private expences', but Garrick was also to be paid a salary of 500 guineas for his services as an actor.[63]

On 4 June 1747 a twenty-one-year patent was issued under the Great Seal to Lacy and Garrick, the term commencing on 2 September 1753.[64] In the autumn they mortgaged their two consecutive patents to James Clutterbuck, mercer, for £12,000[65] in order to discharge the existing encumbrances, and the theatre opened under the new management on 15 September 1747.[66]

This first season ended on 25 May 1748,[67] and a week later the sub-lease under which Lacy and Garrick occupied the theatre expired. This sub-lease had originally been granted by the building shareholders to Theophilus Cibber and his associates in May 1733 for a fifteen-year term (see above). But by the summer of 1748 the building shareholders' own term under their ground lease

from the third Duke of Bedford had only another five and a half years to run, and without a new lease from the fourth Duke they could only offer Garrick and Lacy a short extension. They no longer took any part in the management of the theatre, while the income which they derived from it—about £840 per annum[68]—was a heavy liability on its finances. There was therefore no reason why the Duke, in renewing the ground lease, should depart from the normal policy of his family, which was to renew to the tenant in occupation. Accordingly on 24 August 1748 the Duke granted the new ground lease to Lacy and Garrick for a term expiring at Christmas 1774, subject to a fine of £3,000. Besides the theatre itself the lease included the reversion of several adjacent houses, the existing ground leases of which expired at various dates at or before Christmas 1759. The rent was therefore at first to be £126 per annum, rising ultimately to £210.[69] This enlargement of the site is discussed on pages 32–3.

The grant of the ground lease direct to Garrick, the actor-manager, and his partner Lacy, instead of to the holders of the thirty-six building shares, put an end to the three-sided structure of management which had existed at Drury Lane since the early 1660's. But in addition to holding the ground lease, Garrick and Lacy were also the proprietors of the twenty-one-year patent. The entire ownership of the property (except, of course, the freehold of the site) was thus concentrated in their hands, to the great benefit of both themselves and the London stage in general.

These fundamental changes in the organization of Drury Lane did not become fully effective until 1753, when the building shareholders' interest was finally extinguished by the expiry of their lease. In the summer of that year the financial basis of the management was re-organized. The mortgage to Clutterbuck was paid off,[70] and to take its place Garrick and Lacy assigned their ground lease and twenty-one-year patent to two trustees (of whom Clutterbuck was one) for £10,000. In return the trustees were to receive from Garrick and Lacy a rent of £4 per acting night and the right to forty free seats for each performance.[71] Two days later, on 27 August 1753, the trustees raised the £10,000 by the sale of forty shares at £250 apiece, each subscriber receiving one free seat and one fortieth of the nightly rent (i.e., two shillings). There were twenty-five subscribers, of whom twenty-three bought one share each; John Gastrell and James Gray, both mercers of St. Mary le Strand, bought seven and ten respectively.[72] These arrangements were, of course, restricted to the term of the ground lease expiring in 1774, and there was no provision for redemption of the capital.

Under these more stable conditions of management the theatre entered a period of unprecedented prosperity. In 1762 Garrick and Lacy obtained another twenty-one-year patent extending their rights from 1774 to 1795,[73] and in the same year they also obtained an extension of their ground lease from the fourth Duke of Bedford's son, who then possessed a life interest in this part of the estate. Here again Garrick and Lacy's existing interest was extended from 1774 to 1795 and the site was enlarged by the inclusion of a number of adjacent properties which had not hitherto been leased directly to them by the ground landlord.[74] This greater security of tenure enabled them to make considerable enlargements of the seating capacity of the theatre[75] (see page 45).

In January 1774 James Lacy died and was succeeded by his son, Willoughby Lacy.[76] Shortly afterwards the term of the share capital issued in 1753 expired, and the two proprietors were therefore able to raise a fresh sum, on terms very similar to those of 1753. On 1 September 1775 Garrick and Willoughby Lacy assigned their ground lease to trustees for twenty years for £12,000. The trustees again received a rent of £4 per acting night and were entitled to sell forty free seats at £300 apiece, each subscriber again receiving one fortieth of the nightly rent.[77] Part of the capital thus raised was evidently used for the further enlargement and embellishment of the theatre in 1775–6, Robert Adam being the architect. These alterations included the erection of a splendid entrance from Brydges Street some 60 feet wide (Plate 8).

Garrick was now preparing to leave the theatre, and in 1776, after prolonged negotiations, he eventually sold his half share in the twenty-one-year patent and the leases for £35,000.[78] The purchasers were Dr. James Ford, a wealthy physician, Thomas Linley, a composer and joint manager of oratorios at the theatre, and Linley's son-in-law, Richard Brinsley Sheridan. They divided their half share into seven parts, of which Ford held three and Linley and Sheridan two each.[79] Linley and Sheridan were obliged to enter into substantial mortgages in order to pay for their shares.[80]

Two years later, in 1778, Sheridan contracted to buy Willoughby Lacy's half for £31,500 although it was encumbered by substantial mortgages and two annuities of £500 each payable to Lacy and his wife; the conveyance was not executed until 25 March 1780. Sheridan's share now amounted to $\frac{9}{14}$ of the whole theatre, but it was subject to two mortgages totalling £27,000,[81] and thus his long connexion with Drury Lane was from the start bedevilled by acute financial difficulties.

Between 1780 and 1790 Sheridan and his partners Linley and Ford added to their obligations further outgoings of at least £3 4s. for every acting night. This was done by the sale for £280 each of at least thirty-two rights of free admission, each of which carried a nightly rent of two shillings for twenty-one years from the date of issue.[82]

The entire rebuilding of the theatre between 1791 and 1794 at enormous expense only added to the financial burden, but somehow Sheridan managed to survive until the complete destruction of the building by fire in 1809 virtually ended his venturesome reign.

The changes of ownership during this period may first be described. In 1780 Sheridan sold one fourteenth of his share in what had previously been Garrick's half share (i.e., one twenty-eighth of the whole property) to Dr. James Ford, to whom he was already in debt. His share in the whole property was thereby diminished to $\frac{17}{28}$ ($\frac{9}{14} - \frac{1}{28} = \frac{17}{28}$), while Ford's was increased to one quarter. In 1784 Sheridan sold a further $\frac{3}{14}$ of his share in Garrick's erstwhile half (i.e., $\frac{3}{28}$ of the whole property) to Thomas Linley,[83] and in 1788 he bought Ford's quarter of the whole property for £18,000.[84] Thus Sheridan owned three-quarters and Linley one quarter. By this time another twenty-one-year patent, granted in 1783, had extended the right to act from 1795 to 1816,[85] and in 1791 Sheridan and Linley had obtained an agreement for a new ground lease (see page 35) from the fifth Duke of Bedford, conditional upon their rebuilding the theatre.[86]

Thomas Linley died in November 1795, still possessed of his quarter share.[87] By his will, made some years before his death, he had divided his quarter into five equal parts, one for each of his four children then alive and the fifth to be shared between his grandchildren.[88] But in the meantime one of his daughters, Elizabeth, Sheridan's wife, had died in 1792[89] and her one fifth of the quarter had in consequence become still further sub-divided within the family, one of whom held the minute share of $\frac{1}{150}$ of the whole property.[90] In April 1796 Sheridan agreed with his Linley relatives to buy all their interests,[91] but difficulties seem to have arisen over the funding of the contract—on his own admission the debts on the theatre at this time amounted to £71,000—but another source states that in 1798 he bought part of the Linleys' interests for £30,000. The transactions at this period become so complex as to defy accurate elucidation, and even one of the solicitors engaged in this lawyers' paradise confessed that he had failed to make the elementary distinction between 'one undivided half part' and 'one undivided half part of the remaining moiety'. By 1801, however, Sheridan was claiming to be in possession of the entire property—his three-quarters plus the Linleys' quarter, all still subject, of course, to enormous encumbrances—and therefore to be in a position to make a valid title to sell part of it.[90]

He had already, on 1 February 1800, agreed to sell one quarter share of the property to John Philip Kemble, who had been for many years the leading actor at Drury Lane, but this had been set aside by mutual consent. Instead, Sheridan on 4 January 1802 sold one quarter of his interest in the twenty-one-year patent, the Killigrew patent (of which only $\frac{46}{60}$ had been acquired for Drury Lane, see page 6), the agreement for a ground lease and the wardrobe and other effects to trustees for Joseph Richardson, barrister.[90] Richardson was a minor playwright and Member of Parliament known, apparently, for his convivial propensity 'to flick his snuff about during supper'.[92] He and John Grubb, a keen amateur actor and from about 1796 the treasurer of the theatre,[93] had in 1795 become partners with Sheridan in the management (but not in the patents, leases or theatrical properties) of Drury Lane, the basis of the arrangement being that they were each to pay Sheridan £11,000 and each receive one seventh of the net profits of the business.[90] In 1802 Grubb's share in the partnership was dissolved,[94] while Richardson—'that vile fag end of the Firm', as Sheridan described him[95]—consolidated his position by the purchase of a quarter share of Sheridan's interest in the Killigrew and twenty-one-year patents and other

3—S.L. XXXV

theatrical property for £25,000. He did not of course possess such a substantial sum himself, and in order to raise it he intended to issue fifty debenture shares at £500 each, bearing interest at 5%, payable out of his quarter share of the profits. About twenty-seven such debentures were in fact purchased by a number of his wealthy acquaintances (including the Dukes of Bedford, Northumberland and Devonshire), none of whom, at the time of the fire in 1809, had ever been paid any interest.[90]

Richardson died in June 1803,[96] only a few months after making his purchase. He bequeathed his quarter in five equal parts to his widow and four daughters—such, at any rate, was his intention, but (as he candidly explained in his will) there might be disputes about his daughters' inheritance, and he therefore thought it right 'here to declare that I am perfectly satisfied that they are all my own children, though adverse circumstances [have] for many years deferred my marriage with their Mother'.[97]

On 1 March 1806 Sheridan conveyed another quarter of the patents and theatrical property to his son, Thomas Sheridan.[98] Thus at the time of the fire in 1809 Sheridan still owned half the theatre, and his son and the Richardsons each owned one quarter.

The principal event of Sheridan's reign was the rebuilding of the theatre. In 1789–90 he was negotiating with the fifth Duke of Bedford for a new ground lease of a much enlarged site, but the future of the theatre was greatly complicated by the destruction by fire of the King's Theatre in the Haymarket on 17 June 1789 (see pages 5–6). In order to attract subscriptions for the large capital sum needed for the rebuilding of Drury Lane it was essential for Sheridan to acquire the dormant Killigrew patent and the permanent authority to act which it would confer, for no one would subscribe if this authority remained limited to the term of the existing twenty-one-year patent. In the autumn of 1791 he was negotiating for the purchase of the Killigrew patent with Thomas Harris, its principal owner, and towards the end of the year he published his proposals 'To prospective Subscribers to the Rebuilding of Drury Lane Theatre'.[99]

Sheridan proposed to raise a capital sum of £150,000 by the sale of three hundred rent charges at £500 each. The purchaser of each share was to receive a nightly rent of 2s. 6d. (making, in a season of two hundred nights, a total liability of £7,500) and the right of free admission during the term of the ground lease, which Sheridan and Linley had reason to believe would be extended under the terms of their agreement with the fifth Duke of Bedford to the year 1894. The capital subscribed was to be applied to paying off and extinguishing all the existing mortgages and encumbrances (which Sheridan estimated at £61,000) and then the whole of the surplus was to be applied to the expenses of pulling down and rebuilding the theatre.[99]

To safeguard the interests of the subscribers, Sheridan and Linley in June 1793 assigned their rights in their agreement for the lease, the contents of the theatre and the subsisting twenty-one-year patent to trustees for the shareholders. A proviso in the deed declared that part of the £150,000 should be used to purchase Killigrew's dormant patent in order to guarantee the theatre's acting rights after the expiry of the current twenty-one-year patent, and $\frac{46}{60}$ of it were in fact purchased by the trustees in the same year (see page 6). Sheridan and Linley were to retain their respective shares in the management of the theatre and after payment of outgoings to the shareholders, the actors and all other creditors, they were to keep the remaining profits. The £150,000 was raised by subscription from 143 individuals, many of whom bought several shares.[100]

The architect of the new theatre was the fifth Duke of Bedford's surveyor, Henry Holland, who prepared a sumptuous scheme for the site, with the theatre partially surrounded by uniformly designed 'Taverns, Coffee-houses, Public Houses, and Shops, with Houses, Chambers, and, Apartments proper to be rented by the numerous Persons connected with the Theatre . . . so as to completely insulate the Theatre within its own appropriate Buildings'[101] (Plate 20).

In effect the new playhouse was to form the substantial nucleus of an insular building, regular in appearance and rectangular in plan, having frontages with open arcaded walks similar to those in Covent Garden Piazza, fronting west to Brydges Street, north to Russell Street, east to Drury Lane and south on an intended new thoroughfare to be called Woburn Street, which was to be built on the site of Marquis Court and Little Brydges Street. The original entrance in Brydges Street was to be retained, but the principal

entrances were to be in Russell and Woburn Streets, with spacious vestibules and ample staircases flanking the main shell of the building, containing a vast stage and an auditorium capable of seating nearly four thousand people. Owing to legal difficulties Woburn Street was not formed.

The last performances in the old Wren–Adam theatre took place on 4 July 1791 and early in December demolition began.[102] Although Sheridan and Linley were anxious to complete the new theatre as quickly as possible, all work on the building stopped during 1792 when difficulties arose in the negotiations for the Killigrew patent (see page 6), and it was not until the end of the year that Holland was in a position to order building materials.[101] After this delay Sheridan demanded a speedy completion of the work although he himself did little enough to expedite matters.

In July 1793 *The Theatrical Journal* reported that 'Drury Lane is proceeding rapidly—There are above 300 men at work now and that number will be doubled by the end of the week. Mr. Sheridan was there himself on Saturday and suggested various improvements, such as his superior knowledge of the stage supplied. Kemble too was there all day. Mr. Holland, the architect, exhibited the whole of his plan; and, not being crippled in the means, when executed it will form the finest theatre in Europe'.[103]

Despite a strike of carpenters in September, which Sheridan helped to settle by presenting them with a barrel of ale,[103] progress continued to be rapid and by the end of October Holland was preparing to make contracts for finishing the auditorium. On 27 October 1793 he wrote to Sheridan that 'Altho' I remain unconvinced the original design made two years ago and exhibited . . . to the Subscribers is not by far the best, and altho' I think the late resolves are against the receipts, the accommodation of the Audience, the Grandeur and Splendour of the Amphitheatre and the Scene, yet I am preparing to carry them into execution and propose Friday next to enter into contracts for that purpose with Saunders [the principal contractor] and others but principally with Saunders. I trouble you with this information because after that time it will be very injurious to your interests to adopt any changes that may be suggested by those you now think proper to consult.' This last rebuke was prompted, no doubt, by Holland's having received from

Sheridan's friends, letters offering advice on the internal arrangement of the theatre.[101]

Although Sheridan continued to vex and disappoint Holland by his failure to keep appointments and confirm decisions, the work proceeded with a view to opening the theatre in the spring of 1794. In February *The Theatrical Journal* announced that 'The progress of the workmen is amazing, and that part of the Theatre before the curtain is nearly completed'.[103] The opening took place on 12 March 1794, when a concert of Handel's sacred music (appropriate to the season of Lent) was given on a stage fitted up 'to represent the inside of a Gothic cathedral'. The first theatrical performance was given on 21 April, when the Drury Lane company returned to present *Macbeth* and Henry Fielding's *The Virgin Unmasked*, with an epilogue written by George Colman the younger, during which the curtain was drawn to reveal 'a very fine river on the stage, on which a waterman, in his boat, passed to and fro'.[104]

The interior of the theatre (see Frontispiece) was virtually complete at the time of the opening, but most of the surrounding buildings had not been begun and even within the theatre many of the necessary offices and workshops were incomplete (Plate 21a, b). This was partly the result of delays during the building but a more serious difficulty was the lack of money which in turn was aggravated by Sheridan's insistence on making alterations not provided for in the original estimates.[101]

Holland's estimate of the cost of the theatre building, submitted on 25 November 1791, amounted to £80,000. This figure was itself £11,000 more than Holland's own draft estimates* made earlier in the same month[101] and more than double Sheridan's 'Cursory Estimate' of 1789–90.[105] The final actual cost of the theatre is not known, but by August 1797 nearly £79,000 had been paid out to the builders, con-

tractors, craftsmen and other workmen although the building was still unfinished. This sum included Holland's own fee of £4,250, most of which was paid by rent charges on the theatre.[101]

The balance of the capital sum of £150,000 was of course not available for completing the building because it had already been applied to discharge other debts, principally the outstanding mortgages on Sheridan's and Linley's shares in the theatre, and for the purchase of $\frac{46}{60}$ of the Killigrew patent.[101]

As a result of these financial difficulties the scheme for the whole site as devised by Holland was never completed. Holland protested ineffectually, and claimed that large sums of money had been paid out of the building fund for items such as furniture which had not been allowed for in the original estimates. In theory there should have been over £16,000 still available, 'sufficient to complete the Designs, especially as it was proposed the surrounding buildings should be built by Persons who would take the Ground on which they were to be executed on a building lease'.[101] Sheridan replied that what the architect had contracted 'to finish for £80,000 will not be finished for £160,000'.[106]

It is not known how much more Sheridan expended on the theatre between 1797 and 1809, though it was evidently much in excess of the funds available, for in 1801 he claimed that he had spent 'in the further compleating of the Building a greater sum than the whole net profits of the undertaking since the opening of the Theatre'.[101]

The theatre itself survived for only fifteen years and most of its brief history is concerned with the successive devices by which attempts were made to stave off financial disaster. From 1795–6 Sheridan and the Linleys assigned over fifteen private boxes, each containing eight seats, for fourteen-year terms at a peppercorn, as security for unpaid mortgages.[107]† In 1796

---

* Holland's draft estimates were made up as follows: 'Demolition, clearing site and making drains—£1,000: To build up the new Theatre and its appurtenances, using brick and timber for its walls and supports and covering it partly with the old roof and tyle—£10,000: To fit up finish and decorate the Audience part, to finish the several other rooms and places for their respective purposes, to build the Stage and Flys, form and finish the Orchestra, form and decorate the frontispiece, paint inside, paint the Ceiling—£22,000: To secure the building from fire, put up Stoves to air it, and Ventilators—£1,200: To building the outside wall with Stone as high as the Piazza and brick stuccoed above, to pave the Piazza and form the Shop and other fronts—£4,000: To building one large commodious Tavern . . . next the Theatre and finish the whole of it for use—£7,500: To build ten shops with lodgings on a level of the Piazza and an entresol, and to have complete Houses over them, and finish the whole for use and habitation—£15,000: To build 8 shops and lodgings, having over them the Tavern or some of the appurtenances of the Theatre—£8,300.'[101]

† One of Holland's complaints was that these boxes should have been sold and the proceeds applied to finishing the building. Sheridan claimed that originally the boxes had been reserved 'to meet the extraordinary expences of entirely new Scenery Wardrobe Properties etc. and prevent them falling on the receipts'.[101]

Sheridan and the trustees for the shareholders granted twelve annuities of £50 each, and twelve rights of free admission; six were to the architect Henry Holland (who also held the lease of three boxes, all presumably in lieu of unpaid professional fees), and three each to Harvey Christian Combe (a wealthy alderman and Member of Parliament for the City, a trustee of Richardson's to whom Sheridan was in debt), and to William Adam, a friend of both Sheridan and the Prince of Wales, and later to become Sheridan's trustee.[108]

In the same year Sheridan, several of the Linleys, Combe, Adam, Grubb and Holland executed a trust deed whereby it was agreed to sell thirty-seven rent charges (later increased to forty-seven), each carrying a nightly rent of one pound and the right of free admission during the remainder of the ground lease.[109] It is not certain how many of these charges were actually sold. In 1804 it was stated that there were twenty-six in being, which had apparently been sold at £3,000 each, thereby raising some £78,000 at the expense of an annual charge on the revenue of £5,200.[110] In the meantime, however, the legality of this arrangement had been challenged in Chancery, and in 1801 a receiver of the revenues had been appointed.[111] Three years later the arrears of rent —2s. 6d. per share per night due to the subscribers of the £150,000 building capital fund— amounted to £22,500,[112] and a committee appointed by these shareholders reported that there were no fewer than 475 persons enjoying privileged rights of admission to each performance.[113]

Holland's theatre was burnt down during the night of 24 February 1809. The fire broke out in a coffee house in Brydges Street at about eleven o'clock and soon engulfed the whole building. When the flames were finally extinguished at five o'clock on the following morning little remained standing except the west wall (Plate 21c).[114]*

It was an ironic fate for a theatre for which the architect had wanted and planned elaborate fire-proofing arrangements, only to find that the proprietors were not interested in such precautions. Sheridan had persistently neglected all Holland's measures against the risk of fire, and by 1809 even such equipment as had been installed was useless. The iron safety curtain had been removed and the reservoirs of water on the roof left unattended and probably half empty; the effect of the water was 'like a mere bucket full to the volume of fire on which it fell and had no material effect in damping it'.[117]

The destruction of the theatre, plus all the existing financial problems, would probably have made any other proprietor give up in despair, but Sheridan, with characteristic optimism, at once began to plan for the rebuilding. By mid May 1809 the outline of his scheme was ready. He realized that unless the funds to be raised were large enough to settle all claims upon the old theatre as well as to finance the building of a new one, the project would be 'roofed in with a weight of debt and incumbrance certain to impede its success and ultimately to crush it'. He therefore suggested that a committee of noblemen and gentlemen should be appointed to investigate the accounts and 'assume the principal lead in the erection of the new theatre'. He hoped they could raise £175,000: £40,000 by subscription, £35,000 from the theatre's fire insurance company, £30,000 from a national lottery, £10,000 by loan from the sixth Duke of Bedford, and the rest from the sale of boxes, free admissions and site materials.[90]

A committee of this kind was indeed soon established, but within a short while Sheridan found himself excluded from it. One of its first members was Sheridan's friend Samuel Whitbread, the brewer and Whig M.P. for Bedford, who shortly after the fire had informed Sheridan that he would have 'no objection to being one of a

* Sheridan was informed of the fire while he was listening in the House of Commons to a speech by the Foreign Secretary, George Canning, on the recent campaign in Spain. 'A cry of Fire! fire! frequently interrupted the latter part of the right hon. Secretary's speech, and Mr. Sheridan, in a low tone, stated across the table, that Drury-lane theatre was on fire. Mr. Windham was about to reply when Lord Temple suggested the propriety of adjourning the debate, in consequence of the extent of the calamity, which the event just communicated to the house, would bring upon a respectable individual, a member of that house. Mr. Sheridan observed that, whatever might be the extent of the individual calamity, he did not consider it of a nature worthy to interrupt their proceedings on so great a national question.'[115] Shortly afterwards Sheridan left the House, and 'proceeding to Drury Lane, witnessed, with a fortitude which strongly interested all who observed him, the entire destruction of his property. It is said that, as he sat at the Piazza Coffee-house [in Covent Garden], during the fire, taking some refreshment, a friend of his having remarked on the philosophic calmness with which he bore his misfortune, Sheridan answered, "A man may surely be allowed to take a glass of wine by his own fireside".'[116]

committee' for rebuilding Drury Lane.[118] Whitbread's hopes of political office had recently been disappointed, and he is said to have coveted 'the applause that will come of managing so hazardous a business successfully'.[119] On 28 May 1809 Sheridan accepted Whitbread's offer to serve.[120] It is recorded that on 12 June there was already a general feeling that Sheridan 'should retire altogether from the concern', but at first he refused to comply. In course of discussions with Whitbread, however, he seems to have changed his mind, and by April 1810 he had agreed to end his long connexion with the theatre.[121] His reputation for financial incompetence, whether wholly deserved or not, was indeed an extra liability which the new committee could not afford, and in 1811, when subscribers were being asked to contribute to a new capital fund, Whitbread himself wrote that 'The Question asked before any Man or Woman will put down their Names is this "Has Mr. Sheridan anything to do with it?" A direct negative suffices . . .'.[122]

The aristocratic committee envisaged by Sheridan decided to finance the rebuilding by the formation of a joint-stock company—the first to be established in the London theatre business. This could only be done by royal charter or Act of Parliament, and the Act which was passed in 1810 contains the names of eighty-six noblemen and gentlemen, the nucleus of the new company. There were two Dukes—Bedford and Argyll— one other peer, three peers' sons, four baronets and several Whig M.P.s. The rest included bankers (Thomas Coutts and Thomas Hammersley), City merchants, employees and agents of the theatre's pre-fire administration, and friends of Sheridan. In addition to Whitbread himself, the most important were probably Harvey Christian Combe and William Adam (for whom see above), and Peter Moore, Whig M.P. for Coventry and a close friend of Sheridan. Many of the eighty-six were creditors of the old theatre.[123]

Peter Moore is said to have been 'the most adroit manager of private bills' of the day, and it was he who introduced the Bill in the spring of 1810.[124] It received the royal assent on 21 June 1810, and authorized the eighty-six named noblemen and gentlemen, together with such other persons as should subscribe to the capital fund, to form a joint-stock company for the rebuilding and management of the theatre. The company, to be known as The Theatre Royal Drury Lane Company of Proprietors, was permitted to raise £300,000 by 3,000 shares of £100 each. After paying for the expenses of obtaining the Act this capital was to be applied, firstly, to purchase the still outstanding $\frac{14}{60}$ of the Killigrew patent: secondly, to compensate the subscribers to the £150,000 rebuilding fund of 1791–4, and all other creditors with claims on the old theatre: thirdly, to purchase 'the entire Property and Interests of the present Proprietors' (i.e., R. B. and T. Sheridan and Mrs. Richardson): and lastly, to rebuild the theatre. Ten of the proprietors (of whom Whitbread, Combe, Adam and Moore were the most important) were appointed by the Act to take charge of all arrangements, examine the financial position, and report their findings to a general assembly of all the proprietors.[123]

In May 1811 the new company's managing committee, of which Whitbread was chairman, publicly invited subscriptions for the three thousand shares of £100 each. The management being now incorporated as a joint-stock company, each shareholder would receive his share of the total net profits of the venture, and if he purchased five shares he was also to have the right of free admission during his lifetime only.[125] By the end of October 1811 £120,000 had been subscribed, but by July 1813 (when the new theatre had already been open for nine months) the capital only stood at £194,500. In August 1814 it had reached £205,900, plus £29,506 received on bond,[126] but the intended figure of £300,000 was never reached.[127]

The first general assembly of The Theatre Royal Drury Lane Company of Proprietors was held on 14 October 1811. In its report the committee stated that the resources of the theatre amounted to £56,700 (including £35,000 to be received under the insurance of the old building) and that the debts amounted to £435,000, plus the annual rent of £7,500 still payable to the subscribers to the £150,000 building fund of 1791–4. The committee was nevertheless confident that the entire debt could be extinguished for £143,935, for many of the creditors (led by the sixth Duke of Bedford, who had waived his right to £4,250 in arrears of rent) had agreed to forego a large proportion of their claims. After allowing for the existing resources of £56,700 this would leave an outstanding debt of £87,235, which the committee wisely rounded up to £90,000. If the whole capital of £300,000 were raised, £210,000 would still be left to rebuild the theatre, the cost of which was estimated at £150,000. With an anticipated annual net income of £48,850 the committee forecast that the shareholders would be able to rely on an annual dividend of seven per cent. on their investment.[128]

The actual settlement of all the liabilities in accordance with the Act of 1810 occupied several years. In December 1813 the company bought the outstanding $\frac{14}{60}$ of the Killigrew patent for £9,562 (see page 7), and £46,000 were paid to the old proprietors (i.e. the Sheridans and Mrs. Richardson) for all their interests. Richard Brinsley Sheridan's half share was assessed at £24,000, plus £4,000 for his rights in the sale of fruit in the theatre; the quarter share of his son, Tom Sheridan, was assessed at £12,000, but Mrs. Richardson's quarter was only valued at £6,000 because her husband had not at the time of his death paid the full purchase price of £25,000 for which he had contracted with Sheridan in 1802.* None of these sums were paid in full direct to the three proprietors, all of whom had substantial private debts.[130]

Most of the creditors' claims had been extinguished by September 1814, usually for greatly reduced figures. Nearly all of the subscribers of 1791–4 agreed to forego all arrears due to them— £43,912 altogether—and for the future to accept a nightly rent of 1s. 3d. instead of 2s. 6d., plus the right of free admission.[128] But they insisted that their position should be regulated by statute, and in 1812 an amending Act was therefore passed to safeguard their rights.[131] The theatre was thereby saddled in a season of two hundred nights with a liability of £3,750 per annum, and the failure to extinguish the rights of the subscribers of 1791–4 was bitterly lamented in 1840 by Alfred Bunn, recently the manager of Drury Lane: these rights, he complained, 'were handed over to the [new] proprietors as heirlooms upon the patent and the smoking ruins of the old buildings'.[132]†

Meanwhile the actual rebuilding of the theatre went ahead very quickly. At the time of the opening of the subscription in May 1811 archi-

tects had been invited to prepare plans[134] and in October 1811 the committee of the company had selected the designs of Benjamin Dean Wyatt.‡ The first stone of the new theatre was laid on 29 October 1811.[136] The second general assembly of the company, held on the following day, was informed that Whitbread had already signed a memorandum of agreement with Wyatt and Henry Rowles, the building contractor, and the contract itself, which provided for the completion of the building by 1 October 1812, was to be executed immediately. The total expenditure, so the committee stated, would not exceed £125,000 (including furnishings and architect's commission), of which Rowles would be paid £112,750.[137] By April 1812 Wyatt was reporting that most of the brickwork and roof were complete and that the ornamental work was in preparation.[138] The new theatre opened on 10 October 1812 with an address written by Lord Byron, followed by a performance of *Hamlet*, and a musical farce, *The Devil to Pay*. The seating capacity, according to Wyatt himself, was 3,106, 'exclusive of four Private Boxes in the Proscenium, and fourteen in the Basement of the Theatre, immediately under the Dress Boxes'.[139]

The exterior of the theatre as built differed materially from Wyatt's original plans (Plates 22–9). The Ionic portico intended for the Brydges Street front—perhaps as an answer to Smirke's new portico at Covent Garden Theatre —was not erected, probably for reasons of economy. Many other departures from the first designs testify to the ingenuity engendered by financial stringency. In December 1812 the total expenditure (presumably including furnishings, scenery and the architect's commission) was given as £151,672—only £1,672 more than the sum originally envisaged.[138] One item on which the committee of proprietors did not economise was the new fire-fighting equipment, which enabled water to be pumped in large quantities to any part of the theatre direct from the York Buildings Water Works near the Adelphi.[140]

During the summer of 1812, while the theatre was still in course of erection, the company ob-

---

* Mrs. Richardson survived all the vicissitudes of her connexion with the theatre and in 1824 she was keeping 'a respectable female seminary' in Red Lion Square.[129]

† In 1836, when the company was suffering acute financial embarrassment, the committee of management prepared a Bill to extinguish the rights of these subscribers, but apparently it was never presented to Parliament.[133]

‡ The designs submitted by John Foulston, Rudolph Cabanel, Peter Frederick Robinson, William Wilkins and Philip Wyatt were all highly commended.[135]

DRURY LANE: MANAGEMENT

tained the renewal of both the twenty-one-year patent and the ground lease of the site. The company was authorized by the Act of 1810 to buy the outstanding interest in the Killigrew patent, but this purchase was not completed until December 1813, and in the meantime the twenty-one-year patent which had been granted in 1783 to Sheridan, Linley and Ford for a term extending from 1795 to 1816 was nearing its end. In order to safeguard the company's right to act pending the completion of the purchase of the Killigrew patent, application was made for another twenty-one-year patent, which was granted on 9 June 1812 to Whitbread, Moore and Combe for a term commencing in 1816.[141] On 11 July 1812 the sixth Duke of Bedford granted a new ground lease to the company for eighty-two and a quarter years from 29 September 1812 at an annual rent of £1,703 15s. 6d.[142]

For the first seven seasons the new theatre was managed by a committee appointed by the general assembly of the proprietors. The first committee, elected in April 1812, consisted of Lord Holland, Combe, Lancelot Holland, C. P. Crawford and Whitbread;[138] none of them had had any theatrical experience but they nevertheless decided against sub-letting the theatre to a professional. With Samuel Arnold, the dramatist, as manager this first committee ran the theatre for three seasons and declared a dividend of 5% in 1814,[143] despite the fact that heavy debts were already being incurred, chiefly through the alterations made to the interior in 1814 at a cost of £15,286.[144]

The first committee resigned in the summer of 1815 and Whitbread recommended that the theatre should be sub-leased rather than a new committee appointed. This suggestion was rejected and in June a new committee consisting of Lord Byron, the Earl of Essex, the Hon. D. Kinnaird, the Hon. A. C. Bradshaw and Peter Moore, was elected; at the same time Arnold resigned, and Whitbread committed suicide in the following month. In spite of various economies introduced by the new committee the debts of the company continued to rise rapidly, reaching £84,300 in 1818 and £90,922 in 1819. The position was further aggravated by the numerous Chancery suits initiated both against the company by creditors for the recovery of debts, and against the committee by disgruntled proprietors.[145]

In 1819 the committee were at last persuaded that leasing the theatre at a beneficial rent was the only way to prevent the property being seized and sold under the Sheriff's hammer. In June the chairman of the proprietors addressed a letter to the principal investors explaining the need to raise a subscription loan of £25,000 to discharge the encumbrances which might prevent the theatre from being let.[146]* At the same time the conditions for letting the theatre upon a seven-, fourteen- or twenty-one-year lease from 5 July 1819 were published.[90]

There were four applicants for the lease: Samuel Arnold, whose offer 'required little or no consideration for he was to run no risk'; Edmund Kean, the actor, whose offer 'was soon rejected, as he peremptorily stipulated, to exclude all the committee from interference or access to the Theatre, except through the money-taker—no Green room Loungers'; Thomas Dibdin, the actor and dramatist, who offered an annual rent of £10,100, and Robert William Elliston, the actor, whose offer of an annual rent of £10,200 was accepted.[148] On 7 August 1819 Elliston signed an agreement with five of the proprietors to take a lease of the theatre for fourteen years at an annual rent of £10,200. He further agreed to spend £7,000 in redecoration and to allow the right of nightly free admission to 653 persons.[149] Elliston immediately repainted the auditorium and opened his first season on 4 October 1819.[150]

The decision to sub-let the theatre did not prove successful for the investors. Their dividends were now derived not from the profits, but solely from the rent of £10,200, out of which the Duke of Bedford's ground rent of £1,703 and the rent-charge of £3,750 to the subscribers of 1791–1794 had first to be paid; and even the small sum which remained for distribution after these deductions was often further reduced, in the unstable theatrical conditions of the first half of the nineteenth century, by the sub-lessees' inability to pay their rent.

Elliston remained at the theatre for seven years. During his lease the present portico, the design of which is usually ascribed to James Spiller,[151] was added to the Brydges Street front in 1820 at a

* Subscriptions for this loan apparently came in slowly, but by August 1820 over £20,000 had been received.[147]

cost of £1,050 (Plate 38a).* Two years later Elliston spent £22,000 on remodelling the auditorium to the designs of Samuel Beazley. In the middle of 1825 Elliston seems to have had a stroke which left his hands paralysed and shortly afterwards he delegated the management of the theatre to his son. By 1826 he owed £5,500 in arrears of rent, and on 27 May 1826 the Company of Proprietors demanded payment within three days. Elliston refused to comply because he had spent far more on alterations than the stipulated £7,000, and on 3 June he forfeited the lease.[155]

The committee then advertised for a new lessee and accepted the offer of Thomas Bish, M.P. (who was well known at the Stock Exchange and as a lottery-office keeper) for a fourteen-year term at £10,000 per annum. But within a week of executing the agreement Bish decided to withdraw, and forfeited his deposit of £2,000.[156]

In July the lease was taken by Stephen Price, an American 'of coarse manners, repulsive conduct and vulgar conversation', who had been manager of the Park Theatre in New York. He took the theatre for a term of fourteen years at an increased rental of £10,600 per annum. In spite of his experience in New York, Price's 'want of Theatrical Knowledge soon brought him to a Stand Still'. During his fourth season the committee tried to eject him, but Price, who was a lawyer by training, refused to surrender his lease without compensation, and the committee was forced to pay him an allowance for several weeks. In March 1830 Price vacated the theatre with debts of £2,000 and was declared bankrupt on 7 July.[157]

Once again the committee advertised the lease, which was taken on 29 May by Alexander Lee, 'a broken down singer at the Haymarket and keeper of a music shop in the Quadrant'.[157] Lee was granted a three-year term from July 1830 at an annual rent of £9,000,[158] but being unable to finance such an undertaking by himself he invited Captain Frederick Polhill, M.P. for Bedford, 'a gentleman possessing more money than brains', to take a half share. Polhill had previously employed Lee to teach singing to a young lady whom he was anxious to bring on to the stage; he agreed

to Lee's request, but the partnership was short-lived and when it was dissolved in May 1831 Polhill became sole lessee.[159] In September he appointed Alfred Bunn, who had previously been in charge of the Birmingham theatre, as manager, and this arrangement lasted until the end of 1834. But the increasing financial burden of Drury Lane fell solely upon Polhill, who remained solvent only by drawing upon his large private resources.[160] In July 1833 Polhill renewed the lease for six years, determinable after the first three years, and managed to obtain a reduced rental of £8,000 per annum[161] but in December 1834 he relinquished the theatre, owing £2,500 to the committee[162] and having lost £50,000 of his own fortune.[157]

One permanent feature of Polhill's tenancy remains—the colonnade in Russell Street, designed by Samuel Beazley and erected in 1831, not without some initial opposition from the committee of management of St. Paul's parish (Plate 38b).[163]

In December 1834 Polhill assigned his lease to Bunn, who paid a deposit of £3,000 to the committee.[164] Within a few months he had lost upwards of £2,000[165] and was soon agitating for a reduction in the rent. The committee reacted by proposing to replace Bunn in July 1836, when the first three years of the lease granted to Polhill would expire, and in June advertised the lease once more,[166] but no new lessee could be found.[167]

The problem confronting the committee was that their own fixed annual outgoings of over £7,000, payable whether the theatre was sub-let or not, were greater than the rent which any sub-tenant was capable of paying to the committee.† In 1835 these expenses had totalled £7,139, even after allowance for an abatement of £300 per annum in the ground rent which the sixth Duke of Bedford had granted in February 1835, but the total rent received by the committee from their sub-tenant was only £5,500. Before the lease had been advertised in June 1836 the company's treasurer wrote to W. G. Adam, the Duke's steward, to express the committee's determination not to relet 'until the Rent reserved is found to exceed the permanent charges, or the conse-

---

* In his *Memoirs of Robert William Elliston*, published in 1844–5, George Raymond states that the portico was 'completed under the sole direction and design of Sir John Soane'.[152] Soane had been appointed honorary architect to the theatre in 1819,[153] and occasionally employed Spiller to survey or supervise works in his care.[154]

† The principal items of expenditure were: the ground rent, the rents payable to the subscribers of 1791–4, the bond-holders' interest and the rates.

quence must be again to overwhelm the Establishment with new debts and embarrassments'. He also asked the Duke to remit a further £200 per annum from the ground rent, to which the Duke again agreed.[168]

The committee's good intentions were soon set aside, for in August 1836 they relet the theatre to Bunn at a rental of only £6,000 per annum.[166] Financial disaster did not immediately ensue, however, for the Duke of Bedford's gesture in giving up £500 of his annual ground rent had persuaded others to make similar concessions. The subscribers of 1791–4 gave up threepence of their nightly rent of 1s. 3d. and the bondholders agreed to a reduction of one half in the annual interest on their loans.* In the season of 1836–7 these reductions converted what would otherwise have been a loss of £1,006 into a surplus of £370.[168]

Bunn remained at Drury Lane for another three years. During this time he presented not only opera and drama but also miscellaneous entertainments like lion-taming, tight-rope walking and promenade concerts.[170] This type of presentation did nothing to enhance the reputation of the theatre in the eyes of the committee and provoked from one proprietor an indignant letter to the editor of *The Sunday Times*. He declared that Bunn 'had *disgraced* the boards of Drury Lane Theatre by converting it into a *bear-garden*', and that he had 'subsequently *dishonoured* it by causing it to be designated the shilling theatre'. But there was so little public confidence in the theatre at this time that a block of five £100 shares which entitled the owner to free admission for life could only fetch thirty-five guineas at auction.[171] In the spring of 1839 Bunn was forced to give up the lease owing £12,200 in arrears of rent, and in December 1840 he was declared bankrupt, having lost a total of £23,052 since 1834.[172]

Bunn's precarious finances were a further embarrassment to the company. At their meeting in July 1839 the proprietors were informed that the company owed nearly £18,000, and that Polhill and Bunn owed the company £17,000 in arrears of rent. The treasurer considered that the committee had not sufficiently exerted itself to let the theatre to the best advantage and (very misleadingly) compared Drury Lane's recent record with that of Covent Garden Theatre, which had been let to D. W. Osbaldiston at £7,000 per annum.[173]†

Nevertheless the committee confirmed that the new lessee—J. W. Hammond, an actor and at that time manager of the Strand Theatre—would be paying only £5,000 per annum during his three-year lease.[174] Although Hammond engaged several outstanding actors he was forced to give up after five months, and in June 1840 the committee let the theatre to Edward Eliason, a German violinist, ostensibly to present opera. But Eliason found singers' fees too high and opened the theatre for concerts instead; these did not save him, however, and in the spring of 1841 he too resigned, also in debt.[148]

Next Charles Macready, who had already had two years' experience of financially unsuccessful management at Covent Garden Theatre, was tempted to try his hand at Drury Lane. In February 1841 he was exploring the possibility of taking a lease of the theatre, and by March had agreed to pay a rent of £7,000 per annum.[175] He opened on 4 October 1841, and was soon in debt. He had apparently little idea of the size of the liabilities involved and by August 1842 had lost £8,000, 'the earnings of a life of labour'. Nevertheless he continued for another season and tried to persuade the committee of proprietors to agree to the abolition of the fixed rental. These negotiations were unsuccessful and at the end of the season of 1843 he relinquished the lease.[176]

By August the irrepressible Bunn was again lessee of Drury Lane.[177] He had picked an inauspicious moment to return, for on 22 August the new Act for regulating theatres[178] was passed which destroyed the monopoly (much disregarded) of the patent theatres and only added to their difficulties. Nevertheless Bunn survived until March 1848, presenting mainly opera and sub-letting the theatre to Louis A. Jullien for autumn seasons of concerts. When Bunn resigned Jullien introduced the 'Cirque National de Paris', which ran until March 1849 and was followed by a season of German opera.[179]

In December 1849 James Anderson, an actor at the theatre, took over the lease and management.

---

* The parish authorities were not so sympathetic and could not be persuaded to give any relief from the rates.[169]

† The treasurer evidently did not know that Osbaldiston had been unable to pay his agreed rent to the proprietors of Covent Garden Theatre, or that there too the sixth Duke of Bedford had agreed to reduce his ground rent by £500 per annum (see page 80).

He hoped to profit in due course from the crowds drawn to London for the Great Exhibition, but his productions failed to attract the public and in June 1851 he retired with debts of £5,684, having lost a total of £9,161 in only two seasons.[180] For the next four months Drury Lane was used for an immensely popular American and French equestrian troupe, which was followed by a short season of concerts given by Louis A. Jullien. In December Bunn became lessee again. He redecorated the auditorium in the Louis XVI style and presented a season of opera which lasted until May 1852.[181]

In June 1852 Bunn finally gave up at Drury Lane.[182] He had been lessee of the theatre four times but his persistence had not been rewarded with any sustained success. Writing some twenty years later J. R. Planché described Bunn's management as 'sheer gambling of the most reckless description, in no one instance that I can remember terminating prosperously, what ever might have been the success of certain productions in the course of it'.[183] In July Sheridan Smith, an American, took the lease for 'a brief period'; he proved as good as his word and only survived for one week.[184] Eventually the committee managed to lease the theatre until Christmas 1852 to Frederick Gye and Louis Jullien for their winter concerts;[168] they in turn sub-let for short periods, sometimes to unsuitable tenants such as George Bolton, tailor, who managed the theatre for a week in October.[185]

The difficulties encountered by the committee in finding a reliable lessee had not gone unnoticed by the seventh Duke of Bedford's London steward, Christopher Haedy. In a letter written in August 1852 to the treasurer of the theatre about the arrears of ground rent he warned the company that the theatre might have to be demolished. Haedy himself was sympathetic to the company but as the Duke's adviser he felt that in the long run it would be more advantageous for the Duke to demolish the theatre and let the site on building leases at a lower but more dependable rental.[168]

In September the company found a new lessee to take over from Christmas 1852.[168] This was E. T. Smith, manager of the Marylebone Theatre, who in the course of his remarkable career was lessee of the Alhambra, Her Majesty's, the Lyceum, Astley's and Cremorne Gardens. According to the treasurer, Smith was not a person

the company would have chosen but his offer of £3,500 per annum was the only acceptable one. He subsequently entered into a seven-year lease of the theatre at £4,000 per annum.[186] Haedy then advised the Duke not to take steps to gain possession of the building at least until Christmas 1852, as the treasurer had assured him that the rent to be paid to the company by Gye and Jullien for their autumn season would be used to reduce the arrears of the Duke's ground rent.[168]

The arrears were evidently not paid, however, for in his annual report, written in February 1853, Haedy recommended the Duke to vacate the lease and let the site for building. 'Drury Lane Theatre has held on longer' than Covent Garden, he wrote, 'but there is now strong reason to fear that its days, as a Theatre, are numbered, every attempt to let it as a Theatre ending in failure. The rent payable to your Grace for it is getting into arrear and it appears to be far from improbable that either the Lease of it will be surrendered to your Grace, or that you will have to resort to legal proceedings for vacating it. This has so long appeared to be probable as to have made it necessary to consider what would be the best use it could be put to in the event of the surrender and avoidance of the lease. The result of much consideration is, that it is incapable of being applied as a Building to any profitable purpose, and that the best thing to do with it will be to take it down, sell the materials, and let the site of it as building ground. With that view a Plan for building upon the site of it has been laid down by Mr. Parker [Haedy's assistant], which appears to shew the best appropriation which can be made of the ground as a site for House building. . . .'[187]

Fortunately the seventh Duke was in no hurry to implement his steward's recommendation and the theatre was still standing a year later when Haedy was able to report that 'contrary to what was expected' the arrears of rent had been lessened, and 'for the present at least the necessity for taking steps to vacate the lease has ceased'.[188]

No doubt some of the credit for saving the building must go to the new lessee, E. T. Smith, whose judicious choice for his opening production —*Uncle Tom's Cabin*—took advantage of the current public enthusiasm for the book.[189] But the threat of demolition still hung over the theatre during the 1850's and was occasionally used by the Duke's steward to coax arrears of ground rent out of the company.[168] Smith remained at Drury

Lane for nearly ten years; like Bunn he survived by alternating opera and drama with less serious entertainments such as circuses and Chinese conjuring.[190]

In 1862 Smith assigned his lease to Edmond Falconer, the successful manager of the Lyceum.[191] In 1863 Falconer entered into partnership with his acting manager, F. B. Chatterton,[192] but after three years this arrangement was terminated through 'differences of opinion on the mode of conducting the business of the house' and Chatterton was left as sole lessee.[193] In 1866 he took a new lease of the theatre at a rental of £6,000 per annum, plus £10 per night for every additional performance over two hundred—an indication of the sudden improvement in theatrical business during the previous few years.[194]

Chatterton had mixed fortunes; some of his productions earned record profits whilst others (chiefly of the classics) brought enormous losses. In the summer months he sub-let the theatre to Colonel Mapleson for several seasons of opera. But the committee of proprietors was well pleased and at a meeting of shareholders in April 1873 Chatterton was described as 'the best lessee they had ever had because he made the theatre so prosperous'.[195] In 1876 or 1878 he renewed his lease for another five years[196] but was not able to complete the term, and the theatre was closed in February 1879, when his debts amounted to £36,000.[197]

Later in 1879 the committee let the theatre to (Sir) Augustus Harris at £6,000 per annum.[198] Although only twenty-seven years of age Harris had already had some experience of management at Covent Garden. Within a short while he established the pattern of the Drury Lane melodrama and pantomime which restored the prestige of the theatre and brought it unprecedented success.[199] He remained in charge of Drury Lane until his death in 1896.

In the latter part of the 1880's the future of the theatre began to be overcast by the question of the renewal of the ground lease, which had been granted to the Company of Proprietors by the sixth Duke of Bedford in 1812 and was due to expire at Christmas 1894. Both the company and their tenant, Harris, had submitted rival applications to the ninth Duke for a reversionary lease, and both had been refused. Shortly after the ninth Duke's death in January 1891 Harris renewed his application, and offered to pay a ground

rent of £4,500 per annum and spend a large sum in improvements in exchange for a long lease. But the Duke's steward, Alfred Stutfield, wished to improve this part of the estate by widening Russell Street, and as this would involve the demolition of the theatre he advised the tenth Duke not to accept any proposal for the renewal of the lease.[200]

No decision was taken for two years, partly at least because the future of the theatre during 1891–3 depended upon the future of Covent Garden Market. Demand for the transference of the market to public ownership reached a climax during these years, and in 1893 the London County Council attempted (unsuccessfully) to obtain statutory power to purchase markets compulsorily. In July of that year the Council, still in expectation of the successful passage of its Bill through Parliament, informed the eleventh Duke that if it were empowered to purchase the market it would wish to use the site of the theatre for a much-needed extension. The Council therefore requested the Duke not to renew the lease for a term longer than seven years.[201]

By this time the tenth Duke had died, in March 1893. He or his successor, Herbrand, the eleventh Duke, had evidently decided to reject the increasingly agitated requests of the Company of Proprietors for the renewal of their ground lease. In January 1893 the company had offered a rent of £2,000 per annum for a twenty-one-year lease, and had pointed out that if the Duke refused to renew the lease the company would lose the whole of the capital by which the theatre had been built in 1811–12. The Duke, however, was reminded by his steward that the company had for nearly sixty years past enjoyed an abatement of £500 per annum in their ground rent, and that as Sir Augustus Harris had made a much more advantageous offer there was no reason to depart from the Duke's normal policy of renewing leases to the tenant in occupation.[201] It was to Harris, therefore, and not to the company, that an offer of a new lease was made in August 1893.[202] The company which had built the theatre thereby lost both its assets and its *raison d'être* and on 11 November 1897 the renters and debenture holders closed their account and agreed to a final dividend of £4 9s. on the 293 subsisting shares.[203]

In compliance with the London County Council's request the term to be granted to Harris was for only seven years, at a rent of £6,300 per annum. The agreement, executed in May 1894, contained a number of restrictive covenants designed to prevent the recurrence of some of the worst features of the old company's tenancy. The theatre was not to be used as a circus, music hall, theatre of varieties, or for promenade concerts or dancing, or indeed for any purpose except opera and stage plays, without the Duke's permission; and similarly there was to be no sub-leasing, except for short seasons of opera or drama, without express authority.[204]

Harris died on 22 June 1896, within little more than two years of the signature of the agreement, having in the meantime bought the Killigrew patent from the old Company of Proprietors (see page 7). Within a few months of Harris's death his stage manager, Arthur Collins, acquired from the executors the right to purchase the agreement of 1894 with the Duke, and in October 1896 he submitted proposals for a new lease to the Duke's steward, Alfred Stutfield. The latter replied that the Duke was willing to entertain Collins's offer 'subject to his getting a substantial backer to enter into the Lease with him'.[205] It was probably in order to comply with this condition that on 24 March 1897 a new company to be known as Theatre Royal Drury Lane Limited applied to the Board of Trade for registration, the objects of the proposed company being 'to acquire and take over [the theatre] as a going concern' and to carry on the business of producing musical and dramatic entertainments there. Collins was not one of the signatories of the application, and his exact role is therefore uncertain,[206] but five days later, on 29 March 1897, he signed an agreement with the Duke for a forty-year lease (the London County Council's attempt to purchase and extend the market having now lapsed) at a rent rising to £6,550 per annum. The agreement was conditional upon Collins securing the surrender of Harris's seven-year interest and upon his making the alterations to the building described on page 39. It also contained authority for the committee of the Sir Augustus Harris Memorial Fund to erect the commemorative drinking fountain which still stands against the front wall of the theatre.* On the advice of his steward the Duke contributed £50 to the fund, because Sir Augustus Harris 'By his enterprise and pluck . . . resuscitated Drury Lane Theatre

when it had fallen on evil times and there is no doubt whatever that he has added materially to the market value of the Theatre'.[208]

On 27 May 1897 Collins agreed provisionally to sell this forty-year interest, the Killigrew patent and all fittings, stage properties and machinery connected with the theatre to the new company for £85,000 (a sum probably calculated only for accounting purposes). The certificate of incorporation of the company was issued on 28 May, and on 7 June the agreement between Collins and the company was confirmed.[206] Shortly afterwards Collins obtained the Duke's permission to assign his interest to the company, and arranged for the surrender of the remainder of Harris's seven-year interest.[209] He at once became one of the company's six directors, and by the end of August the company's capital of 125,000 £1 shares had been fully subscribed.[210] The first production of the new régime took place on 16 September 1897.[211]

After the completion of the alterations provided for in the Duke of Bedford's agreement of 1897 with Arthur Collins, the company was in 1900 granted a lease expiring in 1937.[212] In 1903, after further structural alterations had been made, the Duke extended this term to 1977 at an annual rent of £6,450.[213]

Drury Lane Theatre was one of the properties sold by the eleventh Duke of Bedford in 1918 to the Covent Garden Estate Company Limited. In January 1920 this company offered the freehold of the theatre for sale by auction. Bidding reached £134,500, but the reserve price was higher and the property was withdrawn. The freehold was sold privately in March of the same year to the Ellerman Property Trust Limited, which still owns it.[214]

In 1919 there were substantial changes in the ownership of the shares of Theatre Royal Drury Lane Limited, which still held the ground lease, and Sir Alfred Butt became chairman of the company and joint managing director with Arthur Collins.[215] In 1921–2 the interior of the theatre was reconstructed to designs of J. Emblin Walker, F. Edward Jones and Robert Cromie, at a cost of £150,000.[216]

During the war of 1939–45 the theatre became the headquarters of Entertainment National Service Association (E.N.S.A.) and suffered some damage by enemy action.[217] In 1944 Associated

* The memorial was designed by Sidney R. J. Smith; the bronze bust of Harris is by T. Brock, R.A.[207]

Theatre Properties (London) Limited acquired a controlling interest in Theatre Royal Drury Lane Limited.[218] After restoration the theatre re-opened on 19 December 1946 with Prince Littler as managing director.[217] In 1958 Associated Theatre Properties offered to buy all the outstanding £1 shares of Theatre Royal Drury Lane Limited for 22s. 6d.[219] This offer proved successful and by 1966 A.T.P. owned 123,800 of the 125,000 shares.[206]

CHAPTER III

The Theatre Royal, Drury Lane: the Site

THE original Theatre Royal, Drury Lane, was built in an oblong stable yard in the centre of the block of property bounded by Brydges (now Catherine) Street on the west, Russell Street on the north, Drury Lane on the east, and Little Brydges Street and Vinegar Yard on the south (fig. 1). At the time of the building of the theatre in 1662–3 the yard was already surrounded by buildings on all four sides, and the only access to it was by a narrow passage at the west end leading into Brydges Street and by another at the east end to Drury Lane (Plate 1b). When the operations of the theatre required more space, the existence of buildings all around the site made any expansion extremely difficult to achieve. These difficulties were greatly increased by the fact that the ground landlords of the site of the theatre, the Earls of Bedford, who had for many years owned the freehold of the entire block of property described above, had between 1635 and 1659 disposed of the fee farms of most of the ground around the theatre. Until the 1790's the separate fee-farm ownerships thereby established prevented any effective widening of the theatre on the north and south sides, and although enlargements of the site did take place from time to time, notably under David Garrick, Drury Lane Theatre remained hemmed in by the surrounding buildings until Henry Holland rebuilt it in 1791–4. By this time the fourth and fifth Dukes of Bedford had repurchased the freehold of most of these surrounding buildings, and Holland was therefore able to design a much wider theatre with less constricted access. The present theatre erected in 1811–12 now occupies what is virtually an island site, with the principal entrances from Catherine Street and Russell Street (see figs. 1–6).

The site leased by the fifth Earl of Bedford in December 1661 to the building shareholders had some years previously formed part of a strip of land some 60 feet wide, extending westward from Drury Lane to the wall of Covent Garden (later Brydges Street). This strip had been leased in 1616 by Edward, third Earl of Bedford, to Sir Edward Cecil, later Viscount Wimbledon, for a term dependent on three lives.[1] During the currency of this lease part of the site of the future Theatre Royal was occupied by an earlier and probably short-lived playhouse. A survey made in or after May 1635 mentions here a stable, coach-houses, a riding-house and 'A playhouse 31 foote broad & 40 foote longe : boarded walles & sheded with pann tiles'.[2] This may perhaps be identified with the temporary playhouse licensed by the Lord Chamberlain in April 1635 to a group of French players, and which was erected within the short space of seventeen days from the grant of the licence in the 'manage' (i.e. riding school) of Monsieur Le Febure in Drury Lane.[3]

When the lease of 1616 expired in 1652 the middle portion of the strip, comprising the future site of the Theatre Royal, passed into the tenure of Richard Ryder, carpenter, and was described in the fifth Earl of Bedford's lease of 20 December 1661 to the theatre building shareholders as 'the Rideing Yard'.[4] By this time the Earls of Bedford had sold the fee farm of most of their ground surrounding the site of the theatre (see fig. 1).

The lease of 20 December 1661 to the building shareholders was for a term of forty-one years from Christmas 1661 at an annual rent of £50. The site (A on fig. 1) was described as measuring in length 112 feet east to west and in breadth 59 feet at the east end and 58 feet at the west end.[5] Access was by means of two passages, from Drury Lane and Brydges Street. These dimensions were repeated precisely in the later leases granted by the Dukes of Bedford to the building shareholders in 1695, 1710/11, and 1731/2,[6] and it was within the boundaries of this curtilage that the first theatre was built in 1662–3 and (after the fire of 1671/2) the second in 1674. The first theatre did not occupy the whole site; in front of the west end there was a small yard (B on fig. 1) which measured 10 feet by 58 feet.[7]

The freehold of the plot of ground immediately east of the theatre also belonged to the Earl of Bedford, who on 1 May 1662 leased it to William Hewett[8] (see fig. 1, land marked 'leased to Hewett May 1662'). Hewett was one of the two trustees for the building shareholders in their lease of 20 December 1661, but his status in this

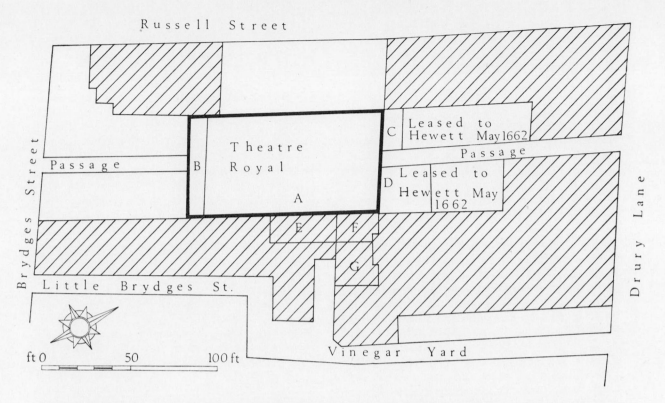

Fig. 1. Site plan, 1661–1748. Based on leases and fee-farm grants in Greater London Record Office. Hatched areas represent land sold by the Earls of Bedford before 1661. Unhatched areas represent land owned by the Earls and Dukes of Bedford

A Site leased for theatre, 20 December 1661 (marked with thick line)
B Yard of first theatre
C Hall

D Sparrow's Nest
E (? Great) Scene Room
F (? Little) Scene Room
G Green Room

second lease is uncertain. However, it seems likely that he was again serving as trustee for the building shareholders.[9] Little is known about what use was made of this site other than that by June 1663 several of the building shareholders and/or actors held a sub-lease of part of it, where then stood several newly built messuages.[10] In a sub-lease of the theatre granted in June 1683 by the building shareholders to Charles Davenant, Thomas Betterton and William Smith[11] the length of the playhouse is given as 140 feet, that is eastwards 28 feet beyond the 112-foot-long curtilage of the theatre site itself. As there is no evidence that the theatre building had been extended eastward, it seems probable that part at least of this second plot was used in conjunction with the theatre even from this early date; but it was not an integral part of the playhouse, and when the

ground lease to Hewett expired in 1702 the second Duke of Bedford granted the new lease not to the building shareholders but to Christopher Rich, who was then managing the affairs of the theatre. This lease states that five houses and other buildings then stood on this eastern plot, and that the passage from Drury Lane to the theatre still extended through the middle of the site.[12]

A lease plan of 1710 shows the plot marked C on fig. 1 (which was later used as a hall to the theatre, see Plate 6) as 'let to players'.[13] By 1739 the plot marked D on fig. 1 was in the tenure of Charles Fleetwood, who was then in control of the theatre.[14] This was then known as the Sparrow's Nest (probably because a John Sparrow had occupied it in the 1670's),[15] and was used for a wardrobe.[16]

It has previously been assumed that the extra

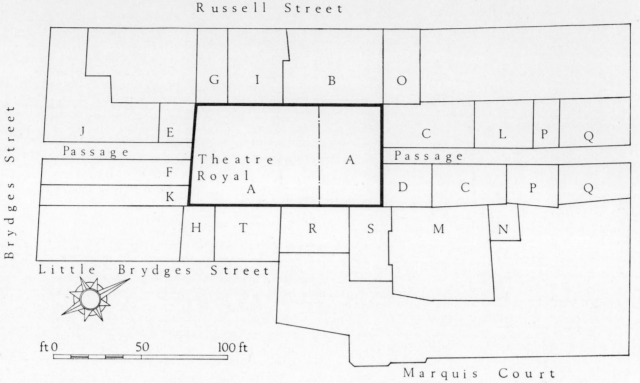

Fig. 2. Site plan, 1748–78. Based on leases and plan of 1778 in Greater London Record Office. The broken line denotes the position of the frontispiece, 1778. By 1778 the whole of the passage from plot A to Drury Lane had been built over

28 feet at the east end of the theatre mentioned in the sub-lease of 1683 (see above) was taken up by a scene room which therefore measured 28 feet by 58 feet.[17] This is not the case; the site of the scene room was on the south side of the theatre on ground the fee farm of which had been sold by the fourth Earl of Bedford in 1635 to Henry Wicks.[18] In about 1662–4 John Higden, who had acquired this fee farm from Wicks,[19] leased part of his ground, of unknown dimensions, to eight of the actors for a term of forty years at an annual rent of £30. In 1684 Higden's son was the defendant in a Chancery suit in which he recited the lease granted by his father to the actors and mentioned that 'the Scene Roome ... did and does stand upon this defendant's father's land'.[20]

In 1683 the actors were ejected from the scene room for failure to pay the rent, and the property (rebuilt after the fire of 1672) was then leased for nineteen years to the directors of the new united company of actors—Charles Killigrew, Charles

Davenant and their principal associates.[20] In 1714 when William Collier, then the sub-lessee and chief manager of the theatre, held the lease of the scene room, it was described as the 'Great Scene Room' (? E on fig. 1) and the 'Little Scene Room'[21] (? F on fig. 1). The plan of c. 1748 reproduced on Plate 6 marks plots E and F as 'taken into the playhouse'. It also marks plot G on fig. 1 as the Green Room, which could be entered from either Little Brydges Street or Vinegar Yard.

Between 1748 and 1791 there was considerable piecemeal expansion of the site of the theatre. In 1748 the fourth Duke of Bedford renewed the ground lease of the playhouse itself (A on fig. 2) to David Garrick and James Lacy for a term of twenty-one years commencing at Christmas 1753. This new lease also included a number of adjoining buildings and houses: three in Russell Street against the north side of the theatre (B), of which the one at the east end was turned into a side entrance to the theatre; six houses in the passage to Drury Lane (C), including a hall to the theatre and the Sparrow's Nest (D); and three houses in the passage to Brydges Street (E and F). These buildings were let for a variety of terms according to when the current leases fell in, but the lease of the whole site was calculated to expire on 25 December 1774; the rent increased as the various buildings became vacant, reaching the maximum of £210 per annum on 25 December 1759.[22]

It was probably about this time, 1748–9, that Garrick and Lacy also acquired the leases of two properties adjoining the theatre which did not belong to the Duke of Bedford. These were a house in Russell Street (G on fig. 2) which is shown on the plan of c. 1748 (Plate 6) as containing a passage to the playhouse and was probably used for the new passage to the boxes made in 1750: and a house in Little Brydges Street (H on fig. 2) which is shown on the same plan as containing two passages into the theatre.[23]

In 1749 the Duke of Bedford granted Garrick and Lacy a lease of two more houses in Russell Street (I on fig. 2) between those they already had.[24] Three years later, in 1752, a new passage into the theatre from Brydges Street (F) was opened on the south side of the old passage.[25] In 1753 Garrick and Lacy obtained a lease of the Rose Tavern on the corner of Russell Street and Brydges Street (J on fig. 2) from the Duke of Bedford.[26]

In 1762 Garrick and Lacy decided to make some substantial alterations to the playhouse and applied to the fourth Duke of Bedford's son, the Marquess of Tavistock, who then possessed a life interest in the property, for a renewal of the lease. The new lease, dated 24 March 1762,[27] extended the site at either end (K and L on fig. 2) and granted a reversionary term of twenty-one years from 25 December 1774 of the theatre and all other buildings leased by the Bedfords to Lacy and Garrick in or since 1748 (A–J excluding G and H on fig. 2). The fine was £2,100 and the new rent £350 per annum from Lady Day 1775.

By this time the Dukes of Bedford were occasionally buying back the fee farms of some of the property which their predecessors had sold in the seventeenth century, and in 1764 the plot marked M on fig. 2, which had been sold in 1642, was repurchased.[28] Two years later the Marquess of Tavistock leased it to Garrick and Lacy for a term expiring at Christmas 1795—the date of expiry of all the other plots in lease to them.[29] This site was later used for scene rooms and a 'Lamp lighting' room.[30] Later in the same year, 1766, Garrick and Lacy also acquired from Jeremiah Percy, plumber, a sub-lease of the adjoining small plot marked N.[31]

In 1775–6 the theatre was altered and embellished to the designs of Robert Adam, and these improvements occasioned the acquisition of yet more property. In 1775 Garrick bought the fee farm of the Ben Jonson's Head Tavern in Russell Street[32] (plot O on fig. 2), 'for the Better accommodation of the said Theatre' and the joint use of himself and Willoughby Lacy. This house was used as a box-office lobby.[33]

The most striking of the alterations made in 1775 was the erection in Brydges Street of an imposing façade (Plate 8) to the two existing parallel passages which gave access to the theatre. On either side of these passages were situated the 'Chair Room', the treasurer's office and a number of lobbies. Some of the more recently acquired buildings surrounding the theatre itself may also have been renovated at this time.[30]

The plan of 1778 reproduced on Plate 7 and redrawn on fig. 3 shows the theatre divided into three parts—the west part, 'from Frontispiece to outside of West Wall, which includes Boxes, Pitt and Gallerys, with the Orchestra and part of the Stage before the Curtain'; the middle part, from 'the Shutter home to the Frontispiece'; and the east part, 'with the two Closets home to the Shutter'. This plan also shows that the theatre had been considerably lengthened since its original erection in 1672–4, for the east wall now stood some 100 feet east of the site of Wren's east wall. Some of this lengthening had probably taken place before 1775—perhaps in 1762.

In May 1776 the site was again extended eastwards towards Drury Lane. This extension was more difficult to achieve because the freehold of the land (P and Q on fig. 2) between Drury Lane and that leased by the Marquess of Tavistock to Garrick and Lacy in 1762 did not belong to the Duke but to one Arthur Jones.* On 1 May 1776 Garrick and Lacy leased to Jones the passage, which had been excepted out of the fifth Earl of

---

* The fee farm of plots P and Q had been sold by the fifth Earl of Bedford in 1656; the freehold was repurchased by the eleventh Duke of Bedford in 1895.[34]

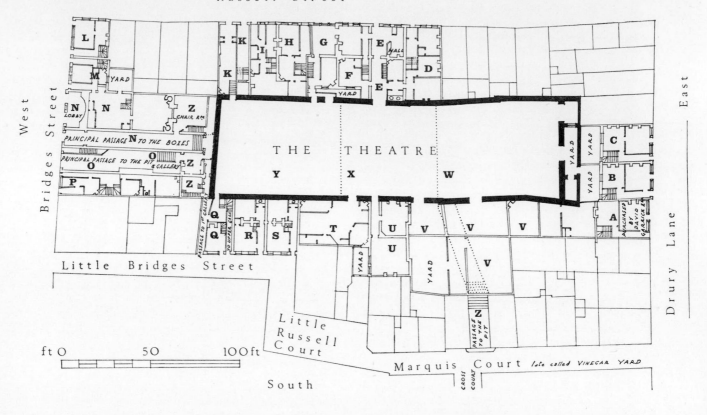

Fig. 3. Site plan, 1778. Redrawn from the plan reproduced on Plate 7

Key

A William Smith now Hughes, house belonging to the Fund
B Jane Garland and Richard Brusby
C William Bayless
    Russell Street
D Thomas Fosbrook. Box Book keeper
E Hall and Entrance in the Theatre
F William Kirk. Housekeeper
G Ditto and dressing-rooms over
H William Pope
I Yearley Waterer
K Francis Heath with the Box passage
    Bridges Street
L Richard Newton
M Ditto next
N John Harrison and the principal passage to the Boxes
O Inmates over and the principal passage to the Pit and Gallery
P Thomas Parsonage

    Little Bridges Street
Q Charlotte Jones with passages to the First and Upper Gallerys
R John Aickin
S Isaac Abrahams
T Property Room, Matted room and Carpenters Hall Building
U Old Green room and New Green room Building
V Scene rooms and Lamplighting room
    The Theatre
W East part with the two Closets home to the Shuttter
X Middle part from the Shutter home to the Frontispiece
Y West part from Frontispiece to outside of West wall, which includes Boxes, Pit and Gallerys with the Orchestra and part of the Stage before the Curtain
Z Treasury. Gallery Staircases and Lobbys from the West Wall of Theatre home to the Rose Tavern and long Passage to the Pit from Marquis Court

(Inscribed) September 1778. J Hele
                          Charlotte Street
                          Pancras

Pencil note written on plots B and C: 'This Plan is certainly wrong as far as relates to Mr. Macnamara, it not shewing it correctly. Ground is not in the Shape here represented. A. R. Brown March 1813.'

Bedford's original grant of the fee farm in 1656, and which still bisected plots P and Q. On 2 May 1776 Jones leased to the Duchess of Bedford (guardian of her grandson, the fifth Duke, who was still a minor) the plots marked P, together with the passage between them, which he had just acquired from Garrick and Lacy. On the following day the Duchess leased the same plots (P), and the passage between them, back to Garrick and Lacy for a term expiring at Christmas 1795.[35] The proprietors of the theatre no longer required the passage from Drury Lane into the theatre, 'a more commodious Passage' having recently been made to it from Marquis Court (see Plate 7). Part of plot P was used for two out-buildings one of which housed the fire engine, and the other was intended to store the organ used in oratorios.[36]

In December 1776 Garrick and Lacy purchased the leases of the two adjoining plots to the east, marked Q. The ground between the two halves of plot Q was described as 'Formerly old Passage to said Theatre . . . with all Tenements . . . afterwards Built or erected Thereon'.[37]

Meanwhile, the lease of the enlarged 'Great Scene Room' (marked R on fig. 2), and of the 'Little Scene Room' (S), the latter now known (probably after rebuilding) as the 'New Scene Room', had been renewed in 1771 to Garrick and James Lacy by Samuel Wegg, the owner of the fee farm. This lease also included both the adjoining plot to the west, marked T, where stood two houses in Little Brydges Street,[38] and the house on plot H. It is not known when the houses on plot T first came into Garrick and Lacy's possession.

Between 1776 and 1791 no additions were made to the site of Drury Lane Theatre. By the latter year both Drury Lane and Covent Garden theatres had become too small to provide for the needs of the increasing London audience and the demand for a third London theatre was growing. Rather than yield to this attack upon his monopoly position Sheridan, who was now the principal proprietor of Drury Lane, sought to forestall the opposition by building a very much larger theatre. For this he needed a bigger site, but even after the various additions made to the site since 1748

the basic difficulty remained—the theatre was still largely hemmed in by ground not belonging to the Dukes of Bedford. It was clearly desirable that the site of the new theatre should not be in several separate ownerships, and accordingly in 1789–90 Sheridan requested the fifth Duke of Bedford to purchase those pieces of ground which would be required and to grant a new ground lease of the enlarged site so formed.[39] The Duke agreed to co-operate, and by the summer of 1791 he had either bought or contracted for most of the properties required. On 30 July 1791 he agreed with Sheridan and Linley that he would before Christmas 1795 grant them a ninety-nine-year lease of all the ground which they wanted. This ground is shown in fig. 4. In order to complete the unification of ownership of the site Sheridan and Linley agreed to sell to the Duke their fee farm of the Ben Jonson's Head in Russell Street (A on fig. 4), which Garrick had bought in 1775.* The lease was to commence at Christmas 1795, the date of expiry of the current ground lease of the site of the existing theatre.[41] On 6 August 1791 the fifth Duke granted Sheridan and Linley a short lease expiring at Christmas 1795 of those pieces of ground of which the conveyances to him had by then been completed.[42]

In the event the Duke did not succeed in purchasing part of one plot in Drury Lane which he had covenanted to buy. The purchase of the free-hold of plot B on fig. 4 was held up by legal difficulties, but as this ground was occupied by old houses in Drury Lane whose site was not immediately required for the rebuilding of the theatre, this delay had no great significance. Ultimately plot B was bought by the theatre proprietors' trustees in 1807, and sold by them to the sixth Duke in 1812.[43]

In the agreement of 30 July 1791 Sheridan and Linley covenanted to rebuild the theatre and to erect new houses on those parts of the site which were not occupied by the theatre itself.† The agreement states that these building works were to be carried out in accordance with the designs prepared by Henry Holland and which had already been approved by the fifth Duke.[41] Shortage of money prevented Sheridan and Linley from fulfilling the whole of their covenant, and the land

* The conveyance of the fee farm of the site of the Ben Jonson's Head to the Duke did not in fact take place until 1814.[40]
† They also covenanted to allow the fifth Duke to choose a box for his own use free of charge—a privilege which had been enjoyed by the Dowager Duchess since at least 1762. The Duke chose the first box next to the stage on the King's side in the second tier.[44] The later history of the ducal box is described on page 38n.

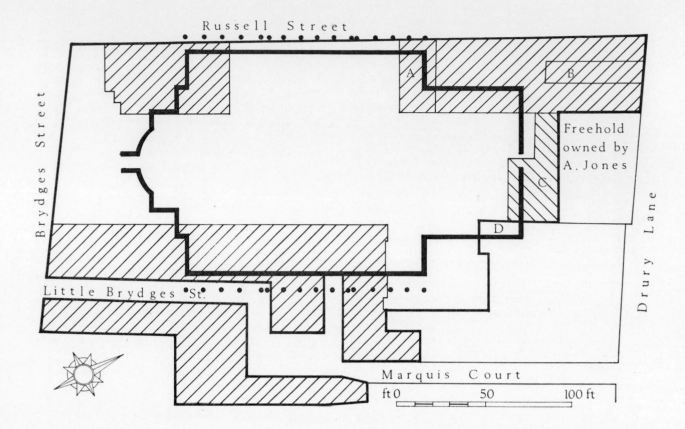

Fig. 4. Site plan, 1791–1809. Based on leases and plans in Greater London Record Office

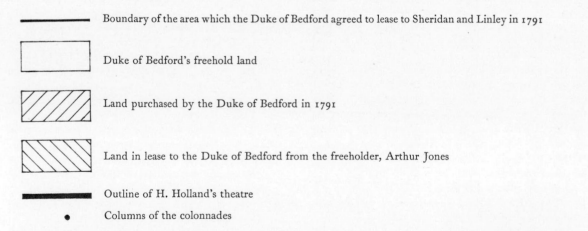

————————   Boundary of the area which the Duke of Bedford agreed to lease to Sheridan and Linley in 1791

Duke of Bedford's freehold land

Land purchased by the Duke of Bedford in 1791

Land in lease to the Duke of Bedford from the freeholder, Arthur Jones

━━━━━━   Outline of H. Holland's theatre

●   Columns of the colonnades

The small plot D within the walls of the theatre but outside the boundary of the agreed site was already held by Sheridan and Linley under a lease granted by Jeremiah Percy to Garrick and Lacy in 1766 (N on fig. 2)

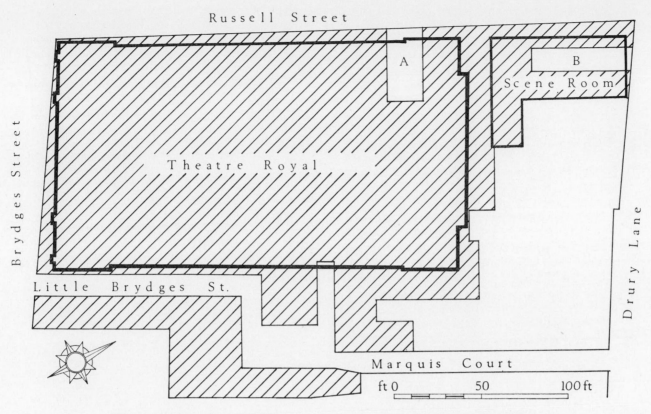

Fig. 5. Site plan, 1812–20. Based on lease plan of 1812 in Greater London Record Office

——————— Outline of Wyatt's theatre

Land leased to the Company of Proprietors by the sixth Duke of Bedford in 1812

at the corner of Russell Street and Brydges Street remained vacant until after the burning of the theatre in 1809 (Plate 21b). Because of their failure to meet their obligations the Duke refused to execute the new ground lease which he had undertaken to grant to Sheridan and Linley, though he continued to receive his rent under the terms of the agreement of 30 July 1791.

The old playhouse closed its doors on 4 June 1791, and the first performance in the new house took place on 12 March 1794.

Fig. 4 shows that Holland's theatre as actually built was not completely restricted to land owned by the fifth Duke of Bedford, for a small piece of the stage was built upon ground which had been leased to the Duchess of Bedford in 1776 by the

then owner of the freehold, Arthur Jones (see page 35). According to Holland's nephew, Henry Rowles, writing in 1815, this mistake occurred because Holland had been misled by the plan of 1778 of Garrick's theatre (reproduced on Plate 7), which purported to show all the ground then occupied by the theatre as being in the ownership of the Duke of Bedford. Even the lawyers were confused, for in the agreement of 30 July 1791 the Duke had covenanted *inter alia* to lease plot C on fig. 4 for a term expiring in 1894, although his own term in it only extended to 1844. In 1800 more of the land owned by Jones was used for the erection of a large carpenter's shop, measuring 60 feet by 20 feet, at the east end of the theatre. This was built by

Mr. John Jackson of Pimlico, upon a platform about ten feet above the ground and on the same level as the stage, for which it was sometimes used as an extension.[45]

As the Duke of Bedford held the ground lease of plot C on fig. 4 from the freeholder, Arthur Jones, the existence of this divided ownership of the freehold of the site of the theatre did not present any problems until the destruction of Holland's theatre by fire on the night of 24 February 1809. But when the present Theatre Royal, Drury Lane, was built in 1811–12, to the designs of Benjamin Dean Wyatt, no part of it stood on Jones's land, which was now owned by a Mr. Macnamara. The latter was left with the ruins of the now useless carpenter's shop and a small part of the old theatre, and he therefore claimed damages for contravention of the lease

against his tenant, the sixth Duke of Bedford. A jury in the Court of King's Bench found for the plaintiff and in 1815 the Duke's steward reported that £1,100 had been paid to Macnamara for the damages awarded to him.[46]

The new theatre was already nearly completed when, on 11 July 1812, the sixth Duke of Bedford granted a new ground lease to the joint-stock company, the Theatre Royal Drury Lane Company of Proprietors, which had been responsible for the rebuilding, for a term expiring at Christmas 1894.[47*] The ground granted by this lease is shown on fig. 5. The plot there marked A, formerly the Ben Jonson's Head (the freehold of which had been bought from Sheridan by the Company of Proprietors and sold to the Duke of Bedford in March 1814) was the subject of a separate lease made to the company in July 1814,

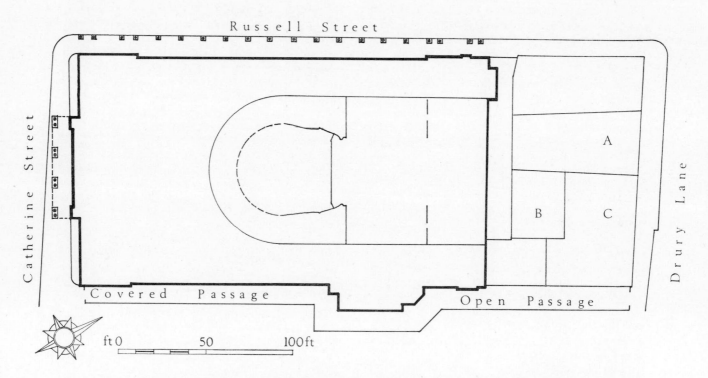

Fig. 6. Site plan, 1903. Based on lease plan of 1903 in Greater London Record Office

* Under the terms of the lease the box in the first tier immediately next the stage, with a lobby, ante-room and a private entrance in Russell Street, was reserved for the sole use of the Dukes of Bedford during the whole term of the lease without any payment.[47] A similar clause appears in subsequent leases. In the lease of 1900 to Theatre Royal Drury Lane Limited the lessees had in addition to employ at their own cost an attendant to look after the box.[48] When the eleventh Duke sold the Covent Garden estate in 1918 he retained his box at Drury Lane subject to his paying a rent of £400 per annum to the purchaser.[49] He eventually gave up the right to the box in 1940.[50]

also for a term expiring at Christmas 1894.[51] The plot marked B on fig. 5 (the freehold of which had been bought by the theatre proprietors' trustees in 1807 and sold to the Duke in 1812) was also the subject of a separate lease to the company in January 1813, again for a term expiring at Christmas 1894.[52] In 1814 the present two-storey building had been erected on this and the adjoining ground at the corner of Russell Street and Drury Lane; it was originally used as a scene room.[53]

On the south side of the theatre there remained some vacant land between the theatre and the north side of Little Brydges Street and Marquis Court (formerly Vinegar Yard). In 1824 this was enclosed by a wall and iron railings and a number of outbuildings were subsequently erected there.[54] The houses on the south side of Little Brydges Street and Marquis Court which had been included in the lease of 1812 were sublet to supplement the company's income.[55] When the ground lease of 1812 expired in 1894 the new lease of the theatre granted by the eleventh Duke of Bedford did not include any property on the south side of Little Brydges Street.

The final alterations to the curtilage of the theatre were made in 1897–1903. As part of his agreement with the eleventh Duke in 1897[56] Arthur Collins, the lessee, undertook to make a narrow private passage extending along the whole of the south side of the theatre and to enclose it with the high wall which now separates this passage from the blocks of flats later built on the north side of the extension of Tavistock Street. In compensation for the resultant loss of some buildings on the south side of the theatre Collins was given permission to rebuild the property room and paint-shop (A and B on fig. 6) at the east end of the theatre, with a front to Drury Lane. This agreement was subsequently taken over by the present company, Theatre Royal Drury Lane Limited,[57] which completed the work and in December 1900 obtained from the Duke a lease embodying these alterations to the site.[58] At the same time the company also obtained a separate lease of Nos. 67–70 (consec.) Drury Lane,[59] C on fig. 6, which had been rebuilt in 1899–1900 to the designs of P. E. Pilditch.[60] In 1903 both these leases were surrendered and the Duke granted a new lease of the whole site for a term expiring in 1977.[61] The company thus obtained possession of all the premises between the east end of the theatre and Drury Lane, and thereby concluded the process of piecemeal enlargement of the site which had been going on ever since the building of the first theatre there in 1662–3.

CHAPTER IV

The Theatre Royal, Drury Lane:
the Buildings

THE BRYDGES STREET PLAYHOUSE OF 1663

Unlike the Duke's Theatre in Dorset Garden, which can be visualized from contemporary external and internal views, the first Theatre Royal in Brydges Street seems to have gone unrecorded except for a few passages of description by contemporary writers. Despite the extensive researches of theatrical historians, the only known facts concern the site in the Riding Yard, a quadrangle measuring 112 feet in length east to west, and 58 to 59 feet in width. Closely hemmed in by built-up properties on all sides, it was approached from Brydges Street by a passage, 10 feet wide, entering centrally on the west side, and by a corresponding passage from Drury Lane on the east. Hollar's map of London's western suburbs (Plate 1a) gives a clear bird's-eye view of the Riding Yard and the entrance passage between the Brydges Street houses. The exact dimensions of the theatre building are not known, but there was an entrance court, 10 feet wide, extending before its west front.

On 8 May 1663, the day following the opening, Samuel Pepys attended a performance at the new theatre. He noted that 'The house is made with extraordinary good contrivance, and yet hath some faults, as the narrowness of the passages in and out of the pitt, and the distance from the stage to the boxes, which I am confident cannot hear; but for all other things it is well, only, above all, the musique being below, and most of it sounding under the very stage, there is no hearing of the bases at all, nor very well of the trebles, which sure must be mended'. To Pepys's account must be added the (freely translated) comments of M. de Monconys, visiting the theatre on 22 May 1663, who thought it to be the most proper and most beautiful he had ever seen, much of it lined with green baize. The boxes were dressed with bands of gilt leather, and the benches of the pit, where persons of quality resorted, were ranged in the form of an amphi-theatre, each higher than the one in front.[1] A later entry in Pepys's diary[2] shows that rain and hail, as well as light and air, were admitted to the auditorium, presumably through a lantern-cupola similar to the one that rose from the leaded platform above the roof of the Duke's Theatre in Dorset Garden, opened in 1671 and reputedly designed by Wren. On 19 March 1665/6 Pepys walked to the theatre, then closed because of the plague, and found it 'all in dirt, they being altering the stage to make it wider'. The last informative comments on the building, made before its destruction by fire in January 1671/2, are those of Lorenzo Magalotti, recording the visit of Duke Cosmo III of Tuscany on 25 April 1669. 'This theatre is nearly of a circular form, surrounded, in the inside, by boxes separated from each other, and divided into several rows of seats, for the greater accommodation of the ladies and gentlemen, who, in conformity with the freedom of the country, sit together indiscriminately; a large space being left on the ground floor for the rest of the audience.'[3]

Several theatre historians, including Professor Edward A. Langhans,[4] have seen a possible connexion between the above-quoted descriptions of the 1663 playhouse, and an unsigned and undated sketch design for an unnamed theatre, volume IV no. 81 in the Wren Drawings at All Souls College, Oxford (Plate 4). This design comprises a geometrically set-out plan, a sketch longitudinal section, and a sketch perspective of the forestage and proscenium. Neither scale nor dimensions are given, but as it can be reasonably assumed that the benches are spaced 2 feet back to back, as in most contemporary and many later playhouses, the plan is contained in an oblong 'shell' having an internal width of 40 feet and a length of 90 feet, almost equally divided between stage and auditorium. The plan is of great interest as an attempt to combine in a Restoration playhouse some of the essential features of an antique Roman theatre, and it demonstrates a knowledge of Vitruvius and

Palladio. The scheme is based on a circle of about 36 feet diameter, placed centrally in the oblong shell. One half of the circle defines the line of a raised barrier dividing the pit from the amphitheatre, while the other half encloses the forestage and is broken by a 20 foot-wide proscenium opening. The pit is furnished with seven semi-circular rows of benches, leaving space for a semi-circular 'orchestra' of only 6 feet diameter, which would certainly have resulted in some of the musicians being placed 'under the very stage', as criticized by Pepys. According to the sketch section, the pit benches are stepped at the relatively shallow rake of 15 degrees, whereas the seven segmental rows of amphitheatre benches are more steeply pitched at 30 degrees. At the back of the amphitheatre, at the same rake, is a circle of five boxes, or loges, with five rows of benches. Behind the boxes is a small foyer or corridor, flanked by staircases which, presumably, serve the amphitheatre and boxes as well as the gallery. The latter, with seven or eight rows of benches, rests on columns in front of the boxes and extends to the front wall of the shell.

A curious feature of the plan is the indication of an enclosure or dais, about 5 feet square, either railed in or surrounded with a wide step, placed centrally and breaking the barrier between the pit and the amphitheatre. This has been generally identified as 'His Majesty's Box', but as it is linked by parallel lines extending from the foyer to the orchestra, it could be interpreted as a vomitory for entering the pit. Above this enclosure, the section shows a suspended object, thought by Hamilton Bell[5] to indicate a canopy or else a corona of lights, or even a central light shaft rising through the roof void. Langhans favours the idea of a corona, but there is also the possibility of its being a horizontal shutter which could be drawn up to close the lantern-cupola, the existence of which is hinted at by Pepys.

The segmentally curved screens flanking the proscenium and forming the sides of the forestage have puzzled most commentators. Each screen is shown on the plan as a series of five small equilateral triangles, impinging so as to present an apparently unbroken face towards the audience. Recalling Magalotti's description, Bell and Langhans see these triangles as a crude representation of boxes, perhaps with proscenium doors below. They are, however, almost certainly 'periaktoi', or centrally pivoted triangular wings which,

turned simultaneously, could rapidly present the three changes of scene appropriate to tragedy, comedy, or the satirical play. As the uncurtained forestage would be the main acting area, 'periaktoi' would offer the best means of changing the scene there, while wings, shutters and drops would be used on the back stage. Furthermore, it was known that these 'periaktoi' were used in similar positions flanking the stage of the Theatre of Marcellus, the influence of which can be seen in this 'Wren' plan. It is true that the sketch section and proscenium view show tiers of arches, suggestive of a Roman theatre exterior, but these could represent the formal 'palace' setting for classical tragedy. The ceiling over the forestage is shown as a flared elliptical arch, serving as a sounding board and, perhaps, painted as a cloudy sky.

The difference between the dimensions of the Riding Yard and those of the 'Wren' plan can be accounted for, since the plan shows only the interior arrangement of the oblong shell, and takes no account of wall thicknesses, nor any side passage or passages, open or covered. No tiring rooms, offices, or scene rooms are shown within the shell, and it is known that there was a 10-foot wide forecourt to the west of the entrance front. Nevertheless, the only evidence relating this design to the 1663 theatre lies in identifying the features delineated with those described by Pepys, de Monconys, and Magalotti. Against this must be set the fact that nothing is known connecting Wren with the project, and it might be thought more reasonable to assume that the King's Company would have turned to John Webb for the design of their new playhouse. The greatly experienced Webb had already reconstructed the Cockpit-in-Court, Whitehall Palace, where the company sometimes performed, and in 1665 he was engaged in remodelling the Great Hall in Whitehall Palace for use as a theatre. The internal dimensions of this hall were nearly the same as those of the 'Wren' shell,[6] and this raises the question as to whether the 'Wren' plan is not, after all, a proposal for a further remodelling of the Hall. Although the seating arrangements proposed might seem more appropriate to a public playhouse than a court theatre, it is recorded that the public were sometimes admitted by payment to the Hall theatre.[7]

It is not impossible that the first Theatre Royal was built, if not designed, by Richard Ryder, the previous tenant of the Riding Yard, a speculative builder of some note who was living from at least 1659 to 1663 in a house on the south side of Russell Street adjoining the Riding Yard. From 1671, or perhaps even from as early as 1660, until 1682 he was surveyor to the fifth Earl of Bedford, the ground landlord of the theatre, and as the King's Master Carpenter, from 1668 to 1683, he would have been engaged on various theatrical projects. He is known, for instance, to have constructed the elaborate scenery designed by Robert Streeter for *Calisto*, produced at the Hall theatre in 1675.[8]

Before leaving discussion of the 'Wren' plan, it must be remarked that the amphitheatrical arrangement of the seating closely resembles that of Vanbrugh's Haymarket Opera House of 1703.

Ogilby and Morgan's map of 1681–2 (Plate 1b) shows on the Theatre Royal site a building which Professor Langhans accepts as a possible representation of one side of the 1663 theatre. The building depicted is of two storeys, the upper one with widely spaced windows. A steeply pitched roof rises to a flat, in the centre of which is a low saucer dome crowned with a finial. The symmetry of the elevation and the central position of the dome would be more appropriate to the exposed west front than the side, which abutting properties would largely have concealed. The 'grass strip' to the north of the elevation is not a path, as Professor Langhans thinks, but is an indication of the gardens behind the Russell Street houses. The value of this particular representation as architectural evidence is very doubtful, though more positive than that of similar 'views' on later maps, generally based on Ogilby and Morgan.

After a relatively brief existence, the first Theatre Royal was destroyed by fire on 25 January 1671/2.

THE PLAYHOUSE OF 1674

Although Dryden, in his prologue for the opening performance, described the new Theatre Royal as a 'Plain built House . . . a bare Convenience only' with a 'mean ungilded Stage', these somewhat deprecatory remarks were probably intended to divert critics from making comparisons with the larger and more lavishly decorated

Duke's Theatre in Dorset Garden. There can be little doubt that the new playhouse was altogether superior, as well as costlier than its predecessor on the same site. Its cost, variously estimated at sums between £3,500 and £4,400, seems to preclude any suggestion that the new building incorporated the galleried western part of the old auditorium, which Leslie Hotson thinks may have escaped the fire of 1671/2.[9] The little that is known of its design is contained in Henri Misson's (translated) description of the Dorset Garden and Drury Lane theatres in about 1698. 'There are two Theatres at London, one large and handsome, where they sometimes act Opera's, and sometimes Plays; the other something smaller, which is only for Plays. The Pit is an Amphitheatre, fill'd with Benches without Backboards, and adorn'd and cover'd with green Cloth. Men of Quality, particularly the younger Sort, some Ladies of Reputation and Vertue, and abundance of Damsels that hunt for Prey, sit all together in this Place, Higgledy-piggledy, chatter, toy, play, hear, hear not. Farther up, against the Wall, under the first Gallery, and just opposite to the Stage, rises another Amphitheater, which is taken up by Persons of the best Quality, among whom are generally very few Men. The Galleries, whereof there are only two Rows, are fill'd with none but ordinary People, particularly the Upper one.'[10] As the audience was seated on undivided benches, it is not possible to determine the capacity of the house from box-office receipts, but it is generally assumed that attendance varied from about five hundred to one thousand. As to the decorations of the auditorium, a reference in Dryden's first-night epilogue to 'the Poets' Heads' is perhaps confirmed by D'Urfey's verse[11]—

'He saw each Box with Beauty crown'd,
    And Pictures deck the Structure round;
Ben, Shakespear, and the learn'd Rout,
    With Noses some, and some without'.*

The design of the new playhouse is traditionally ascribed to Wren, although there is apparently no documentary proof of this. It is, however, noteworthy that Colley Cibber, criticizing some alterations made around 1690, says 'it were but Justice to lay the original Figure, which Sir Christopher Wren gave it'.[12] The tradition was strengthened

* Earlier in his poem D'Urfey describes the theatre as standing 'Upon the Bank of Thame and Isis', and it is therefore possible that these lines refer to Dorset Garden, not Drury Lane.

in 1913, when Hamilton Bell published his reasons for identifying a drawing in the Wren collection at All Souls College, Oxford (Plate 5a), as a longitudinal section through the 1674 playhouse.[5] Except in matters of detail, Bell's findings have never been seriously questioned, and they are partly confirmed by other evidence.

Simply titled 'Playhouse', and bearing a drawn scale, the Wren section shows a substantially built shell measuring about 112 feet in length, excluding the crowning cornice. This length is identical with that of the Riding Yard site, and an equally appropriate width of some 58 feet can be deduced from the slopes of the hipped mansard roof, assuming the probability of a central ridge. From the pit passage and cellar-floor level, some 2 feet 6 inches below ground, the 3 feet thick walls of the shell rise 36 feet to the top of the crowning cornice. Above this is a mansard roof, some 21 feet high and hipped at each end, of which no constructional details are shown. About 8 feet 6 inches inside from the (presumed) west front wall is an inner wall, some 15 inches thick and almost certainly curved on plan, dividing the three storeys of entrance lobbies from the auditorium, and giving support to the joists of the floors and galleries. On the longitudinal axis, it would appear that a ramped approach (in the passage from Brydges Street) leads up to a short flight of five steps ascending through the main doorway into the entrance lobby, where three more steps rise to the back gangway of the amphitheatre. At the (presumed) north and south ends of the entrance lobby are dog-legged staircases, 3 feet 6 inches wide, one flight descending to the pit passages and the other ascending to the lobbies of the first and second galleries.

The auditorium, scaling some 53 feet in length from the back wall to the curtain line, contains an amphitheatre and two galleries above, overlooking a pit and deep forestage flanked by two tiers of boxes. The amphitheatre and galleries alike are 11 feet deep, and have four rows of backless benches raised from steppings 2 feet wide, those of the amphitheatre pitched at 20 degrees, and those of both galleries at 35 degrees. Each gallery is supported by a range of six slender Doric columns rising from the front bench of the tier below, the front gangway and parapet being cantilevered on scroll trusses projecting above the columns. The height of the openings between the tier parapets is only 6 feet, and the headroom at the back of the second gallery is little more than 5 feet. Some 2 feet below the amphitheatre front gangway is the pit, 22 feet deep, with a floor slope of about 9 degrees towards the bowed front of the forestage. The pit's ten rows of backless benches, spaced 2 feet back to back, are reached by passages below the side boxes, leading to doors flanking the front row.

A striking change in the architectural scale of the design is produced by the monumental treatment of the screen walls forming the auditorium sides. Each is divided into four bays by a giant order of Corinthian plain-shafted pilasters, supporting an entablature having a moulded architrave, plain frieze, and scroll-modillioned cornice. The pedestal-like parapets of the amphitheatre and first gallery are continued between the pilasters to divide the bays into two tiers, the lower consisting of two boxes overlooking the pit, and two proscenium doors opening to the forestage. In the upper tier of four boxes the openings are dressed with elliptical arches having moulded architraves, broken by ornamental keyblocks and rising from cornice imposts above plain jambs. While the general treatment of these Corinthian screen walls very probably derived from Jacob van Campen's Amsterdam Schouwburg of 1638,[13] they are designed here to be constructed in false perspective so that the bays, pilasters and entablature diminish in height and width as they approach the inner or scene stage. The vanishing point of this perspective is some 110 feet beyond the curtain line, and level with the floor of the upper tier of boxes. A second pilaster, perhaps on a different plane, marks the proscenium, but the form of the arch or head of the opening is not resolved on this drawing, nor is there any clear indication of the ceiling over the main auditorium, which logic suggests would be flat and gently canted to accord with the rise of the Corinthian cornice.[*]

Measured from the curtain line, the forestage projects 20 feet into the auditorium, its front being formed 'in a semi-oval Figure, parallel to the Benches of the Pit',[12] and only 32 feet distant from the back wall of the auditorium. The

---

[*] The drawing shows no sign of 'the Poets' heads', which might have taken the form of painted trompe l'œil busts on the upper-box parapets, or even as modelled busts placed above the Corinthian entablature, after the manner of the busts surmounting the colonnaded side screens on the stage of the Amsterdam Schouwburg.

middle or scene stage, also 20 feet deep, is shown furnished with four sets of wings and three shutters, all designed to give a much steeper perspective effect than the Corinthian screens of the side boxes. The back stage, 25 feet deep, used for deep vista effects and for storage of scenes and properties, is overhung by two storeys of tiring rooms, the first projecting 10 feet and the second 20 feet from the back wall of the shell. These tiring rooms and offices are presumably reached by staircases which, with the stage-level tiring rooms, reduce the width of the back stage. The floor of the forestage and middle stage rises with a gentle slope to meet the level floor of the back stage.

The Wren section has provided the basis for several conjectural plans of the second Drury Lane theatre, of which at least three have been published—by Richard Leacroft in 1951,[14] Professor Edward A. Langhans in 1964,[15] and Bruce Koenig and Donald Mullin in 1967.[16] To the present writer, however, the fan-shaped auditorium plan evolved by Leacroft, with help and advice from Dr. Richard Southern, seems architecturally the most reasonable of the three, and Professor Langhans's parallel-sided auditorium the least convincing, perhaps because of its structural peculiarities arising from an all too strict adherence to Wren's section, where inconsistencies are obviously present. Koenig's plan effects a compromise between Leacroft and Langhans.

Leacroft's segmentally-curved amphitheatre and galleries are an acceptable interpretation of Wren's section in terms of contemporary construction, whereas Langhans's straight-fronted and wide-spanned tiers are not. The parallel ranges of side boxes, adopted by Langhans and Koenig, ignore one of the basic rules of building in perspective, exemplified in Borromini's Palazzo Spada gallery, in Bernini's Scala Regia, as well as in the streets of Scamozzi's scene in the Teatro Olimpico, where the distance between the two sides of the perspective decreases as the architectural elements decrease in height and width. Not only do the canted side boxes of Leacroft's plan observe this principle, but they demonstrate the probability that the second Drury Lane theatre provided the model for the fan-shaped auditoria of Edward Shepherd's Covent Garden theatre and Goodman's Fields theatre (both 1732) as well as influencing the partial remodelling in

1709 of Vanbrugh's Haymarket Opera House. Furthermore, the fan-shaped auditorium was retained or reverted to by Robert Adam, when he reconstructed Drury Lane in 1775–6. Finally there is some measure of comparative evidence to be found in the Theatre Royal, Bristol, built in 1766 after the model of Drury Lane as it then existed, somewhat altered but still retaining many original features dating from 1674. At Bristol, the two superimposed boxes on either side of the stage are flanked by giant Corinthian pilasters, canted away from the proscenium, and constructed with more than a mere suggestion of perspective in the lines of the box parapets and the architrave of the now incomplete entablature.

Several commentators have not hesitated to recognize a probable representation of Drury Lane's proscenium in the well-known frontispiece to the book of *Ariadne*, an opera by Pierre Perrin and Monsieur Grabut performed there in 1674. This engraving (Plate 5b) shows an architectural setting within a frame or proscenium formed of paired Corinthian pilasters, having fluted shafts and supporting fully modelled entablatures which are returned above the inside face of each inner pilaster, and then continued across the opening in what appears to be a painted valance. Beneath each pair of pilasters is a panelled pedestal containing a musical trophy, and between them projects the bowed apron of the stage, its front also decorated with a large trophy of masks and musical instruments. Despite obvious inaccuracies in the architectural details, and the absence of a deep forestage, the resemblance between the giant Corinthian order of the *Ariadne* frontispiece and that of the Wren drawing can be accepted as favourable evidence that the last is, in fact, a section of the second Drury Lane playhouse.

Before comparing the Wren section, and the conjectural plans made from it, with the drawings and engravings recording the 1674 playhouse as reconstructed in 1775–6 by Robert Adam, it is necessary to take account of the various changes made between those dates. According to Colley Cibber, writing around 1739 and describing the theatre prior to 1696, 'the Area, or Platform of the old Stage, projected about four Foot forwarder, in a Semi-oval Figure, parallel to the Benches of the Pit; and ...... the former, lower Doors of Entrance for the Actors, were brought down between the two foremost (and then only) Pilasters; in the Place of which Doors, now the two Stage-Boxes are fix't. That where the Doors of Entrance now are, there formerly stood two additional Side-Wings, in front of a ful set of Scenes . . . By this Original Form, the usual station of the Actors, in almost every Scene, was advanc'd at least ten Foot nearer to the Audience, than they now can be.'[12] Assuming that the Wren section does represent the 1674 theatre in its original form, Cibber's account may be taken to suggest that the auditorium had been altered before 1696, by curtailing the projection of the forestage, and eliminating all the giant Corinthian pilasters between the side boxes except those flanking the bay on either side of the proscenium. In 1696, it would appear that Christopher Rich further reduced the forestage, by 4 feet, and replaced the proscenium doors by stage boxes. A new proscenium, flanked by splayed faces each containing a proscenium door, was then constructed on the scene stage, eliminating the first set of wing grooves. This last change would have brought the new proscenium or frontispiece to a distance of 70 feet from the west front wall, in fact to the position shown on Hele's survey plan of 1778 (Plate 7). Furthermore, such an arrangement of upper and lower stage boxes flanked by giant pilasters, and a proscenium reveal containing stage doors, is to be seen at the Theatre Royal, Bristol.

Various improvements were carried out during Garrick's régime, beginning in 1747 with the enlargement of the first gallery and 'many other alterations much to advantage'.[17] In September 1750 a new entrance passage to the boxes was opened from Russell Street (marked K on the 1778 survey and G on fig. 2), and in November 1752 a passage from Brydges Street was opened for ladies arriving in coaches[18] (O on 1778 survey and F on fig. 2). The theatre was 'painted, gilded and decorated with new scenes &c' prior to re-opening in September 1753,[19] and in 1762 one of Garrick's major theatrical reforms was accomplished by increasing the seating capacity so as to accommodate all those patrons formerly permitted to sit or stand on the stage. The work involved by making this change was apparently directed by Garrick's partner James Lacy, who 'having a taste for architecture, he took upon himself the enlarging of the theatre'.[20] The interior was again redecorated before the 1771–2 season opened, and during the summer closure of 1775 it was extensively reconstructed by Robert Adam, re-opening on 23

September for what was to be Garrick's farewell season. According to the prompter, Hopkins, the first-night audience signified their approval of the new interior by 'Great applause to the House before the Curtain'.[19]

THE ADAM RECONSTRUCTION OF 1775

The transformation of the much altered 1674 theatre, effected by Robert Adam in 1775, is well recorded in contemporary descriptions, and the graphic evidence, though not extensive, is excellent. First in importance are the Adam–Pastorini engraved views of the new front (Plate 8) and the remodelled auditorium (Plate 9a), which form plates VI and VII of set V in *The Works in Architecture of Robert and James Adam*, volume II. In volume 14 of the Adam drawings in Sir John Soane's Museum, no. 17 is a coloured design for the auditorium ceiling, dated 1775 and as executed (Plate 10a); no. 16 is an alternative design dated 1776 (Plate 10b) and no. 85 in volume 27 is a design for the proscenium frame, dated 1775 and, on the evidence of later interior views, not executed (Plate 11a).

Discounting the false impression of its dimensions, produced by the introduction of undersized human figures, the Adam–Pastorini engraving of the interior gives a comprehensive view of the auditorium as it appeared from the stage. The projecting apron and the pit, with ten rows of benches, were flanked by three tiers of boxes, their straight parapets supported by slender square-shafted wooden columns spaced to form five bays, narrow and wide alternately. At the back of the pit was the slightly raised amphitheatre with, probably, nine rows of stepped benches divided transversely by low partitions into nine boxes, the middle one wider than the rest. Four columns, matching those dividing the side boxes, rose from breaks in the amphitheatre parapet to support the raking joists and parapet of the first gallery, with, probably, eleven rows of benches. Six equally spaced columns rising, presumably, from the curved back wall of the amphitheatre, supported the second gallery which was partly cantilevered and contained, probably, six benches. A second range of six columns, above those supporting the second gallery, rose to the back part of the ceiling, which was at a higher level than the flat ceiling over the body of the auditorium.

The wooden structure of the auditorium was decorated with typical Adam ornamentation, delicately modelled in composition on the tier parapets, which were treated as pedestals or 'dados' above entablatures, and on the front faces only of the supporting columns. The flat plaster ceiling was painted in *trompe l'œil* to represent a shallow dome. A contemporary writer, in *The Public Advertiser* for 30 September 1775, describes the brilliant effect of the transformed interior:

'At first View I was a good deal surprised to find that by some means or other the ingenious Artists had contrived to give an Appearance of greater Magnitude to the House. I knew it was *not* rebuilt, but only repaired; and consequently that there could be no additional Space within the old walls and Roof. Upon Reflection I perceived that one Way by which this was effected, was from having removed the old heavy square Pillars on each Side of the Stage, and by that Means I suppose they have procured more Width from one Side-box to the other.

'I also observed, that the Sounding Board was much raised on the Part next the Stage and that the Height given to it increased greatly the Appearance of Magnitude in the House. This having brought the Ceiling or Sounding Board nearly on a Level, has a wonderful good Effect to the Eye; and what astonished me greatly was to find that the Sound of the Music and Actors Voices both improved by this additional Height. All the People round me agreed with me in this Fact, and owned they thought it a very uncommon Effort of Art.

'Small Pilasters, the Height of which is confined to the different Tiers of Boxes, support and adorn them: They are made more light and more gay by inserting in Front of each a Pannel of Plate Glass, which in the lower Order is placed over a Foil or Varnish of spangled Crimson, which looks both rich and brilliant. The Capitals are gilt, and are what our Artists call the Grecian Ionick. The Glass of the second Order is placed over a green spangled Foil or Varnish, and has an Effect no less beautiful than the former: The Capitals of this Order are also gilt, and are a sort of Corinthian, which I don't recollect to have seen before.

'The upper tier of Boxes is adorned with Therms, of which the Busts are gilt, and the Pannels underneath are filled with painted Ornaments. I admire the Judgement of the Artists for having laid aside Pilasters in this last Tier, it being too low for that Species of Decoration; and besides, the Repetition would have become dull.

'All the ornaments in the Friezes and on the Dados, or Fronts of the Boxes, are elegant and splendid. Nothing can, in my Opinion, answer better than the Festoon Drapery upon the Front of the first Tier. The gilt Ornaments on the Faces of the two Orders of Pilasters (from whence the Branches for the Candles spring) ought not to be omitted in the Catalogue of elegant Ornaments, neither must I omit the Decoration of the Ceiling, or Sounding Board, which consists of Octagon pannels, rising from an exterior circular frame to the opening, or Ventilator, in the Center. The diminishing of these Pannels towards the Center, and the shade thrown next to the exterior Frame give the Ceiling the Appearance of a Dome, which has a light and airy Effect.

'I can never give you a compleat List of all the Ornaments that struck me in this Theatre. The Stage Doors, the spangled Borders on each Side of the Stage, and many other new ornamental Decorations, perfectly answered my Ideas of Elegance and Splendour. Indeed I heard some Cricks alledge, that they thought the Decorations of the House *too* elegant, and too splendid, and that it obscured the Lustres of the Scenery and the Dresses. My Answer to these Observations was, that I thought the Decorations of a Theatre could *not* be too brilliant, and that I did not doubt but, by the Assistance of a Loutherbourg, the Managers could and would soon remove these objections, and bring the whole into perfect Harmony.

'Were I to hazard a Criticism, where almost everything is so much to my Satisfaction, it would be, that the Crimson Drapery over the Stage is too dark for the Objects round it; and that the Gold Fringe has not the brilliant effect it ought to have in such a situation.

'I had almost forgot to observe that the Sideboxes are much improved by the additional Height given to each Tier, which admits of the seats being raised considerably above each other, and consequently gives a much better View of the Stage. The Boxes are now lined with Crimson spotted paper and gilt Border which makes a fine Back Ground to all the Decorations.'[21]

To augment this description there is the evidence offered by the engraved view. This shows that the die of the parapet to the amphitheatre and first-tier side boxes was enriched with figure subjects in oval medallions, interspersed with candelabra ornaments to which they were linked by festooned husk chains. A narrow fluted frieze and delicate cornice underlined the second-tier parapet, where the die of each narrow bay was decorated with a segmental fan motif, and each wide bay with a centrally placed winged figure merging into acanthus scrolls. Below the third-tier parapet was a scalloped pelmet and a narrow entablature, its frieze ornamented with small masks on crossed swords. The parapet die was enriched with circular panels, containing musical trophies, alternating with small lozenges. The terms of the third-tier boxes supported a delicately moulded entablature, its frieze decorated with griffins and candelabra ornaments. An enrichment of festooned garlands and paterae decorated the unbroken parapet of the second gallery. It remains to add that the effect of the plate glass and coloured foil panels of the box pilasters can be gauged from the surviving section of the Glass Drawing Room from Northumberland House, created by Robert Adam in 1773–5 and now in the Victoria and Albert Museum.

The main ceiling, painted in *trompe l'œil*, appears to have been executed in complete accordance with the Adam drawing dated 19 July 1775 (Plate 10a). Save for a long narrow panel of acanthus scroll-work, next to the proscenium, and four spandrel panels, each with an oval figure-subject medallion framed and flanked by husk chains, the decoration was concentrated in a large oval panel treated to present a shallow dome having two rings of octagonal coffers surrounding the central oculus. According to the Adam drawing, the pervading pale green colour of the ceiling was relieved by the bronze-green acanthus scrolls, the blue ground of the figure medallions in the fawn-coloured spandrels, the pink bosses in the coffers of the 'dome', and the gilt mouldings framing all the panels.

It was perhaps intended to repaint the ceiling with another design, according to the Adam drawing dated 1776 (Plate 10b), which was 'contrived to correspond with the inside finishing of the sides, front and Stage'.[22] Here the flat surface is divided by a grid of key-fretted ribs into a series of square and oblong compartments of varying size. Some have a pale green ground

diversely decorated with velarium fans and oblong, oval and circular panels containing figure subjects, some in full colour, others in cameo on a rich green ground. Other compartments are filled with a pattern of octagonal coffers in deep blue with red bosses. The pattern of the grid is dictated by the incidence of the transverse ribs with the vertical lines of the pilasters and terms dividing the side boxes.

The design for the proscenium frame (Plate 11a) is dated 8 May 1775, and it shows the opening flanked by tall panelled pilasters, probably of gilt filigree metalwork over glass and blue foil. The shafts are hidden at the top by a pelmet of crimson drapery, fringed with gold and festooned on either side of a large oblong panel depicting 'The Apotheosis of Shakespeare by the Tragic and Comic Muses',[23] with a profile portrait medallion in gold on black supported by winged figures of the muses on a pale blue ground.

Some idea of the size of the Adam auditorium can be gauged from the following dimensions, scaled off the Adam drawings. The proscenium opening was 28 feet wide and about 21 feet 6 inches high. The ceiling plans show that the auditorium width increased from 30 feet next to the proscenium, to 42 feet 6 inches where the side boxes joined the amphitheatre and first gallery. The splayed fronts of the side boxes were 35 feet in length, the dividing pilasters being spaced so that the first, third and fifth bays were all 4 feet 6 inches wide, the second bay, containing the King's box, was 8 feet, and the fourth bay, which was divided into two boxes, was 9 feet 6 inches wide. The distance from the proscenium to the back wall of the second gallery was probably 70 feet. The height of the auditorium, from the front of the pit to the flat ceiling, scales about 29 feet 6 inches, and the floor-to-floor heights of the first and second tiers of side boxes were 9 feet 6 inches and 8 feet respectively.

As the 1778 survey plan (Plate 7) clearly shows, the space occupied by the auditorium was less than half of that taken up by the stage and its dependencies. Some dimensions of the stage, as then existing, were taken in July 1791. The length from front (apron) to back was 130 feet, and the width between the walls was 53 feet 6 inches. The front (apron) width was 32 feet 6 inches, and the curtain, or proscenium, was 30 feet wide and 22 feet high. From the front to the shutter (opening to the back stage) was 55 feet

4 inches, the width of the shutter opening being 18 feet 2 inches.[24]

Praising the improved approaches to the auditorium, the writer in *The Public Advertiser* observed that 'The Stairs to the second and third Tiers of Boxes I found were projected out of the House beyond the Old Walls, which gives a space to make them much wider and more convenient.

'The Lobby behind the front Boxes is well and agreeably contrived, and is now kept clear of servants by an adjoining Room being prepared for their Attendance: This is a most elegant improvement. The Passages to this Lobby are also much mended, but particularly next to Bridges Street, where the Company are received by three large Arches into a vestibule, or Hall which communicates with the great passage leading to the Boxes.'[21]

The survey plan of 1778 shows that the south arch opened to the 'Principal Passage to the Boxes', while the middle and north arches gave access to the shallow apse-ended lobby. These three large arches, separated by two smaller arches, formed the arcaded ground storey or basement of the new façade with which Robert Adam replaced the old brick front of the Rose tavern. As in similar refacings he used 'a new Composition resembling Stone', in fact, Liardet's Stone Paste, the arcade being coursed to resemble chamfer-jointed masonry, the piers having plain plinths and moulded imposts. Above the ground storey extended a prominent balcony, resting on console trusses and furnished with an elaborate iron railing. The predominantly vertical design of this railing was varied by the large circular motifs in projecting panels, placed in front of the single and paired pilasters of the Grecian Ionic temple front with which the two-storeyed upper face was dressed. There were three bays, each containing a first- and second-floor window set in a face which was plain except for a guilloche-ornamented sill-band below the second-floor windows. The Ionic pilasters, rising from plain pedestals, had fluted shafts and capitals enriched with a band of acanthus leaves above the necking. They supported a pedimented entablature, with the architrave omitted, the frieze containing a long recessed panel flanked by masks in oval medallions, and the cornice enriched with dentils. A martial trophy was placed on a pedestal above the apex, and the Lion and Unicorn on pedestals at each end of the pediment, which had in its

tympanum an oval medallion bearing the royal arms.

Against the general chorus of praise which greeted the Adam transformation of Drury Lane, the author of Ralph's *Critical Review*, 1783, sounded a somewhat discordant note. 'The front of Drury-lane theatre is in a good style, but is incumbered with a large gallery, which is loaded with pots, containing trees and shrubs. We suppose the managers have let the front house to a nursery-man, who exhibits these to allure his customers. The general plan of the interior of this theatre is very convenient, but the ornaments of the galleries and boxes are frippery and unmeaning. Slender columns of glass may strike the vulgar as very fine, but the judicious would wish to see propriety consulted, as well as the rage of gaudy decoration.'[25]

Much of the Adam decoration was removed or obliterated when the auditorium was refurbished in 1783 by Thomas Greenwood and William Capon. From the engraved version of Capon's interior view (Plate 11b) it would appear that the structure was little changed, although the 9 feet 6 inches wide bay in each tier of side boxes was now divided by a pilaster or term inserted to match with those already existing, and the straight parapets of the King's and Prince's boxes were replaced by bowed railings of gilt metalwork. The Adam ornaments having been removed from all the parapets of the boxes and galleries, the first tier was left plain and the rest painted with festooned garlands. According to Capon's own notes 'The ground of this new painting was a very faint kind of pea green or rather a greenish colour, the ornaments *chiaroscuro*'. The boxes were lined with red or a colour between pink and crimson.[26]

A press cutting, undated but probably of 1785, describes how further alterations had made the house 'the prettiest and most elegant theatre that London could ever boast. The back of the front boxes, which, two years ago, by being changed from the old plan into enclosures, became a nest for prostitutes of both sexes, are now entirely opened. The ceiling is raised in order to give room for the lustres to display their lights, and the seats are formed into recesses which communicate with the other boxes, and afford a full view of the stage. There is a circular regularity of arches, from the King's box round to the Prince's, which have a most pleasing effect. These are formed at the back of the boxes from whence the former paper covering is taken, and a wainscot substituted. The wainscot is painted of a crimson colour, in festoons, which gives a richness to the view and deceives the eye into a perspective that makes the boxes look much deeper than they really are. Great pains have been bestowed on the galleries and upper boxes, the fronts of which are newly decorated with festoons, which have a most beautiful appearance. On each wing of the two shilling gallery are placed three pilasters, fluted and gilded, which occupy the spaces formerly filled by false boxes. The pillars through the whole house have changed their whole drapery, and put on new livery; nay even those of iron in the back boxes are capped, cased, fluted, and gilt. The colouring of the boxes and gallery is a new fancy mixture. It is what may be called, in the artist's phrase, a warm lilac, the appearance of which, contrasted with the glowing crimson at the back of the boxes, and the gilded pillars in front, give elegance, beauty, taste, and richness to a scene, which does honour to the painter. The upper boxes, as to convenience of intercourse, remain as formerly. They have been all new painted, and their pillars are richly gilded.' In the same year the stage was illuminated for the first time 'with patent lamps. The effect of this light, which is, in a manner, a new kind of artificial light, was brilliant beyond all expectation'.[27]

During the summer of 1787, the theatre 'though not entirely renovated' was 'essentially altered'. It was now painted a dead white with gilt mouldings and ornaments, the boxes being lined with a rose-coloured paper 'and a white pattern agreeably mixed'. A new act drop was installed, painted to correspond with the architecture, and the opening in the main ceiling was enlarged to give 'a loftier appearance to the whole'.[27] A short while later the proprietors announced their intention to demolish the existing building, and replace it with a magnificent new theatre.

Henry Holland's Theatre of 1791–4

Before attempting a descriptive account of the new theatre, Holland's own account,[28] sent to Sheridan at about the time of the first opening on 12 March 1794, is worth quoting in some detail, with small amendments of spelling and punctuation: 'Drury Lane Theatre was last night opened, having been rebuilt in [blank] months, an expedition which became necessary in order that the public might not be deprived of their Amusement any more of the present Season than possibly could be helped, and on which Account it is opened without the Completion of several Buildings which with it form one great and complete plan, standing foremost in the Rank of Public Buildings in the Metropolis, and with the Aid of the Bill now in Parliament,* the Avenues surrounding it will at once add to its magnificence, and the convenience and safety of the public— the more so, from the footway being covered over with a colonnade of the Grecian Ionic order, affording shelter and convenience below, and forming a Terrace before the Theatre above— intended to be secured by ornamental ironwork and lighted by a number of lamps, also forming part of an elegant design. The Plan includes an Area upwards 300 feet in length and about 155 feet in breadth, and the Building is in heighth from the Substructure to the Roof, 108 feet.

'The outside of the Building, which surrounds the Theatre, is faced with Portland stone, and will be finished with a ballustrade. The Theatre which rises above is intended to be faced with stone, or a cement equal to it, and is also finished with a ballustrade. Through the Roof rises a Turret, including a large Ventilator and a Staircase leading on to the Roof. The Turret takes something of the form of the Octagon Tower of Andronicus Cyrrhestes [i.e., Tower of the Winds] at Athens, and is nearly as large, and on the summit is placed a figure of Apollo, about 10 feet high. From the Terrace on the Roof is by far the finest bird's eye view of London and the River Thames that can be seen from any other place.

'The accommodations for the Stage are upon a larger scale than in any other Theatre in Europe: the opening for the Scenery is 43 feet wide and 38 feet high, after which the painter and Mechanist have a large space in which they may exert their abilities, 83 feet wide, 92 feet long, and 108 feet high. The scenery may be changed or disposed of either by raising it out of sight, or lowering the whole of it, or drawing it off sideways. The Machinery is executed upon the newest and most

---

* This refers to an abortive petition which Sheridan presented to the House of Commons on 4 March 1794 for the purpose of obtaining power to form a new street, to be called Woburn Street, on the south side of the theatre.[29]

approved principles, contrived to be worked by Machinery placed either above or below the stage, thereby preventing the Necessity of having a number of Scene Shifters in the Way of the Performances.

'The Scenes are and must be of course all new, a work that will require some time to bring to perfection, and more especially as the Season of the Year required an Orchestra on the stage for the Oratorios. This has been done by an introduction of Gothic Architecture very well suited to Sacred Music, and forming a striking Contrast to the decoration of the Amphitheatre.

'In the roof of the Theatre is contained, besides the barrel loft, ample Room for the Scene painters, and four very large reservoirs of Water, distributed from them all over the House, intended to extinguish fire. At the same time great precaution has been taken to prevent such a misfortune by the most ample use of all the inventions and contrivances which ingenuity could suggest, and an Iron Curtain is contrived which would completely separate the Audience from the Stage, where accidents by fire usually commence in Theatres.

'The Audience part of the Theatre is formed nearly on a semicircular plan containing a pit, eight boxes on each side of the pit, two rows of Boxes above them, on which level the two galleries open—commanding a full view of the whole stage—on each side of the galleries are two more rows of boxes, rising to a cove so contrived as to form the Ceiling into a complete circle. The proscenium, or that part of the stage contained between the Curtain and the Orchestra, is fitted up with boxes but without any stage door or the usual Addition of large Columns. The boxes are furnished with chairs in the front row, and benches behind covered with blue Velvet.

'The Corridors which surround the Boxes and give communication to them are spacious, having in the Angles of the Theatre, Staircases of communication, and at the West End of the Theatre is a very large semicircular Room, open by an Arch to the Corridors, having fireplaces in it and bar rooms for furnishing the company with Refreshments. There are also large saloons on the north and south sides of the Theatre, as also two handsome square Rooms, one of them intended as an Antichamber for the use of His Majesty, and the other for the Prince of Wales. These Rooms are fitted up in the modern taste with large handsome pannels, chimneypieces, large glasses, and are susceptible of a great deal of decoration which is intended to be introduced as soon as they can be obtained from the Artists who are engaged for that purpose.

'The Decorations of the Theatre are in a Style entirely new, intended to have a richness of Effect and a simplicity that should gratify the Eye without interfering with any decorations that may appear upon the stage, and by forming an agreeable contrast to them render the whole more striking. Accordingly, the Ceiling of the Theatre is painted in compartments of one Colour only. In the same style of painting the galleries are decorated, the fronts and insides of the boxes have for the Ground a clear blue colour, richly ornamented in Chiaro obscuro. The Boxes are supported by silver columns of antique forms, to which columns are attached cut glass lustres by silver brackets. The whole of the Audience part is lighted with very handsome glass lustres, particularly the galleries. In the centre pannels in front of the Boxes are introduced paintings by Rebecca from antique subjects, and more decorations and paintings seem intended to be added when opportunities may offer. Besides the silver Columns which support the Boxes and have a very rich effect, there are four principal square but small pillars which support the Ceiling, decorated with looking glass and with other rich ornaments.

'The sound-board or Ceiling of the proscenium is painted in compartments, and in front of the Proscenium, facing the Audience, are introduced the Royal Arms with Trophies and other grand, magnificent and suitable accompaniments.

'The Entrances to the Theatre must, while the Bill in Parliament is pending, fall short of the intended conveniences. From Russell street there is a box Entrance into a large Hall decorated with Columns, also a private Entrance for His Majesty, and an entrance which leads to the gallery staircases. On the other side of the Theatre, next Marquis Court, the same Entrances are repeated, but till the new street intended to be called Woburn street is opened, the Approach to them can only be for foot passengers in Chairs; as a Chair door the Box Entrance on that side is more complete than to any public Building in London. There are two other Entrances to the Theatre, also incomplete—the one next Bridges street for the pit and Boxes, and the one next Drury Lane to the stage. In these two streets, when the Buildings are completed, will be the handsomest and most decorated fronts. Besides the Ionic portico, always a certain ornament, these fronts of stone will be decorated with pilasters, basso-relievos, trophies, rich iron-work, and other analogous ornaments. . . .'[28]

The graphic evidence relating to Holland's Drury Lane Theatre includes five architectural drawings from his office (Plates 12–14),[30] relating to the auditorium and its approaches, and although sections and elevations are lacking, the whole theatre is recorded in a set of eight plans, taken at all levels from cellar to roof[31] (Plates 15–17). A splendid watercolour by Edward Dayes (see Frontispiece) fully conveys the original appearance of the auditorium in 1794, while its later, altered state is recorded in two unfinished drawings by William Capon[32] (Plate 19), and by the well-known aquatint in *The Microcosm of London* (Plate 18a). There is no really adequate representation of the exterior as Holland intended it to be finished, although his original design with arcaded 'piazzas' is illustrated by the Francia engraving of 1793[33] (Plate 20a), and the final 'colonnaded' design by an unsigned watercolour in the Crace Collection in the British Museum[34] (Plate 20c). The former is similar to the engraved view heading the building subscribers' debenture certificates,[35] made from a perspective drawn by Thomas Malton,[28] which, however, omits the theatre 'shell' (Plate 20b).

Two of Holland's office drawings are now in the Victoria and Albert Museum,[36] both being recorded in Holland's Drury Lane Theatre Catalogue Book of 4 September 1792,[28] where 126 drawings are listed. Holland's no. 15 is a plan of the auditorium and its approaches, taken at pit level (Plate 12b), and no. 16 is a transverse section taken through the auditorium well, looking towards the proscenium (Plate 12a). These annotated and dimensioned drawings probably date from 1792 and show the auditorium as it was then intended to be constructed, but around October 1793 Holland was obliged to make new drawings for completing the interior in accordance with Sheridan's requirements. Three of these later and unlisted drawings have survived and are now in Sir John Soane's Museum. The drawing there numbered 61/36 is a plan at pit level (Plate 13b), no. 61/35 is a longitudinal section of the auditorium (Plate 14), and no. 61/34 is a trans-

verse section towards the proscenium (Plate 13a). The set of eight plans, in Mr. Robert Eddison's collection, appears to be a generally faithful record of the theatre as it was finished in 1794, but was probably executed by William Capon, certainly after 1811 which is the watermarked date on one sheet of paper. Possibly based on originals by Holland, these finely finished drawings are without captions, and as the theatre was destroyed by fire in February 1809, they can only have been prepared as a record or for an intended publication (Plates 15–17).

Although writers have continued to repeat E. W. Brayley's statement that the theatre was 320 feet long and 155 feet broad, with a roof width of 118 feet,[37] all the evidence shows that the theatre formed the major part of a rectangular building intended to be 300 feet long, east to west, and 128 feet wide, excluding the surrounding colonnade which was some 6 feet wide. Within the frame of this vast rectangle, the theatre was planned on symmetrical lines about the long east–west axis, the stage being placed to the east of the auditorium, both encased in an oblong shell which was internally some 176 feet long and 80 feet wide, having its west wall some 70 feet distant from the Brydges Street front. On the north and south sides of the shell, adjoining the auditorium and west part of the stage, were subsidiary ranges, 140 feet long outside and 20 feet wide inside. Each range had a front of thirteen bays, forming the central part of the intended front of twenty-seven bays. In the middle was the box entrance, a spacious and lofty vestibule having over it a handsome saloon, reached by a grand staircase on the west side. East of the box entrance was the vestibule and staircase to the King's box, on the north side, and the Prince's box, on the south. West of the box entrance was the pit vestibule, having on its west side the staircases serving the two galleries. At the east end of each range was a staircase giving access to two upper storeys and a mansard attic, all divided to form dressing-rooms, offices, etc. Adjoining the west wall of the shell was a semi-circular projection, 42 feet in diameter, containing a pit vestibule and a lofty saloon above, both flanked by lavatory accommodation. Entered through a long temporary passage from Brydges Street (apparently not opened until September 1795), the semi-circular pit vestibule opened into a large crescent-shaped foyer, 20 feet wide, contrived in the space behind the pit and below the first tier of dress boxes. Divided by Doric colonnades into a nave and aisles of nine bays, this 'Egyptian Hall' was lined east and west with shops, and ended north and south with a pentagonal apse where stairs ascended north, or south, to the other pit vestibules, and other stairs curved east to enter the pit, and the pit box corridors.

Although its seating capacity, originally calculated to be 3,919,[28] was greater than that of any other contemporary European theatre, the size of Holland's Drury Lane has often been exaggerated. One recent writer has even stated that it was almost twice the size of Novosielski's King's Theatre, Haymarket,[38] whereas the horseshoe well of Holland's auditorium was no wider (both 55 feet), and 6 feet 6 inches shorter, than that of Novosielski's opera house even before the latter was lengthened in 1796.[39] At Drury Lane, the parapets of the three horseshoe tiers all conformed to a semicircle, 55 feet in diameter, which was continued to merge with straight sides canted towards the proscenium, where the auditorium was about 43 feet wide. The pit, including the orchestra, was 51 feet 6 inches deep, and the proscenium with its double boxes flanking the apron stage was 13 feet deep, the curtain opening being 43 feet wide and 38 feet high. Holland's revised plan shows the pit furnished with twenty-four straight rows of backless benches, 9 inches wide and 1 foot apart, placed on a floor of shallow steppings giving a rise of 10 degrees. Supplemented by five short benches on either side of the orchestra, the pit was calculated to seat 974, at 14 inches each person. On each side of the pit and apron stage were eight boxes. The first or dress tier was divided by scroll-profiled partitions into thirty-one front boxes, with three rows of chairs or benches, separated by a cross aisle from the 'basket' or 'back-front' boxes, numbering eleven and containing seven rows of benches. The steppings of this tier were pitched at 7 degrees, and the height of the opening to the auditorium well was 8 feet. The second tier, pitched at 25 degrees, also contained thirty-one boxes, those at the sides having three rows of chairs or benches, and those opposite the stage having six, the height of the opening to the auditorium well being 5 feet 10 inches. Except for eleven boxes on either

side, with three rows of benches and a front opening height of 5 feet 4 inches, the third tier was occupied by the two-shilling gallery, seating 1,100 on sixteen rows of benches on curved steppings giving a rise of 30 degrees. The upper, one-shilling gallery, with its parapet in line above the seventh row of the lower gallery, seated 307 on its seven rows of benches, stepped to a pitch of 35 degrees, and on either side of the horseshoe, at a lower level, was a fourth tier of boxes, nine either side, with three rows of benches. Holland originally calculated that there would be 113 boxes seating a total of 1,538 at 18 inches each person. He also calculated for gallery slips seating 436.[28] As fitted up, there were 129 boxes, this being achieved by the omission of two pit boxes and the substitution of eighteen side boxes for the gallery slips.

The problem of constructing so large and complex an auditorium must have taxed Holland's ingenuity, experienced as he was in building practice. His transverse sections reveal, and various accounts confirm, that the walls of the great oblong shell* were built in brickwork of 4 feet thickness up to the floor level of the first-tier saloons and box corridors, which was 16 feet above the Russell Street pavement and 26 feet above the cellar floor. The cellar was laterally and transversely divided by walls and piers sustaining segmental vaults, floored over at a height of 13 feet above the cellar floor, and on these vaults rested the iron and timber framing of the pit floor and the horseshoe tiers. From the first-tier level, the brick wall of the shell was carried up for another 10 feet with a thickness of 3 feet 6 inches, but above this the shell was framed with huge timbers, the side walls being divided into bays some 15 feet wide by laterally paired posts 36 feet high. To these the joists of the tiers and floors were fixed, and on their heads rested the great roof principals, and the 2 feet thick walls of the attic storey, its parapet being 101 feet above the cellar floor level. The lofty and extensive space above the auditorium ceiling was divided transversely by the roof principals, each consisting of a massive queen-post truss, hipped at the apex and combined with three small king-post trusses, giving the roof three parallel ridges and two valleys.

The early transverse section (Plate 12a) shows

---

* Substantial parts of Holland's lateral walls still survive in the stage cellar of the present theatre. The distance between these walls, which are of identical construction and thickness, precludes any possibility that they are survivals from the theatre of 1674, as claimed by previous writers.[40]

that Holland originally proposed to construct the upper tiers on raking joists fixed to the paired posts framing the shell walls. These joists, additionally supported by the box-corridor partitions, were to be cantilevered some 5 feet 8 inches so that the three rows of benches in each tier would be free from any obstructing columns rising between the parapets. This section also shows an intended fifth tier of side boxes or slips, containing two rows of benches affording a very limited view of the stage through arches groined into the ceiling cove. There were to be only three boxes on each side of the stage apron, stacked above proscenium doors and flanked by massive Corinthian columns on pedestals.

Although Holland reconstructed Covent Garden Theatre in 1793 with partially cantilevered tiers, he redesigned the auditorium of Drury Lane so that the parapets of the three complete horseshoe tiers, and the fourth tier of side boxes, were supported by cast-iron columns. Four of these columns were formed into square-shafted pillars, dividing each horseshoe sweep into three equal lengths, but the rest were designed to resemble antique candelabra with slender fluted shafts rising from tripod feet. These candelabra-columns were spaced 15 feet apart to subdivide each of the three main divisions into three bays, all three boxes wide. The square pillars at the end of each tier were repeated to flank the proscenium boxes, while those between the third and fourth bays on each side were carried up to the roof, forming stops for the canted side walls of the galleries, and for the fourth tier of side boxes. The parapets of the latter were also surmounted by candelabra-columns, two on either side, rising to support the groined cove surrounding the flat circular ceiling. The ceiling above the apron stage was brought down level with the top of the fourth-tier parapet to form a flat sounding board. The vertical face above was formed into three lunettes, or tympana, by arches intersecting the great cove, the wide middle tympanum being treated as a shallow elliptical semi-dome. The back part of the auditorium was constructed so that the raking joists carrying the tiers, and the level joists of the foyer and corridor floors, were supported by three ranges of slender cast-iron columns, arranged concentrically, all rising from the crescent-shaped 'Egyptian Hall' behind the pit. The first range of columns continued up to the underside of the lower gallery, whereas the second and third ranges were carried up to tie in with the roof structure.

Something of the magical effect produced by Holland's elegant and exquisitely decorated auditorium was captured in the superb water-colour view by Edward Dayes (Frontispiece). This shows the pit, where the audience sat on benches covered with red baize,[41] partially enclosed by a low wall painted to resemble rusticated masonry. The parapets of the three horseshoe tiers, and the fourth tier of side boxes, were uniformly treated, each slightly inclined face being divided by upright scroll-consoles into equal lengths containing three oblong panels. Two of these were ornamented with white trellis on a blue ground, flanking a central panel painted with figure-subjects in cameo on a cornelian ground.[42] A list in Holland's writing names the subjects for thirty-five panels, selected from classical mythology, the fine arts and the performing arts, which were executed by Biagio Rebecca.[28] Each tier parapet was supported in turn by a series of silvered candelabra-columns placed over the consoles, those above the fourth tier sustaining the spandrels and arching lunettes of the great groined cove, which were simply painted in beige tones with panels and rosettes from which hung chandeliers, softly illuminating the blue draperies festooned round the arches, and supplementing the lustres that projected from brackets above the candelabra-columns of each tier. The proscenium boxes had bow-ended fronts, dressed with festooned blue draperies, and their openings were framed with silvered trelliswork at the sides and head. Great acanthus scroll-trusses supported the soffit or sounding-board of the proscenium, its surface painted with panels, the middle one containing an Apollo head. The three tympana on the vertical face above were richly decorated, the wide and elliptical semi-dome in the centre with the royal arms against military trophies, and the flat semi-circle on either side with an urn against a musical trophy. The main ceiling over the auditorium was formed into a complete circle by the cove, and its flat surface was painted in 'chiaro obscuro'[41] with a guilloche border framing a pseudo-dome decorated with interlacing ribs, curving to form a pattern of lozenge-shaped coffers. The proscenium opening is shown richly dressed with heavily festooned draperies of a warm golden hue, and a long-standing tradition was observed by placing, on each side of the proscenium, movable figures of Melpomene and Thalia raised on high pedestals. To the general colour scheme of light blue, white, beige and silver, a glittering note was added by the cut-glass lustres, the looking-glass panels set in the side faces of the square pillars supporting the tiers, and the large circular glasses at each end of the first tier of boxes.

Arrangements for public circulation were admirably contrived. Arriving at the north and south vestibules, patrons for the boxes ascended the grand staircases and passed through the first-floor saloons into side corridors within the shell. These gave direct access to the dress-tier side boxes and led westwards, passing a cross-aisle serving the dress-tier front boxes, to the communicating staircases in the north-west and south-west angles of the shell. These staircases were linked by a back foyer, serving the 'basket' boxes and opening to the large semi-circular saloon west of the shell. The upper tiers of boxes were approached by the communicating staircases, which were designed with twin flights rising against the side and end walls of the shell, to meet at a half-landing where a single flight returned diagonally to the next tier level. A cursory examination of the plans will show how Holland sought to avoid the monotonous effect of the usual horseshoe corridors by treating his passages of circulation as a series of linked compartments.

The principal saloons and public rooms were handsomely decorated in Holland's neo-classical manner. The Russell Street vestibule had flanking screens of Doric columns with partly fluted shafts, and the north and south saloons, flanking the dress-boxes tier, were very like the Woburn Abbey interiors, with their panelled walls, lunette overdoors, and cove-surrounded ceilings. The 'Egyptian Hall' behind the pit must have been particularly attractive, with its 'porphyry' shafted Doric columns and its arcaded shop fronts with their fan-glazed lunettes. All of these rooms were well furnished with chairs, velvet-covered sofas, marble-topped pier tables, and jardinières. Large gilt-framed glasses were placed above the chimneypieces and on the piers between the windows, which were hung with crimson morine curtains. A statue of Garrick between Melpomene and Thalia was a notable feature of the semi-circular saloon, which was furnished with two bars for the service of refreshments.[42]

According to the accounts submitted to the proprietors by Charles Smith, upholder, covering a period from February 1794 to January 1795,[28] the King's waiting-room was covered with green cloth, the windows being dressed with curtains and valances of crimson silk-and-worsted damask, and the furniture included three mahogany-framed sofas covered with damask and finished with brass nails. On royal visits the King's box was dressed with a rich canopy, carved with festoons of flowers and gilt in burnished gold, supported by four columns. The inside was lined with rich crimson satin, and the opening was dressed with curtains and festoons of crimson velvet drapery, finished with gold fringe, handsome bows and gold tassels, the royal arms being richly embroidered on the front valance. The box was furnished with two large carved-and-gilt armchairs, six matching chairs without arms, and four stools. The Prince's box was almost as handsome, but finished in blue and silver.[28] The auditorium was also furnished in a luxurious fashion for the time, the box parapets and rails being covered with blue velvet[41] to match with the upholstery of the stuffed chairs, stools and benches. The box doors were lined with cloth or baize, studded with brass nails, and the floors were covered with Brussels or Scotch carpets, printed floor cloths, or matting. The dressing-rooms and offices were adequately equipped with japanned chairs, deal tables with drawers, and looking-glasses. Charles Smith's detailed account for his work at the theatre amounts in all to £2,011 8s. 2d.[28]

The elaborate equipment of the vast stage was designed by Rudolph Cabanel, machinist, of Stangate Street, Lambeth. Holland wrote to him on 4 November 1793, desiring him 'to prepare plans of and for the Stage and Machinery and to let me see them as soon as prepared in order that Directions may be given to forward the Execution of them. It is proposed the opening of the Curtain should be 44' 6" wide by 36' high, to be diminished by a shifting or painted decoration 35 ft wide and 24' 6" high, that the first set of wings shall be close to this painted or shifting decoration, that the openings shall be as follows, clear of the Lamps, 7' 0"–6' 6"–6' 0"–5' 6"–5' 0" –5' 0", that the inclination of the Stage shall be half an inch to the foot, that the floor, traps, placing the Barrels, working the wings and scenes, shall be according to your model—the mode of managing the lights remain yet to be ascertained.'

Cabanel undertook 'to design and direct the construction of the stage . . . and attend as Mechanist for two years at £9.9.0 per week'. Reporting on Cabanel's work in March 1794, Holland noted that 'the preparations which Mr. Cabanel has been ordered to make for Machinery are calculated only for Macbeth, but will answer to any other play where particular Machinery is not required. The whole of the Machinery ordered is prepared and all is ready for fixing; this fixing is entirely prevented by the Stage being occupied. Nor can anything be done in it till the Stage is entirely clear'd and all interruptions removed. When this is done Mr. Cabanel requires nine clear and compleat days and nights to fix and compleat the whole. . . . There is a great quantity of work done and now doing in preparing barrels and pulleys and frames which is not immediately wanted, but this work is doing because the men cannot proceed with fixing the work which is ready.'[28] The plans (Plates 16–17) show quite clearly the layout of Cabanel's stage, the apron with its five traps, seven sets of wings diminishing in perspective, the floor slots for ground rows and descending scenes, and the elaborate system of fly-galleries. At the back of the stage, supported on four massive piers, was a large scene-painting room.

To Holland's lasting disappointment, his fine design for the intended insular building was never realized, for only those parts of the exterior necessary to the theatre were built. Unlike the great Continental theatres, such as that at Bordeaux by Victor Louis, Holland's Drury Lane was intended to be a complex of theatre, taverns, coffee-houses, houses and shops, and it should be regarded as a handsome example of uniform street architecture rather than as a monumental public building. Unified by the colonnade extending round most of the ground storey, with plain-shafted Ionic columns of stone supporting a wooden entablature, the four-storeyed ranges surrounding the lofty theatre shell were conventional compositions designed in a neo-classical style reminiscent of Neufforge (Plate 20c). The long north and south fronts were alike in having severely plain wings, eight windows wide, slightly recessed between a pedimented central feature, five windows wide, and end pavilions, three windows wide, which were emphasized by

their horizontally rusticated faces and the round-arched windows of the first floor. The wings were finished with a cornice and balustrade, this being stopped against the central pediment, and broken above each end pavilion by a pedestal bearing a trophy. On the west and east fronts the pavilions were returned to flank a slightly projecting central feature, five windows wide, its rusticated face divided into bays by pilaster-strips, having fluted shafts extending between patera-stops. Above the cornice extended a tall attic pedestal, its die ornamented with a long oblong panel, presumably for the theatre's name, flanked by wreathed oval medallions, while centred above was a large trophy composed, like those on the pavilions, of a cartouche flanked by flags.* The lofty attic stage of the theatre shell was uniformly arcaded, with eleven equally-spaced arches on the north and south sides, and five on the west and east. Every arch framed a large window, recessed within a marginal surround, and the unmoulded arches rested on wide piers with plain imposts, and had keystones rising to meet the crowning cornice. This was surmounted by an open balustrade broken by wide pedestals containing the chimneys. From the leaded flat roof at the west end rose the octagonal lantern, a veritable Tower of the Winds, surmounted by the statue of Apollo, 10 feet in height, designed and made by Anne Seymour Damer.[43] Holland's first design for the building appears to have been generally similar to the one described above, except that the ground storey was intended to be a rusticated arcade of open arches, and the central feature of the west front was more simply decorated (Plate 20a). The materials used, or intended to be used in finishing the exterior were Portland stone, weather tiles, and brick finished with cement frescoed to resemble stone.

Among the Holland papers in Mr. Robert Eddison's collection is a copy of the printed Proposals for 'building upon shares a spacious Tavern at the West End of Drury-Lane Theatre (To be called The Apollo or Russel-Arms). This Tavern, with Rooms for Parties, public Coffee and Dining Rooms, and Wine Vaults of unparalleled extent, shall be compleated upon an enlarged Scale, yet at the same time on a Plan peculiarly adapted to the accommodation of Frequenters of

* Some idea of the intended effect of Holland's design can be seen in the smaller but similar Grand Front of the Theatre Royal, Bath, designed in 1804–5.

the Theatre.' However, this project failed to materialize, and up to the time of its destruction in 1809, Drury Lane Theatre presented the dismal spectacle of its unfinished west end rising above the untidy hoardings that flanked the insignificant Ionic porch of the pit entrance in Brydges Street (Plate 21b).

Holland's statement of 'Payments made to Workmen & others on account of the New Theatre',[28] made out to 1 August 1797, lists most of the tradesmen employed and the amounts paid to them:

Name	Occupation	£	s.	d.
Saunders, Edward Gray	Builder (general contractor and carpenter-designer of the timber frame-work)	37,201	3	9
Whitehead, William	Bricklayer	7,250	8	11
Harvey, Thomas	Bricklayer	3,263	10	6
W.......	......	2,776	11	10
Westmacott, Richard	Mason	2,302	4	—
Parnham, Robert	Clerk of Works and for sundry disbursements	2,137	2	6
Collins, Samuel	Digger and Carter	1,884	13	2
Rothwell, William	Plasterer	1,616	1	6
Smith, Charles	Upholder for the King's Box	1,187	6	—
Bailey, John	Plasterer	1,160	11	—
Bunn, John	Carpenter	1,066	17	—
Wallis, John	Mason	988	4	10
Copland, Alexander	Carpenter	907	11	—
Wake-Hall	Mason	813	1	—
Hanson, John	Ironmonger for fire plates	740	10	—
Hopkins, William	for Stove Grates	773	1	6
Hollis, John	Bricklayer to the houses set back in Russell Street	663	18	6
Wigstead, Henry	Painter	630	7	—
Oddy, Samuel	Carpenter	417	17	6
Burton, Launcelot	Plumber	408	1	—
Robson & Hale	Paper hangers	405	5	—
Heady, Joseph	Glassman for Lustres	401	12	6
Wood, Henry	Carver	389	4	—
Harris and Bourne	Silkmen	381	4	6
Cabanel, Rudolph	Mechanist to the Stage	355	6	9
King, John	Upholsterer	330	13	—
Oldfield, Thomas	Mason	294	6	—
Smith, D.	for Lamps	271	7	6
Ashlin...	Glassman for Looking Glasses	251	5	6
Hopkins, John	....	246	15	—
Morrell	Upholsterer	244	13	6

Name	Occupation	£	s.	d.
Wyatt, John	Copper Covers	214	8	6
Lacy and Horsley	Founders	212	12	—
Jacobs, Richard	Carpenter to the Stage	201	18	—
Beetham, Nathaniel	Smith	198	10	—
Rebecca, Biagio	Ornamental painter	150	—	—
Holmes, Thomas	Glazier	138	—	—
Barzago, Louis	Ornamental painter	135	—	—
Neilson, Seffron	Carver	128	19	—
Catton, Charles	Ornamental painter	115	15	—
Mutter, George	Purchaser of the lease of the houses set back	110	—	—
Woods, William	Weather tiler	109	—	—
Bottomley, John	Composition ornaments	91	6	6
Cheyne, John	Labourer in trust	90	—	—
Curl, Thomas	Carpenter	82	16	6
White, William	Timber	54	3	—
Hardy, Samuel	Ropemaker	53	8	6
Smith, Joseph	Smith	52	18	—
Brown and Taunton	......	52	10	6
Buckingham, John	......	51	18	—
Brathwate, John	Engine-maker	50	—	—
Daguerre, Dominique	Upholder	50	—	—
Gascoine, Mrs. B.	Locksmith	48	12	—
Nicolls, John	Slater	46	5	—
Decaiz (De Caix)	Metal founder	42	—	—
Tremmells, Roger	Coalmerchant	39	2	6
Willson, Archer	Brickmaker	33	14	3
Morris, George	For cones	32	7	6
Fosbrook, Thomas	......	28	19	6
Johnstone, John	......	27	12	6
Bryan, Michael	Glazier	27	10	—
Younge, John	Charcoal	22	10	—
Banks, Henry	......	17	10	—
Bent, William	Ironmonger	10	8	—

Henry Holland   Architect—Sloane Place
By cash of the Trustees—£1,250 0 0 ⎫
By a rent charge of £1   ⎬ 4,250 — —
per night and privileges— 3,000 0 0 ⎭

                             Total 78,730 10 6

During September 1795 it was advertised that 'The elegant entrance from Brydges-street to the boxes ... will, it is said, be opened for the accommodation of the Public in the course of next week. It is decorated in the Venetian style and will add considerably to the general beauty of our national edifice.' This was apparently the temporary passage illustrated on Plate 21b. At the same time a new Green Room for the actors was added, and a scene room constructed 'to preserve the scenes in prime order for years'.[41]

In September 1797, the following considerable alterations were noted. 'The Pit ... is rendered more commodious as to ingress and regress; there is a passage down the middle . . . ; part of the paling is taken away, and that which remains is considerably lower than before; the seats are newly covered with crimson baize; and the whole is sunk about one foot, and so contrived as to be highly advantageous to hearing and sight. The Orchestra Boxes, which nearly surround the Pit, are increased, three on each side. They are beautifully enriched within by a light elegant paper, and externally by a painted curtain hanging in folds or festoons, which appear through a superb gilt Trielliage. The Orchestra extends from one side of the Pit to the other. The Proscenium or frontispiece on the stage before the curtain, is rendered quite different in its appearance, by the addition of three boxes on each side, rising to the top, enclosed by a cove, admirably decorated by Mr. Greenwood. By this improvement the stage is contracted in its width. There is also a new sounding board, by means of which the voice is distinctly heard in every part of the House. The insides of the Boxes are painted a neat French grey, with crimson furniture, instead of the blue. The fronts of the pannels are nearly the same colour as before, with the addition of a gilt edge round the mouldings. The passages leading to the Boxes are also newly painted. The pillars which support the Boxes are newly silvered; and the whole produce a most charming effect.'[41] The general appearance of the auditorium after these changes were made is admirably recorded in an aquatint in *The Microcosm of London* (Plate 18a) and in the two unfinished drawings by William Capon (Plate 19).

In preparing the theatre for its re-opening in September 1805, the tier parapets were cleaned 'in a manner that renders the painting apparently as fresh as the first season the Theatre was opened'. The candelabra-columns supporting the tiers were now 'richly gilt' and the seats, railings, and box-fronts were covered with new crimson cloth, as were the pit benches. A new drop-scene was painted by Greenwood, enclosed in a frame 'which extends from one side wall to the other'.[44]

During the summer closure of 1806, the pit floor was 'raised bodily' and pitched 'at a greater angle than that of any other Pit in the metropolis'. The stage apron was curtailed 3 feet to increase the depth of the orchestra, the two ends of which were 'appropriated for visitors at the box prices'. To effect the improvement of the pit,

some private boxes were removed, but others were made in the second tier to replace them. In the dress-tier boxes, one row of seats was removed to give greater room and convenience, and to enable an increased elevation to be given to the seats behind. All of this work was 'planned and executed by Mr. Lethbridge, stage carpenter, without the employment of extra labour, and at an expense not much exceeding one half of the annual rent of the two new private boxes'.[44]

Thereafter, no important changes are recorded as having been made to Holland's theatre, which was almost completely destroyed by fire during the night of 24 February 1809. According to Wilkinson's *Theatrum Illustrata* the fire was noticed shortly after eleven o'clock but within half an hour the roof had collapsed. Holland had endeavoured to avoid such a disaster by taking particular precautions against the spread of fire. Four very large reservoirs of water were fixed in the roof and 'supplied by a horse-engine, which will act as a fire-engine, conducting a plentiful supply of water to all parts of the building'. David Hartley's iron 'Fire Plates' were used to protect the timber framing of the shell, and an invention of Lord Stanhope's, 'equally powerful', was introduced in the staircases, wood partitioning, and floors of the boxes, while an iron curtain was made to insulate the auditorium from the stage, where fires usually began.[41] But the iron curtain had rusted and was removed, and the water reservoirs were depleted at the time of the fire which, 'in ten or twelve minutes . . . ran up the front boxes, and spread like kindled flax. This may be accounted for from the body of air which so large a hollow afforded, and also from the whole being a wooden case.'[45]

BENJAMIN DEAN WYATT'S THEATRE OF 1811–12

In the preface to the 1813 edition of his *Observations on the Design for the Theatre Royal, Drury Lane*, Benjamin Dean Wyatt tells how 'In the month of May, 1811, a competition for Designs was opened by the Committee, and in the month of October following, that, which forms the subject of this publication, was adopted. The first stone of the Building was laid on the 29th of October, 1811, and the Theatre was opened to the Public on the 10th of October, 1812.' In refuting an 'unfounded and scandalous insinuation' that his design 'had been borrowed from that of Mr. George Wyatt' for a proposed third metropolitan theatre, Benjamin Wyatt states that he had never seen the latter until it was published in 1812, whereas 'the Design for Drury Lane Theatre, as it is now executed, and as it is exhibited in this Work, was completed, and was shown to several branches of the Royal Family, and other persons of distinction, so early as the month of February, 1810'.[46] There is some measure of confirmation for this statement in the existence of a set of well-finished drawings for the intended new Theatre Royal, designed on a 'reduced scale', signed by Benjamin Wyatt and dated February 1810, now in the library of the Royal Institute of British Architects.

This set of drawings (Plates 22–3) comprises six plans, from basement to gallery, a front elevation, a side elevation, and two alternative longitudinal sections, each supplemented by a perspective view of the auditorium towards the proscenium. Despite its 'reduced scale' this design would have resulted in a larger and costlier theatre than the one eventually built. The exterior, presumably intended to be finished in stone and stucco, is very handsomely treated in the neo-classical style of James and Samuel Wyatt, but the shortened horseshoe plan proposed for the auditorium would have produced many side boxes with only a very limited view of the stage. Basically, however, the plan is very similar in its composition of elements to that finally adopted.

The plan is symmetrically arranged on the long axis of a rectangle some 245 feet in length, east to west, and 140 feet wide. A tetrastyle portico, 56 feet wide and 19 feet deep, projects from the west front to Brydges Street. Within the portico are three doors opening to a spacious entrance hall, 24 feet wide, its great length of 97 feet being divided by three-bay screens to form three compartments, the large middle one being 65 feet long. From the end compartments doors open, north or south, to outer lobbies entered from the side streets. In the entrance hall a door on the main axis opens east to the rotunda, 35 feet in diameter, which has four diagonally-placed apses and axially-placed doors leading north or south to the two grand staircases that serve the four tiers of boxes. North and south of the grand staircases are corridor-like lobbies for the pit and galleries. An U-shaped corridor, 10 feet wide, extends round the pit and each tier of boxes in the auditorium,

the plan of which is a short horseshoe based on a circle, the diameter of the pit and the tier parapets being 64 feet, while that of the enclosing wall is 80 feet. Except for the fourth tier, which contains the lower gallery flanked by side boxes, each tier has four rows of seats or benches divided by carefully angled partitions to form twenty-nine boxes. In addition there are two large boxes in each proscenium splay, stacked above the doors opening to the apron stage, which is 11 feet deep, the proscenium opening being 40 feet wide. The stage, 90 feet wide and 66 feet deep, is flanked north and south by ranges 18 feet wide, containing offices, Green Rooms, dressing-rooms, etc., and at the east end is a 25 foot wide range of scenery workshops, flanking a central entrance.

Externally, at least, the execution of Benjamin Wyatt's first design would have given London a building worthy of comparison with the finest Continental theatres. As already remarked, the style is that of the elder Wyatts, and the manner of its use is quite as masterly (Plate 23a, b). All the fronts are unified by their division into two storeys, the lower having a strongly rusticated face broken by a plain band which serves as an impost for the arches containing the doors and windows. A pedestal underlines the lofty upper storey which has a plain face finished with a frieze, cornice and balustrade. The entrance front to Brydges Street is a simple composition, the ground storey having a central group of three arched doorways, and the upper storey a range of nine windows, all dressed alike with balustraded aprons, moulded architraves, and cornices resting on consoles. The three doorways, and the windows over them, are framed by the equal intercolumniations of the boldly projecting portico, its four plain-shafted Ionic columns rising through the two storeys to support a full entablature and a plain triangular pediment. The long side elevation is more elaborately composed, with an engaged tetrastyle portico in the centre, flanked by wings six windows wide, and ending with pavilions where the upper-storey window has three lights, dressed with a small Corinthian order and finished with a triangular pediment. On this front, the crowning balustrade is broken by panelled attic pedestals extending above the central engaged portico and the three-light windows of the end pavilions. Behind the balustrade rises the simply pilastered wall of the D-ended shell containing the auditorium and stage.

Wyatt's first design for the auditorium is a competent but rather uninspired essay in neo-classical decoration (Plate 23c). The scheme is properly dominated by the segmentally-arched proscenium frame, where the doors and boxes in the splayed sides are flanked by pilaster-strips supporting lintels, the pilasters ornamented with panels containing foliage scrolls, and the lintels with panels containing rosettes between acanthus sprouts. Wide ribs, decorated to match the pilaster-strips, frame the soffit of the arch where a series of five square coffers extends between the plain groined lunettes over the boxes. The wall face above the arch is simply panelled on either side of the royal arms, which, modelled in high relief, rise against the cornice and plain cove surrounding the flat ceiling. While the box parapets within the proscenium have panels of anthemion ornament, those of the four horseshoe tiers are decorated alike with trellised panels above narrow cornices supported by slender cast-iron colonnettes.

There is a later set of Benjamin Wyatt's drawings for Drury Lane Theatre in Sir John Soane's Museum[47] (Plates 24–5). These are signed and dated October 1811, the month when his design was formally adopted by Samuel Whitbread and the committee of proprietors. It is most probable, therefore, that these drawings, or a similar set, were submitted for the competition and, being selected, were used for settling the contract whereby Henry Rowles, the builder, undertook to complete the theatre on or before 1 October 1812.

Although the arrangment of the plan is generally similar to that of the 1810 design, the dimensions of the basically rectangular building have again been reduced, the length to 234 feet, and the width to 129 feet 6 inches. The projection of the front portico has been increased to 25 feet, to provide space for two steps and a landing extending between the antae and screen walls. The entrance hall is now 27 feet wide and 85 feet 6 inches long, while the diameter of the central rotunda is reduced to 30 feet. Separate entrances have been provided, on both sides of the building, for the pit and the two galleries, and the general circulation within the theatre is more skilfully worked out, but the biggest changes are to be found in the form and disposition of the auditorium. The parapets of the four tiers now conform to a semicircle of 61 feet diameter which is continued for some 8 feet on either side before returning, in a reversed quadrant curve, to stop against the enclosing wall of the auditorium, which conforms to a diameter of 107 feet 11 inches. This form of terminating the tiers, probably derived from Ledoux,* was introduced to ensure a better view of the stage from the extreme side boxes. The straight-fronted apron stage is now flanked by concave quadrant faces, without doors below the bow-fronted boxes, and the proscenium opening, which is flanked by free-standing columns, is only 33 feet wide. The stage width is 76 feet and its depth, including the apron, is 68 feet.

The 1811 auditorium contains a pit with nineteen straight rows of benches, ample standing space at the back, and seven private boxes on either side. There are three tiers each divided into twenty-four boxes with four rows of seats, and a fourth tier having seven boxes on either side of the two-shilling gallery which has ten rows of benches. The five back rows are behind the columns supporting the upper gallery, where six steeply banked rows of benches offer a very limited view of the stage through a series of arches intersecting the ceiling cove.

The exterior design of 1810 is retained with some minor changes for the 1811 scheme (Plate 25a, b). In the front elevation, the upper-storey windows are now simply dressed with plain architraves. Similar economies affect the side elevations, where the wings are now five windows wide, and plain niches have replaced the three-light windows of the end pavilions. The engaged portico on the Russell Street side is still shown with three-quarter columns, but that on the south side has only pilasters.

Comparing the 1811 drawings with those of the completed building, as engraved for illustrating Wyatt's *Observations* (Plates 26–8, 29b), it will appear that the only changes that occur in the plans and internal design are such as might normally be made during the progress of a large and complex building operation. The exterior, however, was largely redesigned and completed in an austere Grecian style, presumably to keep the cost of building, furnishing and equipping the theatre within the stipulated sum of £150,000.

In his *Observations* Wyatt relates how, in perfecting his design, it was his 'study to unite a due attention to the profits of the Theatre, with

---

* Claude-Nicolas Ledoux (1736–1806). Designs for theatres at Besançon (1778–84) and Marseilles (1785–6).

adequate provision, in every respect, for the accommodation of the Public'. In this he was guided by four main considerations:

'*First*,—The Size or Capacity of the Theatre, as governed by the width of the Proscenium, or Stage-opening; and by the pecuniary return to be made to those whose Property might be embarked in the Concern.'[48]

According to Wyatt's calculations, given in his *Observations*,[49] the boxes seated 1,286 (excluding the four proscenium boxes and fourteen private boxes flanking the pit), the pit seated 920, the two-shilling gallery 550, and the one-shilling gallery 350. He estimated that this capacity was sufficient to produce takings of £600 per night, thereby ensuring a reasonable return to the investors, consistent with the proper operation and maintenance of a metropolitan theatre 'of a superior order'.[50] The relatively small size of the proscenium was justified by the consequent reduction in size of the scenery, saving canvas, paint and labour, and the fact that such scenery could be changed quickly, with lighter machinery and fewer hands. Wyatt also stresses the saving in expenses by reducing the number of extras required for 'Processions, Scenic Groupings, etc.'[51]

'*Secondly*,—The Form or Shape of the Theatre, as connected with the primary objects of Distinct Sound and Vision.'[52]

The form of the auditorium was settled as a result of experiments in acoustics, carried out on lines suggested by George Saunders, in his *Treatise on Theatres* of 1790, to which Wyatt pays due tribute. By limiting the distance between the front of the stage and the back wall of the boxes to 53 feet 9 inches, he expected to bring all spectators well within the natural expansion of the voice, and enable them to have a clear sight of the stage action. He justifies his choice of auditorium plan, a truncated circle, by remarking 'that the Theatre at Bordeaux is exactly of the same Form as the present Theatre in Drury Lane; and that that Theatre is always quoted as one, in which the voice is better heard, than in almost any Theatre in the world'.[53] It must be observed, however, that Wyatt exaggerates the resemblance between the two theatres. The design of the Bordeaux auditorium is, in fact, based on a square ceiled with a shallow dome and pendentives, one side of the square opening to the box-flanked proscenium, while each other side is expanded to form a shallow semi-elliptical apse which is divided into three equal bays by columns, between which the balconies of loges project.

'*Thirdly*,—The Facility of Ingress and Egress, as materially affecting the convenience of those going to every part of the House respectively; as well their Lives, in cases of sudden accident or alarm.'[52]

In this matter, Wyatt resolved 'to attach similar approaches and accommodation to each side of the House respectively; thus, whatever Doors of Entrance, Staircases, Avenues, &c. are provided for one side of the House, the same precisely are provided for the other side; with the exception only of the upper Gallery, which, from its size, does not require two Entrances'.[54] Here it is worth noting that the 1811 plans show two staircases for the upper gallery, one on the south side and one on the north, but the latter is reduced in the executed plans to a private stair serving only the Bedford and Devonshire boxes. These are shown to be at the north end of the 'First Tier of Boxes' which is above the 'Dress Tier of Boxes', and on the opposite side are two similar private boxes, the larger one allotted to Mrs. Garrick. The lower gallery was served by two triangular staircases contrived within the spandrel-shaped spaces north-west and south-west of the massive semi-circular wall surrounding the box corridors. Access to each of these three corridors was separately arranged through doors or passages leading off the various landings of the 'King's' and 'Prince's' staircases which begin their ascent with a wide central flight, branch left and right to landings at the dress-boxes level, then return in parallel flights to a wide landing level with the saloon, rotunda, and first tier of boxes, whence another central flight ascends to finish at a half-landing level with the second tier of boxes. The pit was approached through corridors entered from capacious vestibules flanking the main entrance hall, and each group of private boxes at pit level was provided with a corridor entered from a vestibule centred in the north or south front.

'*Fourthly*,—Decorum among the several Orders and Classes of the Visitants to the Theatre, as essential to the accommodation of the more respectable part of those Visitants; and consequently of great importance to the interests of the Theatre.'[52]

Wyatt's avowed object here was 'that of protecting the more rational and respectable class of Spectators from those nuisances to which they have long been exposed, by being obliged to pass through Lobbies, Rooms, and Avenues, crowded with the most disreputable Members of the Community, and subject to scenes of the most disgusting indecency'. Knowing that 'an avowed exclusion of any particular class of people from either part of the House, (excepting the Private Boxes) would be utterly impracticable; and therefore that the best plan was to form an arrangement, which should virtually amount to an exclusion of those whom it was desirable to exclude, without any declared intention of doing so', Wyatt eliminated the notorious 'basket boxes', which had been placed behind the front dress boxes in the previous theatre, and placed the crush rooms and refreshment rooms in places sufficiently remote from the dress boxes so that ladies occupying them were 'relieved from the nuisances to which they have hitherto been liable in passing to and from their Boxes'.[55]

Among Wyatt's Drury Lane drawings in the Royal Institute of British Architects is an undated elevation showing the penultimate stage in the design for the entrance front (Plate 29a). The treatment is still neo-classical, with no trace of Greek ornamentation, but the design is bold in scale and austere in expression. The drawing shows a finish resembling ashlar, although cement was probably envisaged. The two well-defined storeys are retained, the lower having three round-arched doorways widely spaced in the middle, and a similar arch framing a smaller round-arched window on either side. Above the upper-storey pedestal, and centred over the arches, are five windows dressed alike with moulded architraves and cornice-hoods. The end windows of both storeys are given prominence by being placed between giant plain-shafted Doric pilasters which rise from the plain plinth, break through the plain impost of the lower storey and the plain members of the upper-storey pedestal, and support an appropriately massive entablature, of which the plain frieze and cornice are returned and continued across the front, above a plain panel sunk in the face over the three windows. Behind the attic pedestal rises the curved wall of the auditorium shell, its face divided into equal bays by small Doric pilasters supporting a frieze, cornice and blocking-course. A festive note is given to the entrance by the four garlanded altars bearing tripod lamps, which are placed flanking the three doorways, these being furnished with handsomely coffered doors below radial fanlights.

Although the entrance front to Brydges Street was built much in the form adumbrated by this drawing, the proportions were changed by a reduction in height, and a Greek flavour was infused by some changes of detail (Plate 29b). The giant Doric pilasters flanking the end windows were transformed into Ionic antae having enriched capitals similar to those of the Erechtheion. In the upper storey, the sill-band was omitted and the windows were given a Greek dress, consisting of a moulded architrave with canted jambs and an eared head, finished with a plain frieze and cornice, the middle three windows having pediments. James Elmes, writing in 1827, states that Wyatt intended to add, when funds permitted, an Ionic portico for which the giant antae were a preparation.[56] This, however, seems most unlikely, for an examination of the front as designed and built will show that if a portico was to be added, having its outer columns responding to the antae, the doors and windows of the inside face would fail to register correctly with any reasonable system of intercolumniation.

Although the entrance front was faced with Roman cement to resemble Portland stone masonry, the other elevations were simply finished in stock bricks, sparingly dressed with cement and stone. For the long north and south sides, Wyatt simplified his 1811 design by omitting the central engaged portico, so that between each end pavilion there now extends an unbroken face of two storeys, the lower having the doors and windows symmetrically arranged in a series of thirteen round-arched recesses. Correspondingly, the upper storey has a range of thirteen straight-arched windows set without architraves in a plain face that is finished with a simple entablature and parapet. The end pavilions, brick versions of those in the 1811 design, also consist of two storeys, the lower having a doorway framed in a round-arched recess, and the upper containing a large niche. Above each pavilion, the parapet is broken by an attic pedestal.

This simple but grandly scaled exterior was designed to form an impressive prelude to a series of finely related interiors, decorated with increasing richness until the full splendour of the auditorium was reached (Plates 27b, 28). Through the three great doors in the entrance front, flanked by tripod-altar lamps on massive pedestals, patrons of the boxes passed into the spacious hall, its length originally extending beyond the side screens, formed of two Greek Doric columns between antae, where a tripod-altar lamp was placed in each narrow side inter-columniation. The two pay-boxes were recessed in the wall opposite the entrances, between three doorways, the middle one opening to the rotunda, the north to the King's staircase, and the south to the Prince's staircase. The ground storey of the rotunda, simply decorated with four niches placed diagonally to flank the doors opening north and south to the grand staircases, originally contained a cast of Peter Scheemakers' statue of Shakespeare, placed on a pedestal-stove opposite to the west entrance door. A stone gallery, cantilevered on scrolled trusses of cast iron and furnished with an iron railing of trellis-patterned panels, surrounds the circular well which opens to the principal storey (Plate 36a). Here the decoration is more elaborate, with three-bay screens of plain-shafted Corinthian columns extending between four diagonally placed piers containing niches, originally furnished with candelabra. The order, based on that of the Temple of Jupiter Stator, Rome, has an entablature with a frieze of acanthus scrolls, griffins and urns, and an enriched modillioned cornice. Above this rises a 'Pantheon' dome with five rings of square coffers, their size diminishing as they near the glazed oculus.

Each grand staircase (Plate 36b) is entered from the hall and rotunda through a colonnade of plain-shafted Ionic columns, five bays wide, which supports the principal-storey landing. Wyatt designed that the walls of the almost square compartment should be plain but for a string-course, enriched with rosettes between acanthus sprouts, at the principal-storey level, and a wave-scrolled impost above it. A simple frieze and cornice surrounds the ceiling, which is divided by enriched beams into a series of coffers surrounding a roof-light. The landings and steps are of stone, the branching and return flights to the principal storey being partly cantilevered and partly supported by light cast-iron cradles, while the central upper flight rests on cast-iron carriages. The iron railings, formed of closely-spaced vertical bars linked by small circles, are finished with a reeded mahogany handrail, and, like the rotunda gallery railing, they originally incorporated slender candelabra-like oil lamps placed above the baluster newels.

Above the hall is the large and lofty saloon, entered by doors from the rotunda and the two staircases (Plate 37a). Here a plain-shafted Corinthian order is employed, with paired pilasters dividing each of the long walls into three equal bays, containing doorways on the east and windows on the west. At each end is a screen, formed of two columns between antae, opening to a segmental apse where a doorway is flanked by niches, designed to contain statues placed above pedestal-fireplaces. Each niche is ceiled with a semi-dome, conforming with the segmentally-arched ceiling of the room. Beyond each apse, Wyatt contrived a small coffee-room, most elegantly designed with Corinthian pilasters on piers supporting segmental arches, below a dome on pendentives (Plate 28a). On the west side of each coffee-room was a 'fruit office', perpetuating the tradition of the Caroline orange-vendors. There is little to record about the original colour schemes of these various interiors, except that the Ionic columns of the staircases and the Corinthian columns of the rotunda had shafts resembling Egyptian granite, or porphyry, while the Corinthian order in the saloon had shafts resembling verde antico marble.[44]

This noble suite of rooms has fortunately survived, with some changes, to constitute an outstanding monument of theatre design in the grand manner, but Wyatt's auditorium was very short-lived and can only be studied in his drawings and a few contemporary views (Plates 27, 32a). These show that the pit was surrounded by thirteen low segmentally-arched openings, the four on either side framing the private boxes. The parapets of the four tiers rested in turn on slender columns of cast iron, having moulded bases, fluted shafts, and simply foliated capitals. The three tiers of boxes were thus divided into fourteen bays, generally two boxes wide. As the dress-boxes parapet projected slightly forwards from the others, the one above it was designed to form a concave hood and decorated with scale ornament. Apart from this, the parapets were ornamented with trellised panels, those of the dress boxes incorporating figure-subject medallions. One of Wyatt's colour studies shows the pit arcade marbled in verde antico, the tier parapets in parchment and gold with red panels trellised in gold, and figure-subjects in green and gold, the walls and partitions of the boxes being a rich crimson. Another study has the dress-boxes parapet resting on caryatids, against a verde antico arcade, while an alternative scheme has porphyry-shafted Ionic columns against the arcade.[57] Instead of proscenium doors on either side of the apron stage, Wyatt introduced a large tripod-altar lamp, raised on a pedestal ornamented with griffins and placed against each concave wall face, where the bowed parapets of the two superimposed boxes projected between a pair of pilasters belonging to the same giant Corinthian order as the free-standing columns and respondent pilasters that flanked the proscenium opening. Although the column shafts were fluted and marbled to resemble verde antico, the pilasters had panelled shafts ornamented 'with concerted rings entwined with grapes and vine leaves, all richly gilt'.[58] The highly enriched entablature was returned above the columns to provide a springing for the richly coffered proscenium arch, but it was continued across the opening, below a segmental tympanum adorned with the royal arms. A winged genius decorated the spandrel on either side of the arch, and in the attic stage of each concave wall face, between panelled pilasters, was a niche containing a statue, Melpomene on one side, Thalia on the other. A frieze decorated with widely spaced wreaths, and a simple cornice extended round the auditorium, below a quadrant cove diapered with small lozenges containing flowers. The almost flat ceiling was painted to resemble a dome, with a border of decorative panels surrounding rings of quadrangular coffers that diminished in size towards the central motif, a circular grille for ventilation, adorned with a rayed head of Apollo.

Crabb Robinson recorded in his diary for 30 November 1812, that he 'went to Drury Lane to see the house not the performance. It is indeed a magnificent object. The Proscenium is the most splendid scene I ever beheld. It is certainly quite enough adorned but it would be absurd to reproach the architect with making a theatre gorgeous. Let the prison be dry and rude so as to excite a sense of severity, let the temple and the hall of justice be majestically simple, but the public theatre should be pompous and profusely adorned. The depth of the proscenium has been objected to as a loss of room, but I suspect this to be an illusion. . . . The boxes capped by a statue of Comedy and Tragedy are placed over an elegant tripod bearing a brilliant white flamed lamp of numerous wicks in a circle. And beyond this on each side a superb column of verde antique . . . the roof displeased me—instead of being arched

and lifted above the walls, it lies as it were a weight upon them. And the shilling gallery is cut out of the ceiling so that the whole produced in me an impression of imperfection and insecurity.'[59]

Wyatt's published plans show that the working area of the stage, about 80 feet wide and 46 feet deep, was originally equipped with six sets of wing grooves, and with two fly-galleries on either side which were connected by narrow bridges against the back wall. The 30-foot wide range to the east of the stage contained a basement, with shops for the stage carpenters and property makers, and at stage level were two lofty stores for scenery, the larger one to the south having a wide opening to centre with the proscenium, enabling the store to be used for deep perspective effects. Above the scenery stores were two painting rooms, the larger one having floor grooves through which the scene-frames could be lowered. The dressing-rooms, Green Rooms, offices, etc., were very capacious and well arranged in the five-storeyed ranges flanking the north and south sides of the stage. Nevertheless, it was found necessary in 1814 to build a detached scene store of L-shaped plan on a site adjoining the north-east angle of the theatre, its front being designed to harmonize with the Russell Street elevation.

When the theatre was first opened 'it was fully foreseen that the embellishments of the interior would not be permanent upon the green walls; the moisture exhaling from the bricks and plaster would certainly occasion a fading in the colours, and a tarnish in the gilding'. In 1814, therefore, the management committee decided 'that the expense of re-painting and re-gilding would be nearly equal to that of a new interior, they therefore determined upon giving a new interior, for in a Theatre novelty has an undisputed sway. The grand saloon is painted with a lilac ground, harmonizing with the columns and pilasters; the great staircase[s] and rotunda are fresh painted and decorated; the corridors of the boxes are divided into pannels of two shades of delicate green, with a white Etruscan border: these lead us into the interior, the basement is painted a rich Scagliola marble. The fronts of the dress boxes are a light blue ground, enriched by a gold octagonal lattice work, with roses in the centres, and a relief of white in the intersections. The canopy fronts of the first tier have an antique projecting scroll, with gold foliage falling upon relieved flutings. The second tier is embellished by a series of classical subjects, painted in relief upon a blue ground, with enriched borders. The third tier of boxes is decorated by a gold scrollwork in relief running from the centre ornament of the same character, to each termination of the sides, upon a blue ground. The prevailing colour, therefore, of the boxes, is blue; but it is relieved, and a warmth of tone produced by the back of the boxes being painted in a light brown colour, divided into pannels by appropriate borderings. The ceiling is new, the dome being divided into alternate compartments of blue vanishing into distance, and scroll enrichments terminating in the centre.

'The hydrostatic lamps placed upon tripods on each side of the proscenium . . . were found, in practice, too delicate in their construction to bear the currents of air to which they were exposed, by the rising and falling of the curtain; they were therefore removed at the close of the first season, and their supports, the tripods, remained as useless ornaments; they are now displaced, and the vacancy filled up by two additional proscenium boxes on each side. . . . The two grand columns have been removed, and the angles left have been filled up by ornaments uniting with the general contour of the House, and affording to the architect the opportunity of indulging the performers in their favourite wish of Stage doors. Above these doors, balconies, with suitable canopies, lattice-work, and galleries are placed, rendering them both ornamental in the general effect, and serviceable in the business of the stage.'[60]

In a description of the theatre, *The Picture of London* for 1818 roundly condemned the management for converting the beautiful saloon into 'what is called a Chinese Temple, with two holes for staircases from the hall below. It is impossible to say whether the man who planned this ridiculous alteration, or the architect who executed it, has shown most want of taste.'[61] During the summer of 1819, the interior was redecorated, the new colour scheme being French grey with gold ornaments, and silver for the pillars of the boxes. Statues replaced the bronze tripods in the niches of the rotunda and corridors, and an ormolu chandelier was suspended from the centre of the dome.[62] Remarking on the declining fortune of the theatre, *The New Picture of London* for 1819 found occasion for favourable comment in remarking that 'the chandelier, hanging in the centre of the ceiling over the pit, and illuminated with gas, is very tasteful and elegant; superior to that in any other theatre'.[63]

Although Wyatt had made every effort to produce an almost perfect auditorium, and despite the alterations made to improve it during the early years of its use, certain striking deficiencies became increasingly obvious. The proscenium was too small for so wide an auditorium, and the acoustics were far from perfect. The manager, R. W. Elliston, therefore decided to overcome these defects, before the 1822 season opened, by employing Henry Peto, an experienced contractor, to construct a virtually new auditorium and improve the stage accommodation, to the designs and under the supervision of Samuel Beazley, then advancing in a career that was to make him the leading theatre architect of his time. This operation is recorded to have involved Elliston in an expenditure of some £22,000.[64]

Beazley completely gutted the auditorium within the wall dividing it from the box corridors, which were to remain structurally unchanged. Four new tiers of horseshoe form were constructed, all with parapets conforming to a semicircle of 51 feet 6 inches in diameter, with each side continued in a shallow elliptical curve so that the width between them, where they adjoined the proscenium boxes, was 46 feet 6 inches. The distance from the front of the apron to the centre of each parapet was now only 48 feet. The apron was 12 feet deep to the curtain, and the proscenium opening was 40 feet wide and 46 feet high to the centre of its arched head. As in Wyatt's auditorium, the first three tiers each contained four rows of seats, divided by low partitions into boxes, but space was now available at the back for some private boxes. According to the account in *Illustrations of the Public Buildings of London*, the dress circle contained twenty-six boxes, each furnished with nine chairs, and ten private boxes each with six chairs. The first circle had four private boxes on either side, between fourteen public boxes extending in front of six private boxes. The second tier was divided into twenty-two double boxes which were separated from the front rows of seats, and at each end was a private box. The top tier contained three large boxes on either side of the lower gallery, with seven rows of benches. The upper gallery had only three rows of benches and a wide standing-space at the back. According to the engraved plan (Plate 30b), the pit contained twenty-one straight benches, whereas the section shows only eighteen. On each side of the pit there were three private boxes, and two large public boxes without seats. In addition there were four private boxes between the columns on either side of the proscenium. The pit seated 800, the lower gallery 550, and the upper gallery 350, which with the seating in the boxes made a total of 3,060.[65]

The view from the stage, given in *Illustrations of the Public Buildings of London*, shows how in decorating the new auditorium Beazley retained much of the general character and some of the original features of its predecessor (Plate 32b). The straight parapets of the boxes flanking the proscenium were recessed between three-quarter columns of a giant Corinthian order, standing on a high panelled pedestal and supporting an enriched entablature, which was surmounted by an attic containing a niche flanked by panelled pilasters. The pedestal panel was, in fact, a removable grille in front of a stage box. The column shafts were hollow and of wood, their apparent flutes being slits through which the stage could be glimpsed from inside the boxes.[66] The entablature of the order provided a springing for the semi-elliptical arch of the proscenium, the face above it being decorated with two spandrel panels. In the niches above the boxes were placed statues of Melpomene and Thalia, salvaged from the old auditorium. The four tier parapets were each supported by a ring of twelve slender cast-iron columns having gilt fluted shafts. Each parapet, however, was different, that of the dress circle exhibiting a series of long panels containing scenes from Shakespeare's plays. 'Grecian ornaments of varied design, in running patterns, with rosettes, wreaths, &c.,' adorned the first and second circles, and the top-tier parapet was treated with a continuous frieze of anthemion ornament. The high wall face behind the top tier was divided into wide bays by plain-shafted Doric pilasters which matched the three square piers supporting the upper-gallery parapet. This formed part of the crowning entablature, its frieze simply decorated with wreaths placed over the pilasters. Bold ribs, enriched with 'roses in annulets' divided the cove and flat ceiling into two rings of panels, the wedge-shaped panels of the ceiling being ornamented with large and small anthemion motifs. At first the prevailing colours of the decorations were warm drab infused with dark red and highly enriched with gold. The proscenium was dressed

6—S.L. XXXV

with a deep valance of festooned drapery, and the opening was provided with a very handsome drop scene of figures against Grecian ruins, painted by Marinari and Stanton, at a cost of some £700.[67] In 1825, however, the ground colour was changed to white, the Shakespearean panels were replaced by others of inferior design, and the crimson furniture of the boxes was replaced by green.[44] Ample light was provided by two tiers of fourteen lustres suspended from brackets projecting above the columns of the dress and first circles, and by the very large gas-lit lustre of lotus form hanging from the centre of the ceiling.

Beazley also made alterations to the stage, by opening up spaces on either side to provide room for 'arranging processions and scenic illusions'. To replace the rooms lost by these changes, he built on the south side a small extension containing a new Green Room and some dressing-rooms.[44] This, however, was not the first change to be made to Wyatt's exterior, for in 1820 a portico had been added to the Brydges (now Catherine) Street front. This much criticized portico, rising only to the first storey, is composed of four pairs of Doric columns, their plain square shafts supporting a simple entablature, originally surmounted by a lead statue of Shakespeare (now in the entrance hall).[68] Although it has been generally attributed to James Spiller, a note in Elliston's account of his outlay in improving Drury Lane Theatre records that it was 'completed under the sole direction and design of Sir John Soane'.[69] In 1831, the long Russell Street front was graced with the addition of Beazley's far more elegant colonnade of a Grecian Ionic order, having fluted shafts of cast iron (Plate 38).

The interior was redecorated before the season of 1830–1, and again before 1836–7, when the lessee, Alfred Bunn, spent £1,500 on an elaborate scheme executed by Crace, who based his designs on Raphael's *Loggie* in the Vatican. The circular ceiling was given a ground of soft cream colour and adorned with emblematic cameo medallions, supported by light gold enrichments radiating towards the centre and connected by festooned garlands of flowers. Round the edge were eight large lunettes, apparently open to the sky, against which were posed groups of children symbolizing the theatrical arts. The cove was separated from the ceiling by a white fret on a lavender ground, and divided into compartments of various colours, ornamented with emblematical devices and bunches of flowers, with gold relief. The Corinthian columns flanking the proscenium were finished in burnished gold, relieved with white, and the box parapets between them had richly gilt ornaments on a crimson velvet ground. The first circle parapet was painted with scenes from Shakespeare's plays, separated by gilt dwarf pilasters on a white ground. The second circle parapet was divided by gilt enrichments into panels, alternately wide and narrow, the former containing a raffle-foliage scroll with birds, and the latter having grotesque masks on a maroon ground. The gallery parapet was painted with a continuous frieze of dancing figures holding wreaths, and festoons with musical trophies.[70] Although Beazley is said to have thoroughly renovated the auditorium in 1841, its general appearance seems to have remained very much as described above, if the evidence of two lithographs, dated 1841 and 1842, is reliable (Plate 33).

In 1847, however, the auditorium was redecorated for the impresario, Frederick Gye. An engraving in *The Builder* shows how each tier parapet was 'laced over with a trellis of large mesh, formed of an engaged moulding gilt' on which were placed 'festoons of detached flowers, very nicely modelled, also gilt'. The Corinthian columns flanking the proscenium boxes were 'entwined by a continuous wreath of flowers gilt', and the cast-iron columns supporting the tiers were similarly wreathed. All these ornaments of *papier mâché* were modelled, gilt and fixed by the specialist contractor, Bielefeld, in five weeks. The ground colour for this display of gilt trellis was a 'faint blossom colour, approaching white'. The circular ceiling was painted to represent a cloudless sky, which was also glimpsed through a series of gilt trellis arches decorating the surrounding cove. In the centre was a group of five flying cupids, apparently supporting the great chandelier of gilt metal and glass lustres, from which projected six flags of glass lustres 'with the lines of the Union Jack marked on them by light'. Additional lighting was provided by a series of small lustres, projecting on brackets from the parapet of the second tier. All the draperies were of bright scarlet cloth 'of which our army officers' uniforms are made', and the boxes were lined inside with 'a yellow patterned paper on a crimson ground'.[71]

A redecoration in 1851, with ornaments in the style of Louis XVI 'selected and executed' by the decorator, Benjamin Hurwitz,[72] cannot have been extensive since two photographs of 1897–8 (Plate 34) show a somewhat arid-looking auditorium that is still recognizably Wyatt's interior as reconstructed by Beazley and redecorated by Bielefeld in 1847. The *papier mâché* garlands had, however, been removed from the trellised parapets and from the slotted shafts of the Corinthian columns flanking the proscenium boxes, but not from the cast-iron columns supporting the tiers. Perhaps to compensate for this loss of ornament, the first-tier parapet had been enlivened with a series of scrolled cartouches, each inscribed with the name of a famous dramatist or composer, placed below the cast-iron columns. The fourth-tier parapet had also been enriched with gilt paterae between panels of trellis.

In 1870 *The Builder* stated that the interior was to undergo a complete transformation to meet the requirements of a new opera company. Drawings by Messrs. Marsh Nelson and Harvey had been handed to Messrs. W. Bracher and Son, who had remodelled the house for Mapleson in 1868.[73] From the photographs already referred to, it would appear that these changes were of a temporary nature. A similar 'transformation' in 1871 was completed by the same contractors in eight days. The work then consisted largely of fitting up temporary partitions in the tiers to provide a circle of pit boxes, a grand tier of private boxes, and an upper tier with ten boxes on either side.[74]

In 1901 it was found necessary to reconstruct the now sub-standard auditorium. Among other improvements carried out under Philip Pilditch's direction, the tiers were reconstructed with steel girders and concrete floors, using only a front row of columns to support them. Two rows of seats were added to each tier, and the box parapets were brought forward. A fire which took place on 25 March 1908 was confined to the stage area.

A photograph taken in 1921 (Plate 35a) shows Pilditch's reconstructed auditorium, opulently decorated by Messrs. Campbell, Smith and Company, in a style somewhat similar to that of Daly's Theatre, designed by Spencer Chadwick.[75] The proscenium frame was composed of marble-shafted Corinthian pilasters which, with scroll-consoles, supported an enriched entablature having a frieze decoration of wreaths. Above this was a broken pediment of semi-elliptical form, the scrolled cornice framing a tympanum containing a richly modelled cartouche with the royal arms, flanked by painted panels of *putti* disporting themselves against a balustrade. The entablature was returned on either side of the proscenium to rest on the fluted Corinthian columns flanking the four stacked boxes. Above the entablature rose a flared and elliptically arched soffit, decorated with two rings of square coffers containing flower bosses. Large pendentives with painted panels, linking the proscenium arch with similar arches on either side of the auditorium, framed the saucer-domed ceiling. The parapets of the four circles were richly decorated with scrollwork and other motifs, such as cartouches, and those fronting the first two tiers projected in a series of shallow segmental curves. It is worth noting that the statues of Melpomene and Thalia, salvaged from Wyatt's proscenium and re-used by Beazley in niches above the proscenium boxes, were now relegated to niches flanking the stalls.

A rebuilding even more extensive than that undertaken by Samuel Beazley in 1822 was carried out in 1921–2, when the auditorium was demolished along with the greater part of the original semi-circular walls, to make way for the present interior, designed by J. Emblin Walker, F. Edward Jones and Robert Cromie, with Adrian Collins as consulting engineer. Representing the best standards in theatre practice of its time, the new auditorium is about 80 feet wide and 85 feet deep. The stalls now seat 883 in three blocks divided by a cross aisle into nine front and sixteen back rows. Above the back stalls are three large tiers, constructed on cantilevered steel girders and completely free of obstructing columns. Each has eleven rows of seats, arranged in three blocks, the dress circle seating 413, the grand circle 446, and the upper circle 435. There are also seven boxes containing six seats, and sixteen with four seats (figs. 7, 8).

The auditorium was decorated in the Empire style to accord with Wyatt's suite of entrance foyers (Plate 35b). The rectangular proscenium has a wide moulded frame of imitated lapis lazuli, below a richly modelled tympanum. Between the proscenium and the three circles are canted faces containing, above stalls level, three tiers of boxes arranged in three bays. The middle bay is flanked by columns and the outer bays by pilasters of a composite order, having shafts of imitated lapis lazuli with bronze-gilt capitals and bases. These columns and pilasters stand on tall pedestals and support an entablature which is surmounted by a panelled attic, broken forward above the middle bay and there crowned with a scrolled motif. In the middle bay of the north side is the lofty royal box, below one having a round-arched opening. The stepped parapets of the first-tier boxes are enriched with cartouches and coats of arms, those of the second tier have Flaxmanesque figure-subject panels, and the third-tier boxes have bowed railings of gilt metalwork. A flared semi-elliptical ceiling links the canted sides and is decorated with a series of octagonal coffers surrounding a large quadrangular panel where a richly framed lozenge contains three circular motifs. From these are suspended three large light-fittings of gilt metalwork and cut glass. Mahogany panelling lines the walls at stalls level, and the side walls of the three circles are handsomely decorated, the first with monochrome panels after Fragonard, the second with marbled pilasters and 'Wedgwood' panels, while the third has a deep band of panels and circular medallions below the entablature which adjoins the flat ceiling. The tableau curtains and box draperies are of Chinese yellow velvet, with Empire motifs in blue.[76]

The stage now has a total depth of some 80 feet, made possible by demolishing the original scene stores and painting rooms at the back. Its floor rises with a gentle slope for a depth of 45 feet and is furnished with a series of lifts. The back part is level and fixed. On either side is a lighting gallery, a fly-gallery, and a loading gallery below the grid. To the east of the stage, and south of Wyatt's scenery store, has been added at various times a large scenery painting room, a property room, and an electricians' workshop.

Drury Lane is unique among London's theatres in many respects, not least in the works of sculpture and painting distributed through the building, notably in the public approaches to the auditorium. At the north end of the entrance hall is a fine statue in lead of Shakespeare inclining against a pedestal decorated with masks, modelled by John Cheere (d. 1787), given by Samuel Whitbread and originally placed above the entrance portico. Statues on pedestals now occupy the originally empty niches in the lower stage of the rotunda. In the north-west niche is a marble of Michael Balfe, composer (1808–70), by

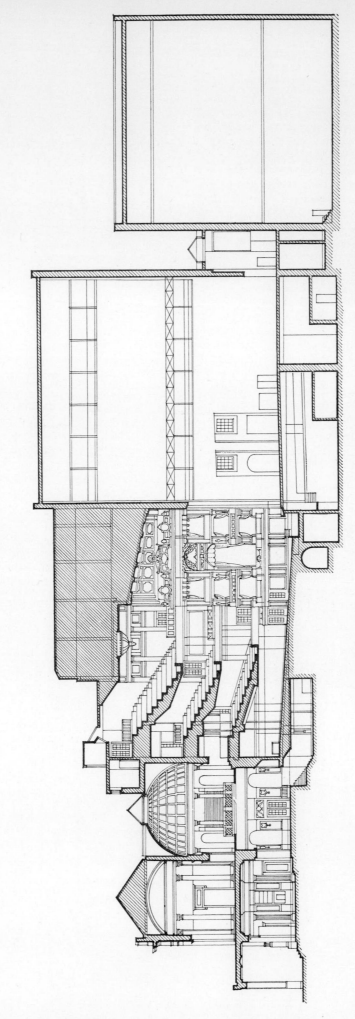

Fig. 7. Section, existing state. Redrawn from a plan in the possession of the Greater London Council

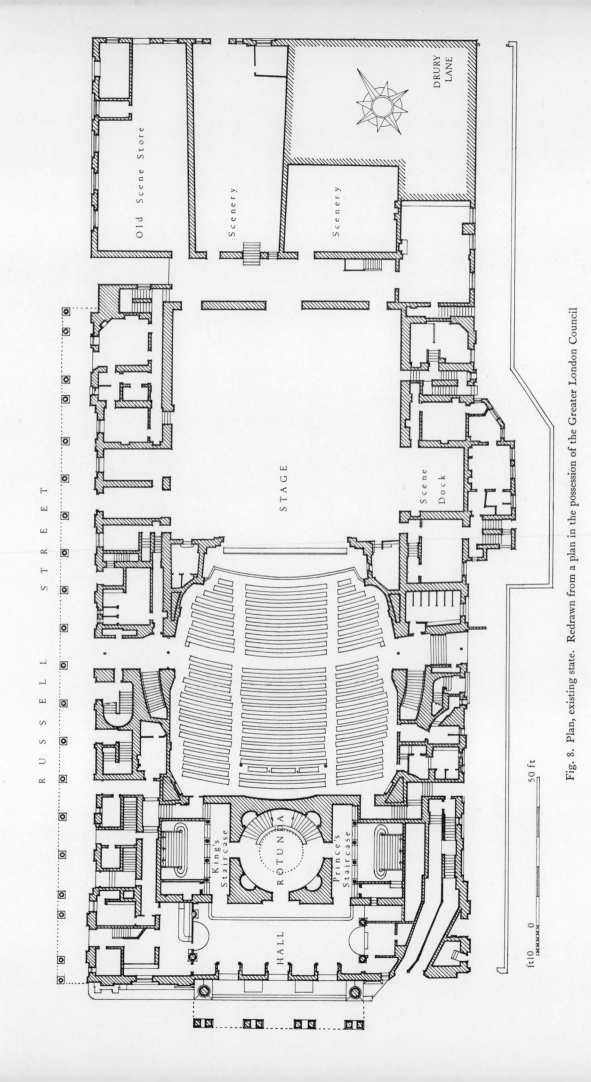

RUSSELL STREET

Old Scene Store

Scenery

Scenery

DRURY LANE

STAGE

Scene Dock

King's Staircase

ROTUNDA

Prince's Staircase

HALL

ft 10   0   50 ft

Fig. 8. Plan, existing state. Redrawn from a plan in the possession of the Greater London Council

M. Mallempré; in the south-west is a plaster version by George Garrard of Roubiliac's Shakespeare; in the south-east is a marble of Edmund Kean, by J. E. Carew; and in the north-east is a plaster statue of David Garrick. The niches in the upper stage of the rotunda now contain portrait busts on pedestals. The north-west niche has Sir Johnston Forbes-Robertson (1853–1937), a marble by C. Rebworth; the south-west has Ivor Novello (1893–1951), a bronze by Clemence Dane; the south-east has Ira Aldridge (1804–67), Negro actor, in coloured marbles; and the north-east has Samuel Whitbread, a marble by J. Nollekens. These busts have replaced the four allegorical female statues representing Tragedy, Comedy, Music and Dancing, each holding a symbolic mask and originally bearing a lamp, that now occupy the niches at each end of the saloon. Among the paintings are several fine portraits of famous players, and scenes from well-known plays. The best of these paintings decorate the staircases, the box corridors, and the Green Room.

CHAPTER V

Covent Garden Theatre and the Royal Opera House: the Management

THE Royal Opera House, Covent Garden, stands upon the site of the theatre erected by John Rich in 1731–2. It is the third theatre to occupy this site, both its predecessors having been destroyed by fire. The first, designed by Edward Shepherd, was burnt in 1808, and the second, designed by (Sir) Robert Smirke, was destroyed in 1856. After this second fire the present building was erected in 1857–8; E. M. Barry was the architect. After nearly two and a half centuries of theatrical usage 'Covent Garden' has earned many claims to fame—as a theatre still acting under the authority of letters patent granted by Charles II, as the scene of the triumphs of many great actors and musicians, and in recent years as the home of both the Royal Opera and the Royal Ballet. Many of these distinctions have been fully described elsewhere,* and the following account has therefore been written from the managerial and architectural viewpoints; it only refers incidentally to the performers and performances which would form an important theme of a comprehensive study of the theatre.

On 16 March 1730/1 Wriothesley, third Duke of Bedford, granted to John Rich, esquire, four separate ground leases of land and buildings at the north-east corner of Covent Garden Piazza (Plate 39). Rich, described as of Southampton Street, Bloomsbury, had managed the theatre in Lincoln's Inn Fields since 1714,[1] and after his recent success there he evidently wished to build a larger theatre.

Before the grant was made Rich had had to purchase the interests of three existing leaseholders, but he already held the ground lease of the fourth piece of ground himself, by direct grant from the Duke in 1726. The four leases,[2] all for sixty-one years from Lady Day 1731, were for the ground shown on fig. 9. There was to be a peppercorn rent for the first year, and thereafter rents of £100, £80, £40 and £30, making a total of £250 per annum. The site had hitherto been occupied by several houses and their ancillary stables and coach houses, most of which Rich covenanted to rebuild. His portico houses at the north-east corner of the Piazza were, however, not to be rebuilt, but to be maintained 'in the like good order, symetry, proportion, forme, plight and condition or better' than they then were. On the principal plot, measuring 120 feet from north to south and 100 feet from east to west, he covenanted to erect 'a new Grand Theatre', with access by three passages some 9 or 10 feet wide—one from the portico walk on the south, another from Hart Street to the north and the third from Bow Street to the east.

News of Rich's plans was first published on 12 January 1730/1, when *The Daily Courant* stated that 'We hear the Subscription for building a new Theatre in Bow-street, Covent-Garden, for Mr. Rich, amounts to upward of 6000l, and that the same will be very speedily begun by that ingenious Architect James Sheppard [*sic*], Esq.'.[3] In fact no money had yet been paid to Rich, and other equally inaccurate accounts continued to appear in the press during the next few weeks.[4] Demolition of the existing buildings on the site of the new theatre was, however, in progress in February 1730/1,[5] and in April the foundations were being dug.[6] By June, when the building contract was signed, a large part of the new brickwork had been completed.[7]

The articles of agreement which John Rich signed with Edward Shepherd of St. George, Hanover Square, architect, on 3 June 1731 provided that Shepherd should complete the building of the theatre 'according to the Dimensions in the Plan or Sections thereunto annexed' by Michaelmas 1732 at a cost of £5,600. Shepherd was to be paid in five instalments of one thousand pounds,

---

* See especially *The London Stage 1660–1800. Part 3, 1729–1747*, ed. Arthur H. Scouten, two volumes, 1961, and *Part 4, 1747–1776*, ed. George Winchester Stone, three volumes, 1962; Harold Rosenthal's two works, *Two Centuries of Opera at Covent Garden*, 1958, and *Opera at Covent Garden. A Short History*, 1967; and Henry Saxe Wyndham, *The Annals of Covent Garden Theatre from 1732 to 1897*, two volumes, 1906.

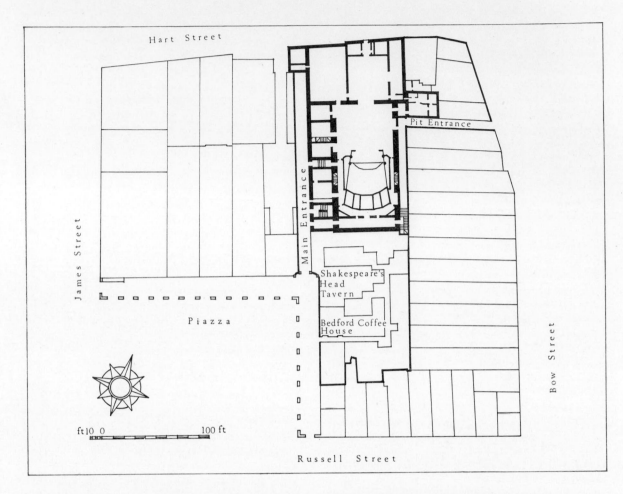

Fig. 9. Site plan in *c*. 1774. Based on a plan of *c*. 1760 in the Greater London Record Office, and on the plan in Dumont's
Parallele de Plans des Plus Belles Salles, *c*. 1774. Heavy lines show Rich's property

which would be due to him when his work reached certain specified stages, and the final six hundred pounds were to be paid on the completion of the building or by 21 December 1732. All disputes were to be referred to Mr. Henry Joynes of Kensington and Mr. Roger Morris of St. George, Hanover Square, both architects, for settlement.[7]*

In order to safeguard Shepherd's interests a second agreement was signed on the same day, 3 June 1731, between Rich, Shepherd and Benjamin Hoare, esquire, the banker, and Christopher Cock of St. Paul, Covent Garden, gentleman. By this deed Rich assigned his lease of the site of the theatre (but not his three other leases of the surrounding property) to Hoare and Cock upon trust.[7] Rich intended to finance the whole venture by the sale of fifty shares, each of £300,

* The text of the articles of agreement is recited in P.R.O., C11/2662/1. Amongst the archives of Hoare's Bank, Fleet Street, there is an abstract of part of the text of the agreement. This document (unsigned and undated) was evidently drawn up shortly after the opening of Rich's public subscription on 11 December 1731, and its purpose was merely to provide agreed formulae whereby Rich, as the building work progressed, was to certify to Hoare's that payment of x pounds to Shepherd had become due, and after Hoare's had made the payment, Shepherd was to sign a receipt for it. This document or memorandum has been wrongly identified as the building contract itself,[8] and this mistake has given rise to unnecessary difficulty over the chronology of events.[9]

making a total capital of £15,000.[10] The money so raised was to be paid into a special account at Hoare's Bank, Hoare and Cock were to issue share certificates to the subscribers, and the money in the account was to be used to pay Shepherd for building the theatre. Rich was to retain the residue, which (if all the shares were sold for £300 each and the contract price of £5,600 for the building were not exceeded) would amount to £9,400.[7]

Within a few weeks of the signature of the two agreements Rich was complaining to Shepherd about bad workmanship and, on 4 September 1731, that 'the workmen were left to themselves not knowing what to do next, but rather than be idle, thought they must do something and so went upon their owne heads'. Shepherd ignored these complaints, and Rich attempted to arrange a meeting with Joynes and Morris 'before things were gone to too great a length to be remedyed'. But Morris was absent abroad, and although the roof of the theatre was covered in on 18 December, whereby payment of no less than £4,000 was due,[11] Shepherd had still not received any money at all.

Rich did not open the subscription list for shares in the theatre (at any rate publicly) until 11 December 1731. The manuscript 'Proposals by John Rich Esq.', which bear this date, recite that Rich had obtained a sixty-one-year lease of a site in Covent Garden and that Shepherd had contracted with Rich to build a new theatre there by Michaelmas 1732. 'Now Mr Rich Proposes to divide the Premises into fifty parts or Shares', and to sell the shares for £300 each to such subscribers as 'do upon the Signing this Proposal pay into the hands of Mr Hoare Banker in Fleet Street one hundred pounds and on Lady Day [25 March] 1732 the farther sum of one hundred pounds, and when the new Theatre Shall be finished the further sum of one hundred pounds.'

Hoare and Cock were (as mentioned above) to pay Shepherd from this fund, 'and the Residue (if any) to be paid to Mr. Rich'. Upon receipt of the last instalment of each share Hoare, Cock and Rich were to assign one fiftieth part of the premises to each subscriber, who was then to lease it back for the remainder of the sixty-one-year term less one month to Rich, who would of course be the manager of the theatre. Each subscriber was to receive a rent from Rich of two shillings 'for every night that Publick Acting shall be performed in the said new Theatre', and the right of free

entry for himself or his nominee 'to see Plays in the new Theatre (without paying anything for the same) in any part of ye House Excepting behind the Scenes'. Rich also covenanted to pay the ground rent to the Duke of Bedford.[10]

There was to be no provision for redemption of the subscribers' capital at the end of the sixty-one-year lease, but in an average season of 170 acting nights[12] each shareholder would receive a rent of £17 (2s. × 170), which would correspond to an annual dividend of $5\frac{2}{3}\%$ on an investment of £300, plus the right of free entry every night. In the event the subscription proved so popular that shares were frequently bought and sold at a premium (on one occasion for as much as £345), and even as late as 1774, when more than two thirds of the leasehold term had already elapsed, a share was sold at par for £300.[13]

The 'Proposals by John Rich Esq.' were signed by thirty-eight individuals, who between them contracted for forty-seven shares.[10] The first subscriber's payment into Hoare's Bank was made a month later, on 10 January 1731/2, and on 28 January the sum of £600, which had by that time been deposited, was paid to Edward Shepherd. Thereafter money continued to come in slowly until 4 October 1733, when the account was closed. By then £6,700 had been received.[14]

This sum of £6,700 represented the sale of only twenty-two shares at £300 each, plus £100 in part payment for a twenty-third share.[7] Previous writers[15] have concluded that 'the subscribers barely paid in enough to satisfy the amount of the building contract' for £5,600 with Shepherd and that Rich's intention to raise £15,000 by the sale of fifty shares ended as no more than 'the ruins of a lovely dream'. But in fact all the shares were sold, for a list of the names of the fifty shareholders in 1744 exists in the British Museum.[16] By this time many of the original purchasers had sold their shares, often at a profit, but this list shows that Rich did raise his £15,000, many of the later payments being probably deposited in Rich's own bank, instead of in Hoare's, which was only used because Shepherd normally banked there, whereas Rich did not.

As stated above, Rich's proposals of 11 December 1731 were signed by thirty-eight individuals, who between them contracted to buy forty-seven shares. Seventeen of these signatories were subsequently credited with deposits of £300 each at Hoare's Bank and on 1 March 1732/3 fifteen of them (or their heirs) each received an assignment of a share of one fiftieth,* although in some cases the payments to Hoare's were not completed until after this date. On the same day Walter Greenwood (a signatory) also received an assignment although only credited with a deposit of £200, and two other assignments were issued to Richard Powell and Edward Wilson, who had not signed, but who are nevertheless credited with £100 each (after 1 March 1732/3) in Hoare's Bank. It is therefore clear that by this date (when the theatre had been open for some four months and some idea of its likely profitability could be formed) the buying and selling of shares had already begun. The names of the persons to whom shares were assigned are listed in the table on pages 109–11.

So far eighteen assignments, representing payments to Hoare's Bank of £4,900, have been accounted for. Seven other signatories were credited with deposits at Hoare's varying from £100 to £400 and totalling £1,500, but as they received no assignment they presumably sold their shares, in most cases only partly paid for; while two other people who did not sign the proposals were nevertheless credited with £200 and £100 each in Hoare's (thus bringing the total payments up to £6,700), evidently after buying a partly paid share from one of the original signatories.

Between 1 May 1733 and 26 September 1734 another twenty-eight assignments were issued, nineteen of them to signatories. In January 1737/8 one more assignment was made, to a non-signatory, thus bringing the total number of assignments up to forty-seven.† None of the recipients of the twenty-nine assignments issued on or after 1 May 1733 were credited with any deposit at all at Hoare's Bank. As they clearly did not receive their shares free of charge the only possible inference is that they paid direct to Rich —and, indeed, there is clear evidence that this was the case, for when Christian Frederick Zincke, a signatory who had received his assignment on 21 September 1733, decided in 1738 to sell his share the deed by which he did so specifically states that

he had bought the share in 1733 by paying £300 to Rich and only a nominal sum of five shillings to Hoare and Cock.[18] The assignment of 1 May 1734 to Thomas Holt also states the same thing.

Under the terms of the proposals it had been intended that all the money paid by the subscribers should be deposited at Hoare's Bank. The reason why this was not done is clear. As promoter of the whole scheme, it was Rich's business to find buyers for the shares, and it was therefore to him, not to Hoare's, that some at least of the subscribers made their payments.[19] At first Rich passed this money on to the account at Hoare's, with the names of each individual subscriber, and Hoare and Cock at once started to pay Shepherd. But when he became involved in disputes with Shepherd about the cost of the building Rich evidently foresaw that if he continued to pay the whole capital of £15,000 into Hoare's Bank, as envisaged in the proposals, he might, pending settlement of the disputes, be unable to draw out 'the residue' to which, after payment of Shepherd, the proposals entitled him. He therefore began to withhold some of his receipts.

It has already been stated that the last payment into Hoare's was made on 4 October 1733 and brought the total payments into the account up to £6,700. But by this time thirty-one assignments, representing £9,300 (31 × 300), had been issued (see the table on pages 109–11), and it is therefore clear that Rich had withheld the difference for his own use. By May 1733 Shepherd had been paid £4,100 out of the Hoare's account towards the contract price of £5,600, and after the last payment into the account in October there remained a balance of £2,600 (£6,700 less £4,100), which would be ample to pay for the disputed balance due to him. And so indeed it proved, for on 7 November 1734 Shepherd's bills were settled by a final payment out of the Hoare's account of £1,550, bringing his total receipts up to £5,650, only £50 more than the original contract figure. The balance of £1,050 (£6,700 less £5,650) which remained in the account was paid out during the same month in

---

* The date of the assignment to William Workman is not known, but as he signed the proposals and deposited his £300 he almost certainly received it on 1 March 1732/3.

† No record has been found of the remaining three assignments, which undoubtedly existed, for in July 1744 there were fifty shares in being.[16] Two of these assignments must certainly have been made to Robert Knight, who signed for one share but paid £400 into Hoare's Bank, and who in 1744 owned two shares. This brings the number of assignments up to forty-nine, with only one unaccounted for. It is, however, possible that Rich deliberately retained one share for himself, and later sold it at a profit. (Philip Elias Turst, who promoted the building of the Pantheon in Oxford Street in 1769–72 by methods very similar to Rich's at Covent Garden, retained one of his fifty shares for himself.)[17]

small amounts to various creditors of Rich's; Rich himself received £200, and the account was closed on 25 November 1734.

By this time the theatre had been in use for nearly two years, the first performance (Congreve's *The Way of the World*) having taken place on 7 December 1732. During this period Shepherd's account remained unsettled. At a meeting held on 8 November 1732 between Rich, Shepherd, Morris and Joynes to settle the disputes, the two arbitrators had agreed (according to Rich) that much of the brickwork was bad and should be taken down, but they had been unable to reach a settlement. At last, in March 1733/4, Rich filed a bill of complaint in Chancery in which he recited numerous building deficiencies and charged Shepherd with having deviated from the terms of the contract. Shepherd rebutted these accusations and claimed that Rich, besides owing him £1,500 under the articles of agreement, also owed him some £575 in interest due for default of payment and for extra works not included in the contract.[7] In May 1734 he filed a counter bill of complaint against Rich,[20] but the dispute was evidently settled out of Court with the final payment of £1,550 in November.[14]

Rich remained the manager of Covent Garden Theatre until his death in 1761. The seating capacity of the theatre was around 1,400 persons, which yielded an average nightly receipt of about £80.[21] Despite the large capital gain which he had made by the sale of the fifty subscribers' shares, the rents which he received from his leasehold premises adjoining the theatre (including the Shakespeare's Head Tavern and the Bedford Coffee House), and from the wine vaults under the theatre[22] he was obliged in 1742 to mortgage his interest in the Killigrew and Davenant patents for £8,000.[16] In the following year he also mortgaged his $\frac{2}{36}$ share of Drury Lane Theatre, his $\frac{7}{36}$ share of the Lincoln's Inn Fields Theatre, and all his property in Covent Garden except the theatre;[23] and in January 1744/5 he had to provide additional security for the mortgage on the patents (on which he had paid no interest) by mortgaging even the theatre and its wardrobe.[16] These mortgages may reflect his expenses incurred in the enlargement of the theatre northward to Hart Street over ground already in his leasehold tenure. A deed of 1760 refers to the wine vaults 'under the north end of the new Building erected at the north end of the said

Theatre in Hart Street',[24] and the extension is shown on the plan reproduced on Plate 39. The date of the enlargement is not known; it was probably after 1740 and certainly before 1760.

John Rich died on 26 November 1761, leaving a widow, Priscilla, and five daughters (one illegitimate). By his will he authorized his wife to sell all his interests in both the letters patent and the theatre, and to divide the proceeds of the sale (subject to a few small legacies) equally between herself and his four legitimate daughters. Until the sale took place the theatre was to be managed jointly by his widow and one of his sons-in-law, John Beard, an actor and singer who had performed at both Drury Lane and with Rich at Covent Garden.[25] For the next six years Beard was the effective manager. In February 1763, during performances of Thomas Arne's opera *Artaxerxes*, a claim to the right to enter the theatre at half price after the third act was enforced by the disorderly tumults shown in the engraving reproduced on Plate 41c, one of the earliest representations of the interior of the theatre.

In December 1765 Priscilla Rich obtained from the fourth Duke of Bedford an extension of the lease of the theatre from 1792 to 1801,[26] and in 1767 she and her four daughters sold the two letters patent and the theatre to Thomas Harris, John Rutherford, William Powell and George Colman for £60,000.[27] Harris, who may possibly be identified with, or related to Thomas Harris, soapmaker, of High Holborn,[28] seems to have been the originator of this partnership. Neither he nor Rutherford, a merchant (probably of wine) of Newman Street, St. Marylebone,[29] to whom he first turned, had any experience of the theatre, and in March 1767 they therefore invited Powell, a successful young actor at Drury Lane, to join them. Powell consented, but after signing a partnership agreement he requested that George Colman, the dramatist, should be admitted to a share in the purchase. Harris and Rutherford first refused, but they agreed when Powell threatened not to proceed with the treaty. Colman at once proposed that he should have a monopoly of the running of the theatre, and at a meeting with Harris and Rutherford at a coffee-house in Dean Street he suggested that Powell's 'vanity, Folly, Expensiveness and other Pernicious qualities' required Powell's exclusion from any share in the management. After much debate it was finally agreed, by articles signed on 14 May, that Colman, with the assistance of Powell where required, should direct the productions and all things 'comprehended in the dramatic and theatrical province', Powell should act, and Harris and Rutherford should control the finances of the concern and have the right to veto Colman's plans. By this time Harris had placed a deposit of £10,000 in the hands of the vendors, and the purchase was completed on 1 July 1767.[30]

The articles of agreement signed on 14 May 1767 gave rise to the much publicized disputes between Harris and Rutherford on the one hand, and Colman, supported by Powell, on the other. Harris and Rutherford claimed the right to be associated in the management of the theatre with Colman, who sought to exclude them from 'the dramatic and theatrical province'. During the autumn of 1767 regular weekly meetings of the four proprietors were held at the theatre on Thursdays, but by December these conferences had been discontinued after 'some high Disputes'. In January 1768 Harris and Rutherford published *A Narrative of the Rise and Progress of the Disputes Subsisting between the Patentees of Covent Garden Theatre*, the first of a score of mutually abusive pamphlets published during the course of this year. In the summer there were unseemly incidents outside the stage door after the carpenter had on Colman's orders 'barricadoed the Doors and Windows . . . by fixing Timbers against them'. Posses of angry men menaced each other across the threshold, but even the intervention (at Harris's instigation) of Justice Spinnage, who 'declared he would order the Doors to be broke upon', failed to produce more than a temporary truce, and Colman, embattled within, retained effective possession of the theatre.[31]

In September 1768 Rutherford, evidently weary of the whole affair, sold two-thirds of his quarter share to Henry Dagge of the Inner Temple, esquire, and the remaining one third to James Leake of the Strand, stationer, for £18,500.[32] In the fourteen months since his purchase of his quarter share from the Rich family in July 1767 for £15,000 Rutherford had therefore made a capital profit of £3,500—a fact which much weakened Harris's case when in February 1769 he filed a bill of complaint in Chancery against Colman (and Powell).[33] Col-

man could hardly be convincingly accused of incompetent management of the theatre, and on 20 July 1770 the Court refused to set aside the articles of 14 May 1767 or to award Harris damages.[34]

Meanwhile Powell had died suddenly at Bristol in July 1769, and for the next five years Colman remained in effective command of the theatre. He appears to have become reconciled with Harris, but ill health and the death of his wife gradually impaired his vitality,[35] and on 1 July 1774 he sold his quarter share to James Leake, for £20,000.[36] He had thus made a capital profit of £5,000 on his original outlay, and had earned for himself the distinction of presenting, on 15 March 1773, the first performance of Goldsmith's *She Stoops to Conquer*.

The management of the theatre now passed to Harris, who retained it, at first absolutely and later in partnership with J. P. Kemble, until his partial retirement in 1809. He began his long reign by commissioning Sheridan to write a play,[37] and the first performance of *The Rivals* was given on 17 January 1775. He continued to work in close friendship with Sheridan, who had purchased part of Garrick's moiety of Drury Lane in 1776. Together they planned to establish a third theatre in London, and in 1778 they bought the King's Theatre in the Haymarket, from which, however, they both quickly withdrew, Harris after the first season and Sheridan in 1781.[38] Meanwhile Harris was consolidating his holding in Covent Garden, and by the complex transactions which have been described on page 5 he had by 1785 acquired $\frac{46}{60}$ of both the leasehold of the theatre and the two patents, plus a twenty-one-year lease (jointly with Sheridan) of the remaining $\frac{14}{60}$ of the patents. The financial resources required for these purchases were provided partly by a long series of intricate mortgages in many of which Harris's brother-in-law, Thomas Longman of Paternoster Row, bookseller, was involved,[39] and partly by the sale, for £250 each, of shares which earned for the purchaser a rent of two shillings for each performance and the right of free entry during the remainder of the existing lease.[40]

With possession of a majority holding in the theatre Harris began in 1782 to improve the auditorium, which had hitherto apparently 'not undergone any material alteration, except in the decorations'. In that year it was 'judiciously widened under the direction of Mr. Richards,* who was confined to the present walls, and therefore could not extend it as he wished' (see Plate 42, fig. 10).[41] In January 1785 Harris opened negotiations with the fifth Duke of Bedford for the extension of the lease, due to expire in 1801, but although terms for a prolongation to 1846 were agreed the matter was eventually dropped, perhaps owing to the objections raised by the minority shareholders.[42]

By about 1790, however, a complete renovation had become essential for the preservation of the theatre's competitive position against that of its rivals. The King's Theatre in the Haymarket was rebuilt in 1790–1 after its destruction by fire, and Sheridan had been working for the rebuilding of Drury Lane since at least 1789.[43] In April 1792 Harris therefore signed an agreement with the fifth Duke of Bedford for the extension of the lease of the theatre from 1801 to 1895. Harris covenanted to spend £15,000 on improvements and enlargements, while the Duke agreed to advance the whole of this sum to Harris at once at 4% interest, in exchange for a very large increase of rent to £940 per annum. Harris was also to pay the Duke a fine of £5,948.[44]

During the summer of 1792 the theatre was very considerably altered, to designs by Henry Holland (see page 91). The auditorium was entirely rebuilt and the principal entrance transferred from the Piazza to Bow Street, where a portico was erected over the pavement and the old passage to the theatre greatly enlarged (Plates 46–8, fig. 11). The total expenditure is said to have been about £30,000.[45]

When the theatre re-opened on 17 September 1792 the price of tickets was considerably increased, and the charge for admission to the gallery was raised from one shilling to two.[46] This raised a tremendous hubbub which continued until the end of the second act, when a member of the company 'assured the audience, that as it seemed to be their wish that a second Gallery, at the usual price, should be continued, the Manager had given directions to build one with the utmost expedition'.[47] Makeshift alterations were carried out within a few days,[48] and in

the summer of 1793 permanent arrangements were made.[49] By this time the Duke of Bedford had granted the new lease (expiring in 1895) to Harris,[50] who had sold his $\frac{46}{60}$ of the Killigrew patent to the trustees of Drury Lane for £11,667 (see page 6). With the help of this windfall further alterations, notably to the ceiling, were made in the summer of 1794.[51] A clause in the Duke's lease of 1793 reserved a box in the theatre for his own private use.

In 1803 Harris, who had by this time been associated with Covent Garden for some thirty-six years, sold for £22,000 a one-sixth share of the theatre and the Davenant patent to John Philip Kemble, the actor.[52] Kemble had performed for many years at Drury Lane, and he now took a share in the management of Covent Garden, at a salary of £200 per annum plus a fee of £37 16s. for three appearances a week as an actor.[53] He celebrated his arrival by making, in the summer of 1803, a number of alterations to the interior of the theatre† (see page 93).

Despite Kemble's assumption of the management the old disputes between Harris and George White (the owner of a small share in the Davenant patent through his father-in-law, William Powell, see page 5) broke out again in an acrimonious correspondence which Harris published in 1804. White accused Harris of financial mismanagement, to which Harris justifiably replied that he had trebled the value of the property, and that White had 'regularly witheld, or refused your consent to every measure that has been, from time to time, proposed'.[55]

In 1806, however, a degree of harmony was restored when Harris sold back to Powell's descendants $\frac{1}{60}$ of the patent which he had acquired in 1781, and a one-eighth share in his lease of 1793 from the Duke of Bedford. They in turn agreed to pay their proportion of the very high rent,[56] and all the proprietors (Thomas Harris, his son Henry, J. P. Kemble, and Powell's descendants George White and Ann Martindale) then agreed that certain liabilities incurred by Harris alone in 1802–3 should be charged proportionately on all their shares.[57]

This unusual harmony proved short-lived, for

---

* John Inigo Richards, R.A., principal scene-painter at Covent Garden.

† According to James Boaden, writing in 1825, William Thomas Lewis, an actor of long standing at Covent Garden, bought a one-sixth share of the property from Harris in about 1799, but relinquished it in the following year after a dispute between Harris and the actors.[54] The conveyances which these transactions must have involved (if in fact they occurred at all) have not been found.

on the morning of 20 September 1808 the theatre was completely destroyed by fire. The performance of *Pizarro* on the previous evening had required the firing of a gun, and it was supposed that the wadding from the gun had lodged in the scenery. The fire was discovered at about four a.m., and within three hours the whole building and several adjacent houses in Bow Street were in smoking ruins. Twenty-three people were killed, most of them by the collapse of the burning roof, and amongst the material losses were Handel's organ and the manuscripts of a number of his compositions.[58]

SIR ROBERT SMIRKE'S THEATRE OF 1809

Nine days after the fire Harris and Kemble called upon the sixth Duke of Bedford's auditor to discuss the rebuilding of the theatre. They had already decided to raise £50,000 by the sale of one hundred shares at £500 each. Each shareholder was to have the right of free admission to all performances and was to receive an annual dividend of £25 for the remaining eighty-seven years of the lease then in being; thus, in theory, he would receive £2,175 (87 × £25), but at the expiry of the lease there would be no repayment of the capital.

Harris and Kemble had also selected their architect for the new theatre, (Sir) Robert Smirke, then aged only twenty-six, and had decided, with the Duke of Bedford's co-operation, to enlarge the site of the theatre by taking in all the adjacent houses on the west side of Bow Street and south side of Hart Street. Several of these houses had been leased for long terms to Harris as recently as 1806, and they and others had subsequently been destroyed in the fire. The Duke evidently proved willing to assist, and the whole of the east side of the new theatre therefore fronted on to Bow Street.[59]

The subscription list for the new shares was filled up by early November[60]—£76,000 was raised, by the sale of 152 shares[61]—and the foundation stone of the new theatre was laid by the Prince of Wales on 31 December 1808.[62] The principal contractor was Alexander Copland, who performed all the bricklayer's and slater's work and some of the carpenter's and mason's; his account was for £127,601.* Smirke's fees amounted to £8,924.[63]

In September 1809, when the theatre was ready to be re-opened, the proprietors announced that as they had spent some £150,000 in the rebuilding, an increase in the prices of admission would be necessary. This gave rise to the famous 'O.P.' (Old Price) riots, which began on the opening night, 18 September, and continued without intermission for nearly three months. At every performance a continuous organized hubbub was maintained which completely drowned the actors' voices. A committee which included the Solicitor General, the Recorder of the City of London and the Governor of the Bank of England was appointed to investigate the accusation that the proprietors had made excessive profits. It reported that since 1803 the proprietors' average annual profit had been $6\frac{3}{8}\%$ on their capital, but if this whole capital had been insured the profit would have been only 5%. For want of full insurance coverage the proprietors had sustained a very heavy loss for which no compensation was payable. With the increased admission prices and the same degree of insurance protection as previously their profit was unlikely to exceed $3\frac{1}{2}\%$ per annum, but with the old admission prices they would make an annual loss of $\frac{3}{4}\%$.[64]

Despite these assurances the disorders continued, and eventually, in December, the proprietors were compelled to restore the old prices.

The new theatre (Plates 49–56, fig. 12) was not a success, at least financially. It stood for less than fifty years, a comparatively short life for such an expensive building, and during most of this

---

* Other tradesmen who worked at the theatre, with the amount of their accounts (to the nearest pound), were:
carpenter, Richard Martyr and Son (£11,927); *carpet maker*, Drury and Son (£514); *carvers and gilders*, J. Lovell (£98), E. Rigby (£67); *chandeliers*, William Collins (£887); *enamellers*, Madgwick and Cooper (£43); *glaziers*, T. and P. Palmer (£1,020); *heating apparatus*, Boulton and Watt (£639); *lampmaker*, G. Phillips (£1,959); *locksmith*, Samuel Lloyd (£452); *masons*, William Peacock (£777), Shell and Milton (£83), Francis Webster (£64); *painter, gilder and paper hanger*, C. Dixon and Son (£8,342); *paintings in bas relief*, Robert Smirke, senior (£379); *paper hangers*, Robson and Hale (£480); *paviours*, H. Brown (£338), William Meredith (£251); *plasterer*, Francis Bernasconi (£6,060); *plumbers*, Samuel Briggs (£1,861), Lancelot Burton (£2,796), William Tarte (£1,878); *smiths*, Armstrong and Company (£1,538), J. Cruckshanks (£803), Cutler and Macnaughton (£2,149), William Feltham (£26), William Morris (£1,895), E. Neville (£44), Robert Smith (£146); *statuaries*, J. Flaxman (£210), B. Papera (£193), C. Rossi (£714); *upholsterers*, Tatham and Bailey (£2,103); *wirework*, Welch and Maddox (£148). Thomas Carpenter was the clerk of works, and John Cantwell the district surveyor.[63]

period the proprietors and shareholders derived little profit from it. This was the age of big theatres, in which the owners of the two patent houses attempted unsuccessfully to preserve their crumbling monopoly rights by building larger theatres whose increased seating capacity would, they hoped, keep pace with the requirements of the growing numbers of theatre-goers in ever-expanding London. The new Covent Garden normally accommodated some 2,800 people[65]* and (according to a contemporary abstract of bills) cost £187,888, exclusive of wardrobe, stage equipment and ancillary costs incurred in the adaptation of various adjacent buildings.[63] By 1832 Francis Place, in evidence before a Select Committee of the House of Commons, accurately summed up the plight of both the patent theatres in his statement that 'It is the excessive outlay, and the high prices of admission, the consequences of the monopoly, inducing them to build houses which cannot be filled, which has ruined them'.[66]

In the years between Thomas Harris's partial retirement in 1809 and his death in 1820 the management of the theatre appears to have been shared with his son Henry Harris and with John Kemble. In 1812 they and the other proprietors (i.e., George White and Mrs. Martindale, descendants of William Powell) agreed that the funds for the theatre should, after payment of all outgoings, including the dividend to the 152 shareholders, be applied to the payment of certain specified debts. This agreement appears to have been observed 'for a year or two, and then to have been abandoned'.[67] By 1817 the Duke of Bedford was complaining that his rent was in arrears, to which Harris replied that he and his partners had not taken a shilling profit on their investment.[68]

Thomas Harris died in October 1820, and soon afterwards John Kemble transferred his one-sixth share to his younger brother, Charles Kemble.[69] Henry Harris, with $\frac{7}{12}$, was now the principal proprietor, and therefore succeeded to the management. His partners, Kemble ($\frac{1}{6}$), and George White's sons-in-law and heirs, John Willett ($\frac{1}{16}$) and John Forbes ($\frac{1}{16}$), soon became dissatisfied with his arrangements, however, and in March 1822 they entered into an agreement

with Henry Harris by means of which they were to have control of the theatre for ten years. But one proprietor was not a party to this agreement. This was Francis Const, a lawyer, who at about this time inherited a life interest in one eighth from Mrs. Martindale, recently deceased. When he heard of the agreement he filed a bill of complaint in Chancery in which he correctly asserted that some of the debts mentioned in the agreement of 1812 were still unpaid, and therefore prayed for the appointment of a receiver of the profits of the theatre. This plea proved successful, and on 19 February 1824 a receiver was appointed. Four days later Kemble, Willett and Forbes repudiated their agreement of 1822 with Harris on the ground that they had entered into it without knowledge of the existence of the agreement of 1812. Harris then filed a bill for performance of the agreement of 1812.[70] After three hearings the case was ultimately decided in 1831 against Harris.[71]

With this contentiousness among the proprietors Covent Garden did not prosper during the 1820's,[72] and in 1829 payment of the rates and taxes was so far overdue that a magistrate's warrant was issued and a tax-collector put in temporary possession. In addition to the extravagance and incompetence of Kemble, Willett and Forbes[73] the proprietors were facing the challenge of changing social and religious attitudes. Charles Kemble stated in 1832 that 'The late hours of dining take away all the upper classes . . . from the theatre; religious prejudice is very much increased, evangelical feeling, and so on; and they take away a great number of persons from the theatre who formerly used to frequent it'. But above all, the ancient monopoly rights of both the patent theatres were being steadily eroded by the competition of the ever-growing number of new and smaller theatres licensed by the Lord Chamberlain. In 1832, the centenary year of Covent Garden's career, when the total encumbrances on the property had risen to the enormous sum of £256,496, the proprietors decided to relinquish the management and to secure what they hoped would be a reliable revenue by sub-letting the theatre. P. F. Laporte, who had formerly managed the King's Theatre in the Haymarket, was granted a seven-year sub-lease

---

* This figure of 2,800 excluded spectators in the private boxes. The amount of accommodation available was frequently varied. When George IV visited the theatre in 1823, 4,255 people paid for seats, and this figure again excludes the occupants of private boxes.[65]

at an annual rental of some £10,000, payable to the proprietors.[74]

This important change of managerial policy did not succeed. Laporte departed after only one year, and for the next ten years there was a series of short and financially (though not always artistically) unsuccessful sub-tenancies—Alfred Bunn 1833–5, who was also managing Drury Lane, D. W. Osbaldiston 1835–7, W. C. Macready 1837–9, and C. J. Mathews 1839–42.[75] By 1843, when the Act for regulating theatres finally abolished the monopoly rights of the two patent theatres, Covent Garden had virtually ceased to be a place of dramatic or musical entertainment and had become the *venue* for a series of meetings of the Anti-Corn Law League, whose long campaign was finally successful in 1846.[76]

The sub-tenants' failures had, of course, involved both proprietors and the holders of the £500 shares issued in 1808–9 in further difficulties. In 1832 the shareholders, who were entitled to an annuity of £25 on each share but who had not received a single shilling during the previous seven years, agreed to forgo part of the arrears and for the future to accept only £12 10s. per annum until all outstanding debts had been paid.[77] In the same year the sixth Duke of Bedford agreed to reduce the ground rent payable to him by the proprietors by £300 per annum,[78] and in 1837, when the proprietors had had to forgo part of their rent from their sub-tenant (Osbaldiston), the Duke agreed to another reduction, this time of £200 per annum.[79] Despite these concessions the total charge upon the building stood at about £5,000 per annum (consisting of ground rent, rates and taxes, salaries of treasurer and firemen, and provision for gradual repayment of outstanding debts), and for three years, 1843–5, the theatre was virtually unused, apart from occasional short bookings.[77]

At this point Covent Garden Theatre was rescued from its parlous position by the discontent which prevailed among the musicians at Her Majesty's (formerly the King's) Theatre in the Haymarket, hitherto the principal home of opera in London. In 1846 the Italian composer Giuseppe Persiani, piqued, it is said, at the refusal of Benjamin Lumley, the manager of Her Majesty's, to accept an opera of his composition,[80] took a lease of Covent Garden from the delighted proprietors at a rent of £6,000 per annum.[77] He obtained the assistance of Frederick Beale, a member of Cramer, Beale and Company, the music publishers, and of (Sir) Michael Costa, the disgruntled conductor at Her Majesty's,[80] and towards the end of 1846 he engaged Benedict Albano, who had hitherto been known chiefly as a civil engineer, to reconstruct the theatre for opera.[81] Work began in December, and during the next four months up to 1,200 men worked day and night in what amounted to the complete rebuilding of the interior of the theatre (Plate 57). The total cost of the alterations and re-equipment was variously estimated at £27,000 and at upwards of £40,000; the contractor was Henry Charles Holland.[82]

The theatre, now known as the Royal Italian Opera House, re-opened on 6 April 1847 with a performance of Rossini's *Semiramide*.[83] A large loss was made during the first season, and Persiani fled abroad. Changes were made in the management,[84] and by March 1848, when further alterations were being made to the auditorium, Frederick Gye had become 'the general controller'.[85]

Gye was the son of the proprietor of Vauxhall Gardens, and had first been associated with Covent Garden in 1843.[86] This connexion lasted until his death in 1878, and during this long and eventful period he proved to be one of the theatre's most successful managers. In 1849 the proprietors granted him a seven-year lease at a rent related to his gross receipts[87] and after an uncertain start[88] he was greatly assisted by the closure of Her Majesty's Theatre, his principal rival in opera, from 1852 to 1856.[89] But in January of the latter year he unfortunately subleased the theatre to J. H. Anderson, known as 'The Wizard of the North', for a six-week run of conjuring and pantomine.[90] Anderson, it is said, had already burnt down two theatres over his head, and was now to add a third to his remarkable record.[77] During the concluding moments of a disorderly *bal masqué* sponsored by Anderson, fire broke out in the theatre at about five o'clock on the morning of 5 March 1856, and within a few hours the whole building had been destroyed[91] (Plate 58).

THE BUILDING OF E. M. BARRY'S ROYAL ITALIAN OPERA HOUSE AND THE FLORAL HALL, 1856–60

Within five days of this disaster Gye was discussing the new situation with the seventh Duke of Bedford's agent,[92] but rebuilding did not begin for almost nineteen months.[93] The proprietors now (i.e., the owners of the patent and the existing lease, of which thirty-nine years remained unexpired) were Henry Harris's two daughters, represented by William Harry Surman, $\frac{7}{12}$, the late Charles Kemble's representatives, $\frac{1}{6}$, Captain Forbes, $\frac{1}{8}$, and John Willett, $\frac{1}{8}$.[92]* Henry Harris had died in 1839 leaving private debts of £50,000, none of which had been repaid, while the affairs of Charles Kemble, who had died in 1854, were in Chancery, where his share in the theatre had been valued at £500. The proprietors' debts on the property had by now been reduced to the comparatively small sum of £9,000, but even so they were quite unable to rebuild the theatre from their own resources.[77] The 152 shareholders (i.e., those who had in 1808–9 subscribed £500 each towards the rebuilding then in progress, in exchange for the right of free entry and an annuity of £25 for the rest of the term of the lease) were in no better position. Since 1832 they had agreed to forgo half their annuities, and the value of their shares had declined from £500 to £120 each. At a meeting of both the proprietors and the shareholders held on 15 March 1856, Surman, as the representative of the principal proprietors, flatly stated that he and his partners were 'not in a condition to rebuild the theatre' unless the shareholders were able to raise £100,000.[94] This they proved unable or unwilling to do, and on 10 April the Duke of Bedford therefore obtained an order in the Court of Queen's Bench by which he resumed possession of the site.[95] The shareholders of 1808–9 lost all their money and rights of free entry; the proprietors forfeited their lease, but presumably retained possession of the now almost valueless patent. The way was now clear for Gye to make a completely fresh start, and to erect the opera house which still stands.

In his negotiations with the seventh Duke of Bedford Gye's position was strengthened by the fact that he was the sole applicant for a new lease. At first even he thought that it would be impossible to raise the money to build a new theatre or opera house, and he therefore proposed to erect 'a Concert Room of large dimension and a Building (which he proposed to call The Floral Hall) for the sale of Flowers upon an enlarged scale'. This pro-

posal involved the purchase and demolition of the Piazza Hotel (the easternmost house in the portico walk on the north side of the marke square) in order to provide the Floral Hall with a front to the square. When the Duke's agent mentioned the rent that would be expected Gye broke off the negotiation, 'stating that owing to the principles of free trade having been brought to bear upon Theatrical property through an end having been put to the Monopoly so long enjoyed by Drury Lane and Covent Garden Theatres, it had become impossible to raise the funds necessary for rebuilding a Theatre unless the site for it could be obtained at a much more moderate ground rent...'.[96]

Gye was an extremely able man of business and it is therefore very remarkable that he should have clung to his ill-conceived scheme for a Floral Hall. While quite a young man he had, in about 1842, 'projected a scheme for connecting the different parts of the metropolis by means of a gigantic arcade', and in 1845 he had read a paper on the subject. The arcade, of iron and glass and 70 feet in height, was to extend from the Bank to Trafalgar Square and was to be of the same width as a first-class thoroughfare; it would combine 'the grand desideratum of a covered communication with a spacious and luxurious promenade', and at some point in its course there was to be 'an extensive flower market, constructed entirely of glass'.[97]

Only four months before the fire at Covent Garden Theatre he was evidently still hankering after this idea,[97] and so, when the Duke of Bedford's expectations of rent had somewhat abated and negotiations had been resumed, Gye stuck to his Floral Hall. He also hinted that he might at some future date convert the proposed concert room into a theatre or opera house. Terms were at last agreed; early in 1857 the Duke's agent gave the lessee of the Piazza Hotel notice to quit (for which substantial compensation had to be paid)[98] and on 18 February he and Gye signed an agreement for a ninety-year lease to be granted to the latter, who covenanted to erect two buildings, to be known as the Royal Italian Opera House Concert Room and the Floral Hall.[99] The rent was to be £1,150 per annum.[100]

In order to raise the money for the rebuilding,

* Between 1825 and 1832 Forbes and Willett had each become possessed of half of Francis Const's $\frac{1}{8}$, thus increasing their respective shares from $\frac{1}{16}$ to $\frac{1}{8}$ (see page 8).

Gye on 1 October 1857 conditionally assigned the agreement for a lease to three trustees[101] to hold on behalf of a group of about fifteen wealthy gentlemen, each of whom lent substantial sums totalling about £80,000. These mortgagees included the architect of the new theatre, E. M. Barry (£1,500), the principal contractors, C. and T. Lucas (£21,159 jointly), the sub-contractor for the ironwork, Mr. Henry Grissell (amount unknown) and the Duke of Bedford[102] (£19,600). Building work had already begun, on 23 September 1857.[103]

The new theatre was built within less than eight months, and at a contract figure of £60,000 plus another £10,000 for extra works,[104] its cost was less than half that of its predecessor. Although the site leased to Gye was larger than that occupied by Smirke's theatre, a substantial portion of the new site was to be used for the Floral Hall, and the area of ground available for the new house was therefore much reduced. By greatly increasing the height of his building (eight storeys of rooms on either side of the main block) and by placing it on an east–west instead of a north–south axis, Barry nevertheless contrived to design a theatre with almost as many seats as its predecessor and with a larger stage and auditorium[105] (Plates 59–67, figs. 13–15).

Most of the bricklayer's work had to be done during the unfavourable winter season. In order to avoid delay Messrs. Lucas, the contractors, supplied their employees with special waterproof clothing, 'and the men, while working in this black-hooded costume, reminded [E. M. Barry] of nothing so much as the story-book pictures of the familiars of the Inquisition'. Much of the joiner's work was prepared at Lucas's Lowestoft works and brought down to London.[103] With mounting costs and shortness of time Gye attempted to put off the erection of the portico in Bow Street, but the Duke of Bedford and his agent insisted, 'knowing how generally the completion of buildings of this kind, once postponed, never takes place (it was so with old Drury Lane Theatre, the appearance of which in Brydges Street remained through this cause, an eyesore till that Theatre was burned down)'.[106] The order for the construction of the portico was not given until 27 March 1858, but Messrs. Lucas rose to the occasion, and the last stone of the architrave was fixed complete on 8 May, one week before the opening of the theatre.[103] Over £100,000

were staked, it is said, in bets on whether the theatre would be ready by the appointed day; even on the very morning 'the confusion seemed to be increasing instead of diminishing; and persons, tempted by curiosity to visit the scene of their expected evening's amusement, were inclined to wonder how they could ever get into the house'.[107] But all was well, and the theatre was opened on 15 May 1858 with a performance of Meyerbeer's *Les Huguenots*.[108]

Three weeks later, on 7 June, the seventh Duke of Bedford executed the lease to Gye. Specifically excepted from it was one private box, plus its own lobby, retiring room, fireplace, chimney-stack, staircase and entrance, which were retained for their own use by successive Dukes, until 1940.[109] The contrivance of this tiny enclave, reminiscent of the 'peculiar jurisdictions' sometimes found in the complex field of medieval ecclesiastical law, had occasioned the architect much trouble, for the retiring room could only be placed behind the curtain, and the approach to the ducal box had therefore to be by means of 'a sort of bridge thrown over a corner of the stage'.[105]

Owing to shortage of money the erection of the Floral Hall had not yet begun,[106] but in April 1858 the site was being prepared by the demolition of the Piazza Hotel and the passages which had formerly provided access to the old theatre from the Piazza.[110] In July Gye mortgaged his lease of the whole site, this time to the Rock Life Assurance Company[111] and the Duke of Bedford advanced him a further £7,500.[106] Building work presumably began soon afterwards, the architect again being E. M. Barry and the contractors C. and T. Lucas, with Mr. Henry Grissell responsible for the ironwork.[112] The hall (Plate 68) extended some 230 feet westward from Bow Street. On its north side it abutted on the opera house, and on the south and west sides the walls were of brick; the remainder of the fabric was of glass and iron. At the west end a short arm extended southward to obtain a frontage to the market square, and the intersection of the two arms was covered by a glass dome. Gye intended to lease stalls for the sale of flowers, plants and seeds,[113] but the Duke of Bedford did not welcome such competition for the business of his market, and in 1860 he therefore provided new accommodation for some of the flower dealers at the south-east corner of the Piazza. The Floral Hall was first used on

7 March 1860,[114] when a grand Volunteers' ball took place there.

For over twenty-five years the Floral Hall proved to be a white elephant. Unable to use it as he had originally intended, Gye and his successors repeatedly attempted to obtain the permission of successive Dukes to use it in other ways—as a drill hall,[115] for concerts and exhibitions, and even as a music hall.[116] Occasional licences for concerts were granted, but the neighbours' objections were considered to be reasonable[117] and standing permission was never conceded.[118] In 1865 the West London Industrial Exhibition was held there,[119] but in 1872 Gye was still, according to the Duke's advisers, 'disposed to be troublesome as to making proper application for licences'.[120] In 1882 the ninth Duke, who was constantly on the look-out for a chance to relieve the endemic congestion of the market, proposed that he should buy the leasehold of the Floral Hall from Gye's heirs. Terms could not be agreed, however,[121] and it was not until 1887 that the Duke, now desperate for space, finally did so. He paid £20,000 for his purchase[122] and agreed to a reduction of £435 in the annual ground rent payable to him under the lease of 1858 for the site of both the opera house and the hall.[100]* The Floral Hall was at once incorporated into the market as a foreign fruit mart. It is still used for this purpose, but the roof and the dome were destroyed by a fire in April 1956.[123]

THE ROYAL ITALIAN OPERA HOUSE FROM 1858

Gye continued to hold the ground lease of the theatre, heavily mortgaged, until his death on 4 December 1878, when his personal estate was valued at under £35,000.[124] In 1873 most of the subscribers to the building fund of 1856–8 agreed to accept about half of the amounts still due to them in exchange for the free use of specified seats or boxes in the theatre during the unexpired residue of the lease.[102] But a number of mortgages and other encumbrances remained outstanding, and by 1875 they had all been bought by or transferred to Andrew Montagu of Melton Park, an exceedingly wealthy Yorkshire landowner, for the enormous sum of £105,000.[125]

Gye bequeathed all his interest in the theatre to his five children, one of whom, Ernest, had already been concerned in the business and now assumed control.[126] Opera in London was, however, being gradually ruined by the excessive salaries demanded by the foreign 'star' singers.[127] Ernest Gye proved unable to bear this load for long, and in 1883 he and his brothers and sister (evidently with Andrew Montagu's concurrence) assigned all their interest in the ground lease to the Royal Italian Opera Covent Garden Limited.[128] Gye continued as manager for another season, but in 1884 this company was wound up.[129]

From 1888 until his death in 1896 Sir Augustus Harris presented seasons of opera with the powerful financial backing of a group of aristocratic patrons.[130] In 1895 Andrew Montagu, who had become the outright owner of the ground lease (evidently by foreclosure on the equity of redemption), had also died. He had bequeathed all his enormous real estate to George Denison Faber,[131] who was then the registrar of the Privy Council—a post from which he speedily resigned on this sudden access of good fortune.† Faber was in 1918 created Baron Wittenham of Wallingford; he was an enthusiast for grand opera, but he was also, according to *The Times*, 'a financier of the first order',[133] and in 1899 he therefore sold the ground lease for the useful sum of £80,000, to the Grand Opera Syndicate Limited.[134]

This Syndicate consisted of the wealthy patrons who had hitherto supported Sir Augustus Harris. Its directors immediately raised a working capital of £60,000 by the issue of 600 mortgage debentures of £100 each.[135] Substantial alterations (including the rebuilding of the stage to the designs of Edwin Sachs) were made to the interior of the theatre in 1899–1901 and in 1911,[136] and under the Syndicate's auspices 'fair but intermittent' profits were made until the war of 1914–18.[137]

In 1914 Sir Joseph Beecham (owner of the

---

* The ground rent for the combined site of the opera house and the hall was £1,150 per annum. After the ninth Duke's acquisition of the lease of the hall in 1887 the ground rent payable for the opera house alone was £715 (£1,150−£435).[100]

† It may be noted that a small part of this inheritance consisted of the original of the Davenant letters patent.[132] In the complete absence of any evidence on the point it may be surmised that Frederick Gye had acquired it from the pre-1856 proprietors, and that it had later passed from Gye to Montagu.

famous proprietary brand of pills and father of Sir Thomas Beecham, the conductor, who had first appeared at Covent Garden in 1910) had entered into an agreement with the eleventh Duke of Bedford to buy the whole of the Covent Garden estate, including the opera house. Sir Joseph had died in 1916 before the completion of the contract, and in 1918 the whole estate was conveyed to a private company controlled by the Beecham family, the Covent Garden Estate Company, of which Sir Thomas was a director. However, this change of ground landlord was no help to the theatre, which the Grand Opera Syndicate had been compelled, in 1917, to mortgage to Coutts and Company, the bankers.[138] In 1919 the Syndicate presented a season under the direction of Sir Thomas Beecham, but in the more straitened financial circumstances of the post-war period it had lost much of its vigour. From 1925 to 1927 summer seasons of opera were given by the London Opera Syndicate, which had been formed by Samuel Courtauld, the industrialist, and had taken a three-year sub-lease from the Grand Opera Syndicate. The latter, 'though still alive, had ceased to function, [and] the "Phoenix" seemed really dead' when yet another syndicate, called the Covent Garden Opera Syndicate, appeared and was granted another short sub-lease.[139]

Opera in London was thus in an already precarious position when in February 1929 the Grand Opera Syndicate surrendered the ground lease of the theatre to the ground landlord.[140] This was now Covent Garden Properties Company Limited, to which the market and part of the old Bedford estate (including, of course, the opera house) had passed from the Beecham family's private company. It was a public company, dealing exclusively in real estate, and by 1930 rumours were circulating that after February 1933, when the short sub-lease to the Covent Garden Opera Syndicate expired and the Covent Garden Properties Company would obtain possession, the theatre would be demolished.[141]

The interim period between 1930 and 1933 was chiefly remarkable for the grant of the first state subsidy to opera in England. In November 1930 Philip Snowden, Chancellor of the Exchequer in the Labour administration then in power, announced that the British Broadcasting Corporation having recently launched a scheme for the promotion of grand opera, the government intended to assist the Corporation by an annual grant of £17,500 for five years.[142] Much public criticism of this then novel action ensued, and one outraged taxpayer even attempted to obtain an injunction to prevent payment of the money.[143] In the more stringent financial conditions of 1932 the subsidy was suspended, but the precedent had been established.[144]

In the same year 'A certain melancholy interest' attached to a brief season of grand opera under Sir Thomas Beecham, for it had now been 'more or less definitely decided' that after the next summer season the theatre would be demolished.[145] In December 1932 Covent Garden Properties Limited submitted plans to Westminster City Council for the formation of a new street extending across the centre of the site of the opera house, and in the same month *The Times* lugubriously accepted the inevitability of demolition.[146]

The existing sub-lease of the theatre, originally to expire in February 1933, had been extended for another five months, to 31 July.[147] At the annual general meeting of Covent Garden Properties Company Limited, held on 14 July, the chairman, Philip E. Hill, stated that while the directors of the company did not wish to take 'a merely mercenary view' of the question, it was nevertheless 'quite impossible, in fairness to the shareholders, to continue to let the Opera House at a rental which was admittedly only a fraction of its true normal value'.[148] This rental had, since the previous February, been £1,000 per month,[149] compared with the £715 per annum which had been paid since 1887 under the lease granted by the Duke of Bedford in 1858.

But the theatre was rescued yet again. By December 1933 a new company, the Royal Opera House Company Limited, of which Philip Hill himself was one of the directors,* had obtained an agreement for a new lease, and Covent Garden Properties Company Limited had undertaken to make important improvements to the theatre. These works, which ultimately cost some £70,000, included an entirely new wing of offices, dressing and rehearsal-rooms in Mart Street.[150]

The Royal Opera House Company Limited continued as lessee until 1938, when it was

---

* The other directors were Lord Allendale (chairman), Lord Lloyd, Lady Cunard, Lord Esher, Lord Stonehaven, Ronald Tree, Benjamin Guinness and Geoffrey Toye (managing director).[150]

wound up.[151] By 1939 the position was critical once more, and the annual report of Covent Garden Properties Company Limited stated that 'unless more satisfactory arrangements for letting or for a sale of the property can be made, the board must develop the property in the best interests of this company'.[152]

During the war the theatre was leased to Mecca Cafés and used as a *palais de danse*.[153] In July 1944 it was announced that Leslie Boosey and Ralph Hawkes, the music publishers, were to take a five-year lease of the opera house,[154] and that a number of persons eminent in the arts had been appointed to a committee of management.[155] From this evolved the Covent Garden Opera Trust,[156] under whose auspices, and with the help of a regular subvention from the newly established Arts Council of Great Britain, the opera house embarked on its immensely successful post-war career. The first post-war performance took place on 20 February 1946, with a performance by the Sadler's Wells Ballet of *The Sleeping Beauty*.[157]

In July 1948, when Boosey and Hawkes's lease was drawing to an end, Covent Garden Properties Company Limited announced their intention of granting a new and much longer lease to a new tenant. This would have ended the promising post-war departure inaugurated by Boosey and Hawkes in conjunction with the Covent Garden Trust and the Arts Council, and was therefore opposed by the Council. The government then issued a compulsory purchase order against the ground landlords and eventually, after prolonged negotiations, Covent Garden Properties Company Limited granted to the Ministry of Works a forty-two-year lease commencing on 25 March 1949. The Ministry then sub-let the theatre to the Covent Garden Trust, which subsequently became the Royal Opera House Covent Garden Limited.[158] This arrangement still exists, and has been severely criticized by the Arts Council on the ground that during the forty-two-year lease well over one million pounds of public money will be spent on the maintenance of a building still in private ownership.

CHAPTER VI

Covent Garden Theatre and the Royal Opera House: the Buildings

EDWARD SHEPHERD'S THEATRE OF 1731-2

The most important item of graphic evidence relating to the first Covent Garden Theatre is Gabriel-Martin Dumont's highly informative plan and section of *c.* 1774.* This engraving (Plate 40) was probably based on a careful survey of the building after an extensive addition had been made north of the stage, but what is shown of the auditorium is largely confirmed by the documentary evidence, and by some early engravings of performances showing the proscenium and flanking boxes.

On 2 March 1730/1 *The Daily Advertiser* reported that 'the New Theatre which is to be built in Covent-Garden will be after the Model of the Opera-House in the Hay-Market; and by the Draught that has been approved of for the same, it's said it will exceed the Opera-House in Magnificence of Structure'. On the other hand, the articles of agreement, signed on 3 June 1731 by John Rich and Edward Shepherd,[1] seem to suggest that the new theatre was to be modelled on the Lincoln's Inn playhouse, rebuilt in *c.* 1713-14 by Christopher Rich, although this in turn probably derived from Wren's Drury Lane of 1672-4 and Vanbrugh's Haymarket opera house of 1704-5 as altered in 1707-8. Dumont's plan and section show that Covent Garden was basically similar to the earlier theatres except for the greater depth and capacity of its two galleries.

In his bill of complaint against Shepherd, Rich refers to the articles of agreement whereby Shepherd covenanted that he would before Michaelmas 1732 erect and build a theatre with all the appurtenances thereunto appertaining 'with the best of Materialls and Workmanship and according to the Dimensions in the Plan or Sections thereunto annexed†... and (among other things)

That the Stage the Front and Side Boxes Gallarys and Benches should be finished in as good a manner in all respects as those at the Theatre in Lincoln's Inn Fields (Except the Lineing of the Boxes and Seat Coverings History Painting Gilding all Glasses which were not to be done by the said Edward Shepherd but by your Orator) [i.e. Rich]. That the Vaults under the intended Great Lobby and the Boxes and Passages leading thereto should be Joyced and boarded. That the outside Passages where no Rooms were intended to be built over should be Roofed and Tyled with Glazed Pantiles or plain Tiles ... and should be paved with Purbeck Stone from end to end of the East and West sides of the said intended Theatre. That the Lodgements above the Stage for the flyings should be framed with good yellow Joysts to be Seven Inches by Nine Inches and the common Joysts Seven Inches by Three Inches covered with Yellow Deals without Sap on each Side of the Stage fifteen foot wide. That the Boxes over the Stage Door and the Boxes over the two Side Boxes adjoyneing to the Kings and Princes Boxes should be ornamented with Entabliture (as delineated in the said Plan). That there should be in and about the said Theatre as many staircases as designed by the said Plan.... The Musick Room Treasurers Box Keepers and other Offices and all other conveniencys necessarily appertaining to a Theatre (and as that at Lincolns Inn Fields) should be done and finished with good and substantiall yellow boarded floors without sap. And that a Carpenters Workshop a Painteing Roome Such Wardrobes and other conveniencys (as should be required by your Orator) should be made in the roofe of the said intended Theatre.'[1]

Dumont shows the stage, auditorium and great lobby contained in an oblong shell, internally some 112 feet in length north to south, and 56 feet

---

* The engraving as reproduced in Dumont's *Parallele de Plans des Plus Belles Salles de Spectacles d'Italie et de France* was printed in reverse. In the reproduction of this engraving on Plate 40 of this volume of the *Survey of London* this error has been corrected.

† This plan has not survived.

wide, its massive brick side walls rising some 50 feet to support the timber-framed roof, pitched at 45 degrees and extending between the gabled north and south end walls. The west wall of the shell was adjoined by a four-storeyed range of the same length, some 20 feet wide, containing the theatre offices, Green Room, dressing-rooms and, at the south end, the entrances and main staircases to the boxes and galleries. The doors and windows in this range opened to a 10 feet wide passage, entered through the grand entrance in the north-east angle of the Piazza. A similar passage along the east side of the shell was joined at its north end by a branch leading to Bow Street, this serving as the pit entrance.

The north part of the shell was allotted to the stage, about 42 feet deep to the proscenium and 55 feet to the apron front. Dumont shows a raked floor with five sets of wing grooves, a wide trap for scenes at the back, and fly galleries some 20 feet above the floor. The forepart of the fan-shaped auditorium contained the apron stage, an orchestra enclosure or 'musicians room' of roughly semi-elliptical shape, and a pit furnished with twelve rows of benches on a raked floor. The pit was approached by corridors under the side boxes, linked by a cross passage beneath the amphitheatre, a tier raised some 4 feet behind the pit and having six stepped rows of benches, divided by low partitions to form four narrow boxes on either side of the wide 'King's front box'. These amphitheatre or front boxes were served by a cross corridor entered directly from the great lobby, 56 feet long and 10 feet wide, which Dumont shows divided into three compartments, the large middle one furnished with two bureaux, presumably pay-boxes. Above the amphitheatre were the two large galleries, all three tiers having their front parapets at the same distance of some 40 feet from the proscenium. There were fourteen stepped rows of benches in the first gallery, which was pitched at an angle of 25 degrees, and sixteen in the second, pitched at 40 degrees. Both galleries were constructed of wood, with raking joists resting in front on four wooden posts, having iron cores,[2] spaced at nearly equal centres in line with the first row of benches. The rakers of the first gallery were supported at the back by the brick inner wall of the great lobby, and those of the second gallery by a row of wooden columns above the wall. Except for the back four rows, the second-gallery benches had

the advantage of freedom from these sight-obstructing posts. To avoid the costly curved construction used in Vanbrugh's opera house, the steppings and benches at Covent Garden were formed in straight lengths, five to each row, joined at angles to conform with shallow curves struck concentrically from a wide radius. The back-to-back spacing of the benches appears to have varied from about 2 feet 6 inches in the front boxes to 2 feet in the second gallery.

On either side of the auditorium were three tiers of shallow boxes, their generally straight fronts being canted away from the proscenium at an angle of 97 degrees to allow for the expansion of sound. Each upper tier was divided into seven boxes, three single and two double, but at stage level the first box was replaced by a proscenium door. Next to this was a stage box (the King's and Prince's boxes) forming the centre of a three-bay decorative feature, the box parapet projecting between two giant Corinthian plain-shafted columns rising through two tiers of boxes to support a cornice which extended above a festooned frieze-band and across each flanking box, resting at either end on a carved term placed above a small Ionic column. (In Shepherd's answers to Rich's charges of neglect and bad workmanship, reference is made to these 'Thermes', which Rich had ordered to be done by his own carver.[1]) The second-tier box parapet in the middle of this feature was decorated with an enriched lunette panel and the flanking boxes had balustrades, but elsewhere the gallery and box parapets were simply treated as panelled dadoes above cornices. To improve the passage of sound, the plain plaster ceiling above the auditorium was formed in three sloping planes, their pitch increasing towards the back of the house. The front slope, which formed a sounding-board above the apron and orchestra, was decorated by Jacopo Amiconi with a history painting in distemper, depicting Apollo and the Muses awarding the Laurel to Shakespeare.[3] The conjunction of this ceiling with the wall face above the three-bay feature left a triangular face which Dumont shows decorated with drapery festoons between husk pendants, the latter being continued down the pilasters dividing the third-tier boxes. Above the double boxes next to the second gallery were 'slips', affording a very limited view of the stage.

A satirical engraving of c. 1760, by Gerard Vandergucht (Plate 41b), gives a convincing picture of the proscenium and flanking boxes. The proscenium opening, 26 feet wide, was framed with giant pilasters having panelled shafts capped with scrolls, supporting an architrave adorned with a cartouche inscribed 'VIVITUR INGENIO' and flanked with festooned garlands. Against the pilasters stood movable figures of Melpomene and Thalia, raised on *bombé* pedestals. This proscenium frame, seemingly derived from those created for the Stuart masques by Inigo Jones and John Webb, may well have been, like those, painted in *trompe l'œil* on a flat face partly cut in profile. The engraving confirms Dumont's section by showing an Ionic column against each proscenium door, while the box above has a balustraded parapet and a carved term supporting the crowning cornice.

The well-known engraving depicting the rioting in February 1763 (Plate 41c) shows some of the features referred to in Rich's bill of complaint, such as the gilded iron scrolls guarding the stage apron between the orchestra and the boxes, and the iron spikes on the parapets of the stage boxes. It confirms the general appearance of the proscenium, described above, and shows that the auditorium was illuminated by candle-branches on the columns and posts supporting the tiers, while the stage was lit by four coronas or hoop-candelabras.

In accordance with Rich's requirements, a carpenter's work-shop, scene-painting room, male actors' wardrobe, etc., were constructed in the lofty roof space above the auditorium. This somewhat cramped and inconveniently situated accommodation was later supplemented by the very spacious back-stage premises shown by Dumont and probably added between 1740 and 1760. Extending some 60 feet north of the main building, and having a frontage of 105 feet to Hart (now Floral) Street, this deep range provided three large rooms at stage level. The middle one, 34 feet wide and 43 feet deep, had a wide opening to the stage to which it formed an extension for deep perspective scenes, and for the spectacular processions for which Rich's productions were famous. At the north end was the stage door, flanked by dressing-rooms. An even larger room on the west side, 50 by 36 feet, was designed for use as a scenery store, and beneath it was a large rehearsal room. On the east side was a scene-painting room, 54 by 15 feet. Additional space for storing scenery was provided by building a long and narrow room extending above the pit passage on the east side of the shell.

The 'great entrance' to the theatre was located in the east end bay of the north side of the Piazza, and closed the vista along the east arcade of the portico buildings (Plate 41a). The panelled double doors to the entrance passage were hung in a large opening, almost square, set in an elaborate 'frontispiece' composed of two concentric arches, the inner recessed within a quadrant-curved reveal framed by the outer. These arches were dressed with moulded archivolts and engaged Ionic columns, their shafts broken with plain blocks, and the entablature-impost was carried across the doorway, below a tympanum decorated with a relief of the Royal Arms. Each side of the curved reveal contained a plain niche, and its soffit was enriched with two rings of coffers. This 'frontispiece' found little favour with contemporary critics, one describing it as 'a very expensive Piece of Work, but highly condemned by good Architects, as full of Absurdities'.[4] One 'good architect', William Kent, expressed his opinion in a letter to Lord Burlington, dated 16 November 1732, 'as for what you and I do, it may be esteem'd a hundred year hence, but at present does not look like it, by what I see doing in ye Arcad's in convent garding, Inigo thought proper to add a portico of the Tuscan order, but these wise head's have put an Ionick expencive portico in the rustick arches, for an Entrance into the absurd Building they have made'.[5]

The altered auditorium of 1782

The alterations and additions made to the theatre during its first fifty years of existence seem to have been generally directed towards improving the accommodation behind the scenes. As to the auditorium, *The Town and Country Magazine* for September 1775 remarked that 'Few alterations have been made ... except the converting the slips into boxes, new painting it, and other necessary decorations'.[6] During the theatre's closure in 1782, however, Shepherd's fan-shaped auditorium was gutted to make way for a new one of parallel-sided plan. A long and laudatory notice in *The Morning Chronicle* begins by declaring that the new interior 'not only forms one of the most elegant, and beautiful *coups d'œil* that was ever seen within the walls of a playhouse, but is, taken altogether, as worthy of admiration, for its peculiarly nice adaptation to the purposes of a

Theatre, as far as the skill and contrivance of Mr. Richards* (the artist who formed the design, and carried it into execution) in making so capital an improvement within the old walls of a House, now proved to have been built on erroneous principles'. Contrasting the advantages of the new auditorium with the defects of the old one, the writer noticed that 'the ground plan of the late Theatre was eight feet three inches wider at the back row of the pit, than at the curtain; in consequence of this error, all the spectators in the side-boxes were turned away from the stage: In the present Theatre, the back of the pit and the front of the stage are nearly parallel. The sound-board and pit cieling were formerly divided into two parts, making an obtuse angle inclining upwards from the front of the stage, where the curtain drops; this is now raised eight feet, and makes one entire level cieling.'[7]

The new floor below the pit benches was raised to give the occupants of the front rows a better view of the stage than they had previously enjoyed, while the surrounding gangway was sunk one step below the new floor level so that those standing there would not obstruct the view from the front boxes, where the seats were also raised by about 5 inches. Eight 'enclosed boxes', entered directly from the back lobby, were introduced behind the front boxes.† The first (two-shilling) gallery was raised by 2 feet 6 inches to provide more headroom in the boxes below, whereas the upper (one-shilling) gallery was 5 feet lower than its predecessor, the depth being reduced by five rows so that it no longer overhung the five front rows of the lower gallery, which were also free from obstructive columns. The three tiers of side boxes were equally divided into compartments containing the same number of benches, all of the same length and breadth, except that the second-tier boxes next to the lower gallery were 'considerably enlarged and made much more commodious'. Above the side boxes were slips, reached by way of the new lower gallery entrances in the Piazza and Bow Street. A new entrance to the upper gallery was provided 'within three yards of the gate in the Piazza'.

The first-tier front and side boxes were arranged in pairs behind a widely spaced colonnade of the Ionic order, the slender-shafted columns supporting a balustrade which formed the lower-gallery parapet. Columns of the Corinthian order were similarly used to divide the upper tiers of side boxes, and the slips were 'bounded in front with a ballustrade'. All the columns were painted a light pearl colour, the fluting being 'a degree darker (of a green tint)', with gilding applied to the capitals and fillets. The balustrades and other ornaments were also gilt, as were parts of the mouldings. The ceiling was painted to represent 'a serene sky, in imitation of the Roman theatres'. Crimson festoon curtains ornamented the side and upper front boxes, which were

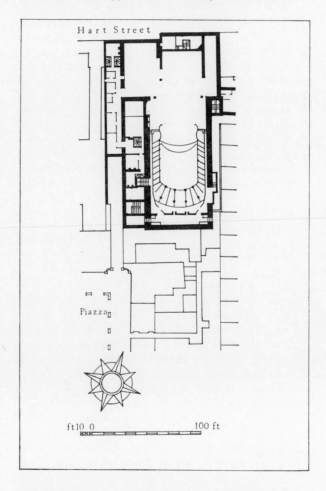

Fig. 10. Plan, after John Inigo Richards's alterations of 1782. Based on plans in Mr. Robert Eddison's collection, and on George Saunders, *A Treatise on Theatres*, 1790, Plate X

* John Inigo Richards, R.A., principal scene-painter at Covent Garden.
† These were probably the first example of the so-called 'basket boxes' that were a prominent feature of Henry Holland's Covent Garden and Drury Lane auditoria.

lighted by small lustres suspended by chains in front of each column. The front boxes were illuminated by 'four lustres, and a large girandole ornamentally placed at each end'. An important change in the presentation of plays was made by removing the entrance doors to the stage from their original position below the side boxes, and placing them, below balconies, in the splayed sides of the proscenium frame 'at such an angle, as to be seen by the spectators on the same side'. An interior view (Plate 42a), possibly by Van Assen, conforms in most respects with the above description, although it shows the first colonnade with Corinthian instead of Ionic columns.

In his *Treatise on Theatres*, published in 1790, George Saunders includes two plans of the reconstructed auditorium, which he wrongly dates as 1784. The first plan shows the pit with the amphitheatre and side boxes, and the second shows the lower gallery (Plate 42c). Encroaching on the former stage space, the new auditorium was 86 feet deep from the proscenium to the back wall of the old shell, 56 feet wide between the shell walls, and 31 feet 6 inches high from the stage floor to the ceiling 'which slopes upwards to make room for the upper gallery'. The front part of the auditorium was no longer fan-shaped but uniformly 38 feet 6 inches wide, the side boxes having been rebuilt so that their straight parapets were parallel with the shell walls. The two upper tiers each contained five pairs of boxes, and the lower tier a royal box and four pairs, all furnished with three stepped rows of benches. The stage apron and orchestra projected some 20 feet in front of the proscenium, leaving space for a pit 36 feet 6 inches deep, with seventeen rows of benches on its raked floor. Behind the pit was the raised amphitheatre, more capacious than before, being 18 feet deep and having eight stepped rows of benches divided by low lateral partitions into nine boxes. The first (two-shilling) gallery, with its parapet in line above that of the amphitheatre, was increased in depth to 30 feet 6 inches, with sixteen stepped rows of benches. The first five rows were free from obstructing columns or overhang by the second (one-shilling) gallery, which was now reduced to a depth of 21 feet 6 inches, with only eleven stepped rows of benches. Saunders' plans show that each gallery, in turn, was supported by two rows of four widely spaced columns. All the new benches were set out to concentric curves but with uniformly cramped spac-

ing, Saunders commenting that 'the public should not submit to be crowded into such narrow seats: 1,foot 9 inches is the whole space here allowed for seat and void'. He gives the capacity as—second gallery, 384; first gallery and slips, 700; front and side boxes, 729; and pit, 357, this making a total of 2,170.

With regard to the decorations, Saunders observed that 'Mr. Richards would have acted judiciously had he introduced more painted ornaments in lieu of projecting ones, which as a scene-painter I am rather surprised he did not. For example, the parapets of the gallery-fronts and upper boxes, which afforded opportunities for plain surfaces, are filled in with solid balusters; the others are divided into panels and tablets, with carved ornaments in the friezes; pilasters are placed at the sides of the gallery without the least apparent necessity, and the like all round the lower range of boxes, with decorative arches over; and all the partitions are lined with paper, and festoons of drapery hang in front; than which nothing can be more injurious to the progress of sound. . . . The frontispiece is such an one as no architect would have applied. Were a painted frame to be proposed for a picture, how would a connoisseur exclaim!' This last would seem to suggest that the old tradition persisted, of having a proscenium frame painted in *trompe l'œil*.[8]

Although he shows four instead of five bays of paired side boxes, Rowlandson's very comprehensive view of Covent Garden, published in 1786 (Plate 42b) almost certainly represents the auditorium described by Saunders. As in the plans, the stage box shown by Rowlandson has a segmental parapet and a canopy above, while the columns supporting the box tiers and galleries rise from pedestals breaking each parapet. The balustraded parapets of the two galleries, and the panelled fronts of the boxes with festooned draperies below them, are just as Saunders describes them. The proscenium splay, with its door and balustraded balcony, is much as shown on Saunders' plan.

The auditorium plans published by Saunders correspond in all important respects with two plans of the whole complex building, probably drawn from a survey made at an unspecified date but possibly around 1791, and forming part of a series of five drawings, now in the possession of Mr. Robert Eddison, which are attributed to William Capon, the scene painter and theatre architect (Plate 43). One of these plans, taken at basement level, shows the pit and its seating exactly as in Saunders. The other plan, of the first (two-shilling) gallery level, differs from Saunders in showing five wide boxes on either side instead of ten paired ones, while between the smaller end box and the canted partition wall on each side of the gallery is a space without seating, perhaps a 'slip' for standing spectators. This plan also shows how the new auditorium's encroachment on the former stage area had been amply compensated by demolishing the north end wall of the old shell, and extending the working stage by taking in part of the three large rooms in the Hart Street extension.

Henry Holland's reconstruction of 1792

The survey from which these plans were drawn may well have been made in connexion with Henry Holland's first proposals for another, more extensive reconstruction of Shepherd's building. This scheme is illustrated by the remaining drawings in the Capon set (Plates 44, 45b), one of which is entitled 'Design for a Model to be made on a scale of 4 inches to ten feet for the proposed new Theatre erected in 1792', although the drawing is inscribed November 1791. Holland proposed building within the old shell a deeper and wider auditorium of horseshoe plan, having a greatly increased capacity. The pit was to contain nineteen straight rows and one curved row backing against the wall below the first of the four horseshoe tiers. These were intended to be spaced at vertical intervals of 8 feet, below a flat ceiling covering the auditorium well. The front part of the first tier was to be three rows deep and divided by low partitions into twenty-three boxes, extending between the large King's and Prince's boxes flanking the stage apron. Behind the middle boxes was to be a slightly raised amphitheatre of eight rows, divided into seven large boxes, between standing spaces against the side walls. The second tier of three rows was to be divided into twenty-seven boxes, but both the third and fourth tiers were to have ten boxes on either side of a gallery of fourteen rows. The massive side walls of the original building were to be penetrated with openings formed at intervals, providing access to the boxes and galleries from new corridors extending along either side of the shell. The new coffee room, already added to the south end of the shell, was to be flanked by two staircases, the

west ovoid and the east circular in plan, and a capacious new box entrance was to be constructed within two existing houses fronting to Bow Street.

Holland's 'model' design represents a fusion of the established English and Continental auditorium forms by combining the deep galleries of the former with the horseshoe-shaped box tiers of the latter. Although no plans of the executed work appear to have survived, it is clear from descriptive accounts, and the well-known interior view in Robert Wilkinson's *Theatrum Illustrata* (Plate 46b), that the 'model' design was considerably modified in execution, although its most important feature, the horseshoe plan of the tiers, was retained.

The following description of the theatre as reconstructed by Holland has been based on the lengthy but often obscure account given in *The Public Advertiser* for 18 September 1792, which has been checked with Wilkinson's interior view. The 'model' design provided the general form of the new auditorium, which contained a pit and four straight-sided horseshoe tiers, the first three entirely given up to boxes, and the fourth to the two-shilling gallery. The straight-fronted apron stage was deeper than before, and the orchestra was 'very roomy, and more commodious than the old one, having a place for an organ, and the floor laid on an arch . . . to assist the general sound'. Wilkinson shows the pit furnished with twenty rows of seating as in the 'model' plan, all straight benches except the curved back row. The boxes in the first three tiers, or circles, were divided by console-shaped partitions, low in front but rising in a concave curve to meet the side walls or the slender cast-iron columns that were ranged in a semicircle to support the partly cantilevered upper tiers. The parapets were formed with a cyma-curved profile 'very accommodating to those who sit in the front rows'. In the first-circle front boxes the first row was separated from the back rows by a low partition 'and a passage of communication', presumably a cross-aisle, 'yet the back rows look over them, and are as good a place for seeing and hearing as any in the house, though not so good for being seen and heard'. As Wilkinson's view shows, the second and third circles of boxes differed from those below 'only in respect of their height'. The fourth-tier, or gallery, seats were 'considerably elevated so as to give a complete uninterrupted view of the Stage'.

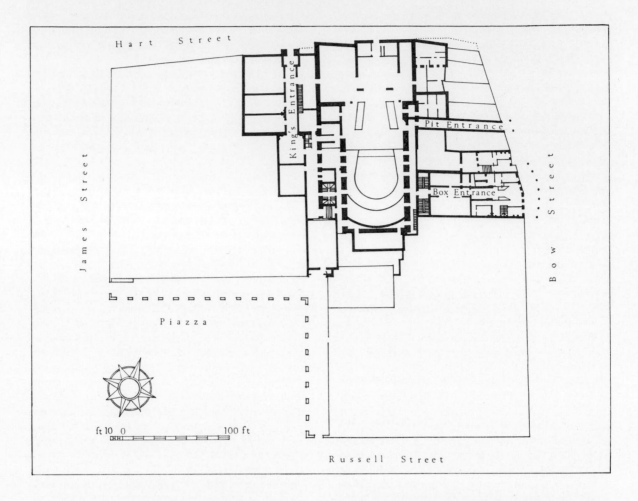

Fig. 11. Site plan in *c.* 1808. Based on a plan in the British Museum, Crace Collection Maps, portfolio xiii

According to *The Public Advertiser* 'The general effect is that of a small Theatre, and we understand it is not calculated to hold many more than the old one. Every part of it is lined with the thinnest board, painted in water colours, as a means whereby the sound may come improved to the ear. The decorations are considerable, though not overcharged; a Theatre calls for dress as much as a Stage. The cieling [*sic*] is painted as a sky, the opening to which is surrounded by a ballustrade, supported by rich frames, which have their bearings on the walls, and on the proscenium. The proscenium is composed of pilasters and columns of the Corinthian order, fully enriched, having between them the stage doors, over which are the balcony Boxes. In the entablature to the order

is introduced the old motto, "Veluti in Speculum", and over the entablature is a cove enriched with antique foliage on each side of the Royal Arms. The soffit of the entablature forms the sounding board to the proscenium, and the cove is calculated to throw the voice forwards.' The 'swelling' fronts of the tiers had decorations 'of white and gold forming compartments, in each of which is a painting of gold colours on a pearl ground'. Throughout the house, the boxes were 'lined and ceiled with wainscot ... not papered for the advantage of sound' but 'coloured red as suiting best the audience'. As to the gallery 'its decorations have been sufficiently attended to; it is neat, airy and lofty, and has a proper degree of elegance'.

The account in *The Public Advertiser* concludes with a description of the circulation and amenities of the now very extensive theatre premises. 'Round every circle of Boxes, and to the Gallery, are very spacious corredors accessible by roomy staircases. In Hart Street a very large building has been erected for the Scene Painters, Scene Rooms, Green Room, Dressing Rooms, etc.' Through this building there was a private entrance for the royal family to the state box. The stage door and box office were also in an additional building in Hart Street. 'The whole of the avenues to the Theatre have been altered and improved. The principal and new entrance is in Bow-street, under an antique Doric Portico, leading through a large and spacious staircase Saloon, handsomely fitted up and warmed by stoves, to the lower circle of Boxes, and to a double staircase that leads to the upper circles. In Bow-street the old way to the Pit and Gallery is preserved. From the Piazza in Covent-Garden the old Box entrance is preserved, leading by the Front Boxes round the House, and to the old Coffee Room, which is likewise preserved. . . . A new entrance is made to the Pit, and a new double staircase to the Gallery.' These improvements and additions are clearly delineated on an undated plan[9] (Plate 45a) showing the whole complex of buildings belonging to the theatre, of which the original shell of 1731–2 now formed a relatively small nucleus. Much of Holland's work involved altering and extending existing houses in Bow Street (Plate 48), but the building on the west side of the stage was entirely new. The Hart Street front (Plate 45b) was a simple and elegant composition, three storeys high and five windows wide, the ground floor dressed with a Doric order and the lofty first floor having round-arched windows.

The absence of a second, one-shilling, gallery in the new house gave rise to riotous scenes on the opening night of 17 September 1792, which were only ended by the management's promise to reinstate that accommodation as soon as possible. Within a fortnight a temporary measure was effected by partitioning off some seats in the two-shilling gallery.[10] When the theatre re-opened for the season in September 1793, it presented 'a still more beautiful face to the Public than it did before. The mode of introducing an Upper Gallery, the elegance of the Ceiling, and the lightness of the decorations, added to the uncommonly convenient space allowed those of the audience who sit aloft for breathing room, contribute much to the general effect of the coup d'œil, and give a relief and wholeness to the appearance that render it striking, beautiful and grand.'[11] Further changes, mostly affecting the decorations, were made in time for the re-opening in September 1794, when it was reported that the 'frontispiece', or proscenium, was new 'and a pelastre [sic] next the green curtain, instead of a column as formerly, with different ornaments, it is now of a delicate fawn colour with green gold panels, and a beautiful troylage [i.e. trellis] of gold on the pannels of the pilastres and front of the boxes over the stage doors—green satten wood doors and gold mouldings. The ceiling is entirely new, and the painted gallery which impeded the sight from the one shilling gallery, is removed by a slope.'[12] In 1796 the centre boxes in the second and third tiers were enlarged, and the entrances and lobbies improved.[13] After this, apart from the annual redecoration, no changes worth recording were made in the auditorium until 1803, when it was reported in September that 'all the front boxes on both tiers have been enlarged by the addition of one seat capable of accommodating each with ease, six persons more than they held last season. The slips, or rather the side continuation of the two shilling gallery to the stage, are now converted into boxes. The frontispiece has been raised ten feet, and sixteen private boxes have been added. . . . The ceiling is ornamented in the antique manner, without any of its heaviness. . . . All the improvements have been made under the direction of Mr. Creswell [a scene painter] and Mr. Philips.'[14] The effect of these latest changes is admirably depicted in the aquatint by Pugin and Rowlandson in the first volume of *The Microcosm of London* (Plate 47b).

The theatre was completely destroyed by fire on 20 September 1808.

SIR ROBERT SMIRKE'S THEATRE ROYAL OF 1809

Built in the remarkably short space of ten months, the Covent Garden Theatre Royal of 1809 was (Sir) Robert Smirke's first important undertaking, and one of the earliest Greek Revival buildings in London. Among the finest and largest theatres in Europe, it was, unlike its predecessor, fully insular, almost completely covering a site measuring some 218 feet north to south, and 166 feet east to west. Whether by intention or coincidence, the basic disposition of elements forming the old accretive theatre was repeated in the arrangement of the well-balanced but asymmetrical plan of the new building (Plates 52–3). A lofty oblong shell, internally some 152 feet long and 82 feet wide, contained from north to south a three-storeyed range of scene painting and storage rooms, a stage 56 feet deep, and a five-tiered auditorium of horseshoe plan having side and back corridors. On either side of this shell was a lower range, about 35 feet wide, divided into dressing-rooms and scene-recesses flanking the stage, and public entrances, lobbies and staircases contiguous to the auditorium. The main entrance hall and principal staircase were on the east side, entered through the great portico in the middle of the Bow Street front. The royal saloon and staircase, and the secondary staircase to the boxes, were on the west side, reached by a private passage linking Hart Street to the Piazza. Entrance to the pit corridor was through a spacious loggia, forming the ground storey of a range, about 20 feet wide, at the south end of the main shell. Above the loggia were two saloons, a lower and an upper, serving the boxes. Below the pit floor, which was raised above ground level, was an extensive and lofty basement designated for use as stables.

The principal front, facing east to Bow Street, was 209 feet 3 inches long and 50 feet high (Plates 49–50). Symmetrically composed, it was dominated by the Doric tetrastyle portico which projected between wide flanking wings and narrow end pavilions. According to contemporary accounts 'the Temple of Minerva, in the Acropolis of Athens, suggested the design for the portico . . . which is pure Grecian Doric'.[15] Raised on a podium of three steps, the fluted stone columns rose some 30 feet to support an entablature, having triglyphs and plain metopes, and a pediment having a plain tympanum. The flanking wings, of stucco-faced brick dressed with stone, were divided by a moulded stringcourse into two storeys. The low ground storey of each wing contained three plain segmental-arched openings, equally spaced at wide intervals, and in the lofty upper face were three corresponding windows, dressed alike with a moulded architrave, narrow frieze, and cornice. In the wall face above these windows extended a long panel containing a bas-relief of figures carved by J. C. Rossi from models

by John Flaxman, described below (Plate 51b). The end pavilions echoed the theme of the portico with their dressing of two plain-shafted pilasters supporting a triglyphed entablature, framing a wall face containing a large plain niche underlined by a continuation of the first-floor stringcourse. Each niche contained a stone statue carved by Rossi, the tragic muse Melpomene in the south, and the comic muse Thalia in the north (Plate 51a). Only the cornice of the crowning entablature was continued across the wings, and the whole front was uniformly finished with a tall parapet of pedestal form. This was returned all round the building, underlining the seven windows in the north face of the lofty attic stage of the main shell (Plate 51c). The long east and west faces of this attic were screen walls, penetrated at equal intervals by six wide segmental-headed openings, through which projected sections of the main roof's eaves.

The Flaxman bas-relief panel in the north wing symbolized ancient drama, and that in the south wing modern drama (Plate 51b). A contemporary account states that Greek tragedy is represented by Aeschylus, with Minerva, Melpomene, and Bacchus, while two Furies pursue Orestes who implores the aid of Apollo, seated in his chariot. Aristophanes and Menander represent Greek comedy, and are attended by Thalia, Polyhymnia, Euterpe, Clio and Terpsichore, with Pegasus attended by three nymphs. Modern drama has Shakespeare and Milton. Shakespeare summons characters from *The Tempest*; beyond them is Hecate's car, with Lady Macbeth, and Macbeth recoiling from the murdered Duncan. Milton contemplates Urania and the chained Samson, and behind them are characters from the masque *Comus*.[16] These bas-reliefs are now arranged in one long and two short panels on the front of the present opera house.

Inside the portico were three doorways that opened to the main hall, of oblong plan divided laterally by Doric piers into a nave and aisles of three bays. Against the north wall of the nave stood a Grecian stove, and at the south end was a short flight of steps beginning the grand staircase. The first landing was flanked by wide piers with niches containing pay-boxes, near each of which was a 'Grecian lamp, elevated upon a column of [imitation] porphyry'. The staircase continued its rise southwards in a lofty oblong compartment, with two long flights extending between plain

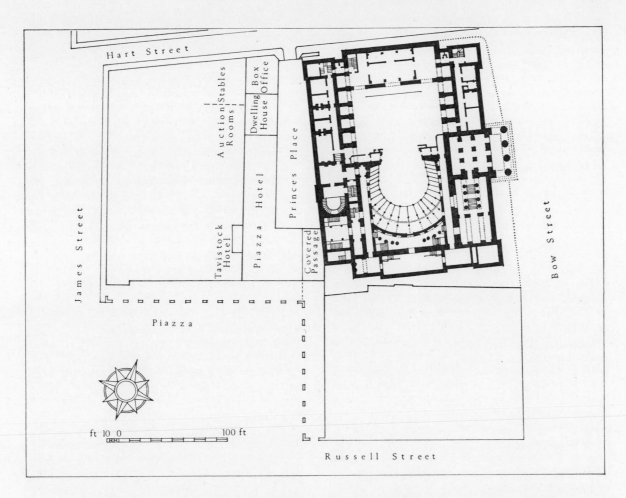

Fig. 12. Site plan *c*. 1842. Based on a plan in the Greater London Record Office and on the plan in Clement Contant, *Parallèle Des Principaux Théâtres*, 1842 ed., plate 56

walls surmounted by colonnades of five bays, screening the side galleries extending from the top landing at the principal-floor level. The columns, of the Ionic order, had unfluted shafts 'imitated from porphyry', and in every intercolumniation was suspended a 'superb Grecian lamp' (Plate 56a, b). Each colonnade supported a plain architrave, from which rose a segmental barrel vault, its surface divided by guilloche bands into bays, all modelled with five oblong panels framing two square coffers containing flower bosses. At the head of the staircase, in the south wall of the compartment, was a handsome doorway giving access to an ante-room, ornamented with pilasters of imitation porphyry and containing a focally-placed statue of Shakespeare, carved by Rossi in

yellow marble. On the west side of the ante-room were folding doors into the long corridor on the east side of the auditorium, giving access to the boxes in the first circle. At the south end of this corridor was an entrance to the semi-circular cross-corridor, with two staircases linking the three circles of boxes, and a central entrance to the lower saloon, a narrow oblong room decorated with pilasters of imitated porphyry and 'eight beautiful cast statues from the antique'. Of similar form, and 'originally appropriated to the private boxes', the upper saloon had at either end a stove recess flanked by Doric columns of imitated porphyry[17] (Plate 56c).

The west side entrance to the boxes, with twin staircases linked by a wide central landing space, was 'handsome, but not so elegant as that from Bow Street'. Adjoining to the north was the large D-shaped King's staircase and the King's saloon, adjacent to the King's box. These entrances, the pit entrance, and the gallery staircases, were approached by way of the old entrance in the north-east angle of the Piazza.[17]

The auditorium (Plates 54–5) contained a raked pit with twenty-three straight benches, surrounded by four tiers of true horseshoe plan, the semi-circular sweep facing the stage having a diameter of 51 feet 6 inches, the same dimension as the depth of the auditorium well from the apron front. The first three tiers, or circles, were each divided into twenty-six boxes, the side ones three rows deep, and those in the centre varying from five to six rows. The first- and second- circle boxes were of the loge type, with low partitions, but those in the third tier were originally made more private by their ceiling-height partitions and anterooms, an innovation of Continental origin which provoked a storm of criticism.[18] The fourth circle was mostly allotted to the two-shilling gallery, with ten rows of benches extending between the two groups of eight boxes at the sides of the horseshoe. The one-shilling gallery, with four rows of benches, partly overhung all but the front three rows of the lower gallery and extended above the side corridors to the boxes, its benches affording a very limited view of the stage through a series of thirteen semi-circular arches groined into the cove surrounding the main ceiling. The apron stage extended between the reveals of a deep proscenium arch, each reveal containing a stage door and two boxes superimposed between giant Doric pilasters, their plain shafts painted to resemble Siena marble. These pilasters supported simple entablatures from which rose an arch of elliptical profile, its soffit painted with three rings of thirteen square coffers. The front face of the arch was decorated with a winged figure painted in pseudo-relief on each spandrel, and the Royal Arms were placed against an attic pedestal above the crowning entablature. This last was continued round the whole auditorium to form the parapet of the upper gallery, and to provide a springing for the groined arches and cove surrounding the ceiling, its slightly concave surface painted to resemble a saucer-dome with radial coffering and an outer ring of arabesque panels. The wall face behind the fourth-circle boxes appears to have been painted to resemble festooned

red drapery: the circle parapets, painted with continuous bands of palmettes in gold on a dove-grey ground, were supported by slender fluted columns of gilt cast iron; and the pit wall was painted to resemble Siena marble. Except for the private boxes in the third tier, which were painted dove-grey, the prevailing background colour of the auditorium was pink, accentuated by the box doors of plain mahogany. Illumination was by chandeliers of glass and gilt metal, suspended from scrolled brackets of gilt ironwork projecting from the parapets of the second, third and fourth tiers, and centred above the supporting columns. The stage had a raked floor with six sets of wing grooves, a proscenium of adjustable width, a mezzanine and cellar basement, and fly-galleries at two levels.[19]

Smirke's lack of experience in theatre design led to serious defects in the auditorium, which had to be remedied during the seasonal closures of the theatre. On 10 September 1810 it was reported in *The Times* that the staircases linking the circles of boxes had been made 'much more commodious', and that the twelve centre boxes of the third tier had been 'thrown open' to accommodate 120 persons. The two-shilling gallery was given improved headroom, but the upper gallery and the side 'pigeon holes' in the ceiling cove were not altered until 1812, when *The Times* of 8 September remarked that the 'range of dens, sometimes tenanted by no unfit inhabitants, has now been thrown open, the arches removed, and those over the boxes, which only disfigured the house, judiciously closed altogether'. In 1813, or possibly in 1819, the proscenium was altered by removing the arched soffit and substituting an elliptical semi-dome, thus greatly improving the sighting from the upper parts of the house (compare Plate 54 with Plate 55b). All these changes brought the theatre to the state in which it was recorded around 1825 by Britton and Pugin, in *Illustrations of the Public Buildings of London*, where the auditorium is described as follows:

'The appearance of the house is very imposing: the colour is a subdued yellow, relieved by white, and superbly enriched with gilding. Around the dress circle are wreaths inclosing the Rose of England, in burnished gold; the first circle displays the Thistle of Scotland, and the second circle the Shamrock of Ireland: and these three emblems are alternately placed, with fancy devices, in rich borderings, &c., in every part of the Auditory; which, from the reflection of the lights, gratifies the prevalent taste for splendour with one blaze of refulgence. The back and sides of the pit are decorated by the representation of dark crimson drapery, as are the interiors of all the boxes; which produces a very effective contrast to the brilliancy of the front. The boxes are supported by small iron columns, fluted, and gilt. The ceiling, over what is called the slip boxes, exhibits pannels of blue, relieved by white, and enriched with gold. The middle part of the ceiling is circular; in the centre of which, from a richly-gilded glory, surrounding a circle of golden lyres, &c., is suspended a chandelier of glass, of the most superb description; illumined by two circles of gas lights: the remainder of the ceiling is a light blue sky, relieved by delicate white clouding. The cove of the proscenium, in the segment of a circle, contains the moiety of a rich gilded glory, and sky to match the ceiling, surrounded by a bordering of gold; in which, as well as round the ceiling, either fancy flowers are introduced, or representations of those national emblems, the Rose, &c. The proscenium is supported by four pilasters, painted to imitate Sienna marble. Stage doors are wholly dispensed with. The top of the proscenium, from whence the curtain descends, is an arch of about thirty-eight feet wide and three feet deep; surmounting a superb drapery border of crimson, white, and gold, elegantly disposed upon a transverse bar of gold, terminated on each side with a lion's head: in the centre of this drapery is the King's Arms. For the green curtain is substituted a drop, representing a luxuriant profusion of drapery; crimson, white, and gold, (to match the borders,) drawn up by cords and tassels; and disclosing part of the interior of a palace, supported by numerous Ionic columns; which has a most imposing appearance. There are also pilasters, imitative of Sienna marble, which slide backward and forward, in order to widen or contract the stage.'[20]

The public, or open boxes in the theatre contained about 1,200 people, the pit 750, the first gallery 350 and the second gallery 500, making a total of 2,800, exclusive of those in the private boxes.[21]

Benedict Albano's reconstruction of 1846–7

The ever declining fortunes of the proprietors and lessees prevented any further changes of importance being made to Smirke's theatre between 1819 and December 1846, when the auditorium

area was gutted from roof to cellar to make way for a new interior designed on Italian principles. Benedict Albano, a civil engineer, was engaged by the promotors of this undertaking. 'He submitted three plans—one by which it would have been transformed into the largest theatre in the world, surpassing San Carlo and La Scala; a second smaller than those theatres; and a third which, though it gave additional tiers of private boxes, left the theatre of its original size. The second plan was adopted.'[22]

This skilfully organized operation, completed in four months, was fully described in *The Builder* in April 1847, in an account here summarized.

On 2 December 1846 the contractor began clearing the building of rubbish preparatory to demolishing the entire auditorium and the inner foundation walls, vaults, etc., to the depth of about 22 feet below the pit-corridor level. Some three weeks later work was begun on the walls carrying the cantilevered stone staircases linking the new box corridors, and the foundation walls bearing the two rings of cast-iron columns supporting the new lyre-shaped tiers, which were set out on a wider radius than before. The columns, 6 to 8 inches in diameter, were equally spaced, the front ring being 10 feet 4 inches and the back ring 11 feet 6 inches apart. The sixth tier of columns had flanges to which were fixed storey-posts, framed into the existing roof structure and supporting the cantilevered wooden framework for the new ceiling. This was constructed of thin battens nailed to ribs, forming a shallow dome of parabolic section and elliptical plan, some 70 feet long and 60 feet wide. The depth of the auditorium well was about 80 feet from the curtain line, its greatest width being 62 feet and its height 54 feet. The tier parapets, moulded to a serpentine profile, were successively recessed so that the topmost tier was 2 feet 3 inches behind the lowest. The proscenium opening, 46 feet wide, was framed by a deep splayed reveal, with three superimposed boxes on either side, flanked by Corinthian columns some 26 feet high, supporting entablatures and an arched soffit of elliptical form. The curved front of the apron stage projected 9 feet in front of the curtain line, and the orchestra pit, 12 feet 6 inches deep, accommodated eighty-five musicians.

There were 188 boxes in all, thirty in the first tier, thirty-four in the second and third, twenty-eight in the fourth, fifth and sixth, and six in the proscenium. With six seats in each, the boxes held 1,128, the stalls seated 256 and the pit 263, the seven-row amphitheatres in the fourth and fifth tiers each seated 148, and the gallery held 300, bringing the total seating capacity to 2,243. With extra seats in the boxes, and standing patrons, the capacity could be increased to some 4,000, as it was on the opening night of 6 April 1847.

The auditorium (Plate 57) was opulently decorated in a florid Italian Renaissance style by Albano, who made considerably greater use of modelled ornament than had been the custom hitherto, thereby disregarding the observations and advice given by writers on theatre construction such as Patte and George Saunders. In spite of this it was generally agreed that the acoustics were well-nigh perfect. For the ornamental work he used a new material having a hemp basis and called Canabic, for which he held the patent. Female terms were used to encase the cast-iron columns supporting the tier parapets, each of which was enriched in a different way. The second tier exhibited a rich and continuous band of tall acanthus leaves; the third, fourth and fifth tiers had basically similar motifs composed of scrollwork and foliage flanking a central medallion, a lion's head, or a satyr's mask; while the sixth tier had a festooned floral garland with pendants below the columns.

The Corinthian columns flanking the proscenium boxes had fluted and cabled shafts, and the arched soffit, edged with enriched mouldings introducing naturalistic ornaments such as flowers and squirrels, was decorated with two large shaped panels containing painted medallions and arabesques, with a relief of the Royal Arms in the centre. Linking the arch with the main ceiling were two large spandrels adorned with figures on a gold ground, Britannia on the left side and Italia on the right. Except for the colourful main ceiling, the painted panels of the proscenium arch, and the turquoise ground of the medallions on the tier parapets, the auditorium was decorated in white and gold and dressed with red draperies set against a background of red walls, box partitions and seats.

The ceiling had at its centre a large circular ventilation grille of ornamental scrollwork in a richly moulded frame, surrounded by festooned garlands and linked to the outer frame by cabled mouldings. These divided the intervening space into four large quadrant-shaped panels, painted with cloudy skies and grouped figures symbolizing Music, Lyric Tragedy, Comedy and the Visual Arts. The rich architectural frame to the ceiling was broken at equal intervals by eight motifs, six large and two smaller, all composed of ornamented pedestals flanked and surmounted by standing or seated figures symbolizing the Arts and Sciences, and the Seasons. These painted decorations, executed on paper and then affixed to the ceiling, were by Italian artists named Ferri, Verardi and Zarra. It remains to add that the auditorium was brilliantly illuminated by an immense crystal chandelier lit by gas and suspended centrally from the ceiling. Supplementary light was given by candle branches projecting from the second- and third-tier parapets.

The public approaches were improved by making a new box-office and entrance, and by closing the loggias behind the Bow Street front to increase the width of the rooms within. The grand entrance hall was materially altered by raising the ceiling, which was now divided into compartments and supported by Doric columns instead of the original piers. The short flight of steps beginning the grand staircase was moved back, reducing the first landing but greatly improving the headroom, and the barrel vault over the staircase was replaced by a flat ceiling. The arcaded loggia at the south end of the building was enclosed to form a crush-room for the pit, entered from a vestibule replacing the south-east staircase to the gallery. The upper part of this staircase was floored over to form an extension of the grand-tier saloon, which was further improved by removal of the double staircase and by redecoration. A green watered paper on the walls provided a ground for the Siena-marbled columns and pilasters, and for the white and gold surrounds of the doors, which were grained to simulate satinwood. Behind the scenes, a new stage entrance was formed, and a large retiring room for the musicians was provided below the apron stage.

On 5 March 1856 the theatre was again destroyed by fire, for the second time within less than fifty years (Plate 58).

E. M. BARRY'S ROYAL ITALIAN OPERA HOUSE OF 1857–8

The present opera house (Plates 59–67, figs. 13–15), built in 1857–8, is a smaller building than its predecessor, although the stage is larger and the auditorium more spacious. These improvements could only be effected at the expense of circulation space, which is barely adequate and seems cramped when compared with Continental examples. Nevertheless, Barry's theatre has the advantage of a compact and well-arranged plan (Plate 62), asymmetrical in its layout though balanced about an east–west axis. Excluding the portico, projecting about 18 feet from the Bow Street front which is canted in a north-west direction, the building is 210 feet long on the north side, fronting Floral Street, and 219 feet long on the south side, adjoining the Floral Hall, while the uniform width is 123 feet 6 inches. The 89 feet deep stage and

its dependencies occupy the west part of the site, and the entrance foyers form a 25 feet wide range extending along the east front to Bow Street.

As in the previous theatres, stage and auditorium are enclosed by a massive brick-walled shell, 90 feet wide inside. This leaves space on either side for a narrow range containing a basement and seven storeys, divided to form the staircases, ante-rooms, lavatories, etc., required for the audience, and the staircases, dressing-rooms, offices, and workshops appertaining to the stage. A buttressed wall of semi-circular plan links the side walls of the shell, rising to the underside of the fourth tier and defining the basic horseshoe form of the auditorium. The fourth tier, originally

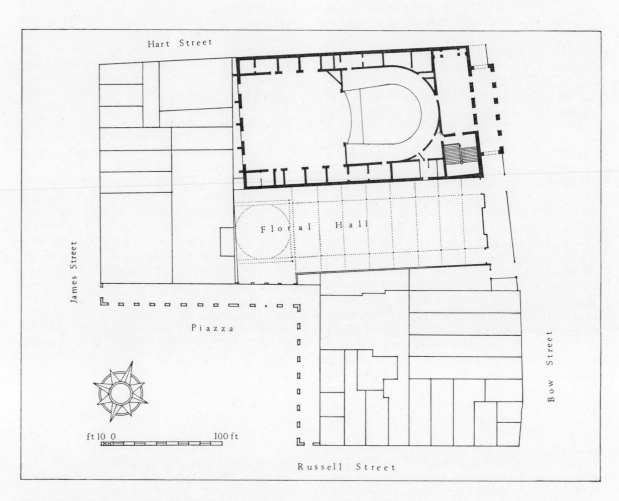

Fig. 13. Site plan in *c.* 1866. Based on a plan of 1866 in the possession of the Trustees of the Bedford Settled Estates

divided into amphitheatre stalls and gallery, extends in depth to the Bow Street front, above the 25 feet wide range containing the entrance hall with the grand staircase to the south and the crush bar or saloon above.

The three tiers of boxes and the amphitheatre stalls were originally served by two staircases, one in the north side range and one in the south-east spandrel space, both being approached at ground level by way of the stalls corridor. The amphitheatre-gallery staircase in the north range is entered from Floral Street, as are the royal and the Duke of Bedford's boxes, the ante-room to the last being reached by a passage slewed across the north-east angle of the stage. On either side of the stage is a staircase serving the dressing-rooms, offices, workshops and flies. Alterations have been made from time to time, bringing the building into conformity with safety regulations, the most notable change being the provision of ample exit staircases on the south side of the auditorium, discharging into Bow Street.

The building was strongly constructed and as fireproof as contemporary practice could render it (Plate 63). The load-bearing walls of the inner shell are about 85 feet high, and their thickness decreases from 3 feet 4 inches in the basement to 3 feet in the first tier, and 2 feet 8 inches above. The external walls, 95 feet high from the foundations and 2 feet 4 inches thick, are linked to the shell walls by cross walls of 2 feet thickness, strengthened at 12 feet intervals by horizontal tie-rods of iron. These cross walls form fireproof divisions between the various rooms in the side ranges, and enclose the public and private staircases which are constructed with steps and landings of York stone. The main roof structure consists of a series of eight wrought-iron trellis girders, 9 feet high, spanning the 90 feet wide void of the shell and spaced approximately at 20 feet centres, leaving a bay some 30 feet wide at either end. Each bay, except that at the west end, has a light iron roof, slated and furnished with skylights, which rests on low-pitched triangular trusses spanning between the trellis girders. The four bays above the auditorium ceiling were provided with floors and used as carpenters' workshops, the auditorium ceiling of saucer dome, pendentives and arches being suspended from the trellis girders, as are the two tiers of flies on either side of the stage. The large and lofty scene-painting room over the rear part of the stage has a lean-to roof with ample skylights, resting on trussed rafters.

Exterior

The exterior of the theatre is a competent but uninspired essay in the Roman Renaissance manner of the mid nineteenth century (Plates 59–61). The Bow Street front is dominated by the grandiose Corinthian portico, hexastyle with plain-shafted columns, which rises loftily above the low and simply rusticated ground storey, and projects for one intercolumniation from the main wall face of seven bays. The exposed bay on either side of the portico is flanked by pilasters, which are paired at each end of the front. Barry's original design shows the ground-storey piers with a face of seven jointed courses, between a low plinth and a simple cornice, and there are openings in all five bays of the carriage-way. As built, there are only five courses to the piers, between a high plinth and a narrow entablature, and each front bay of the carriage-way contained a deeply recessed window, the middle three now altered to form doorways into the extended entrance hall. The Portland stone columns of the portico are 36 feet high and 3 feet 8 inches in diameter at the foot of the shaft. They rise from pedestals, linked by open balustrades, to support a pedimented entablature having a moulded architrave, plain frieze and a dentilled cornice framing a plain tympanum. (Barry's design shows the Royal Arms within the pediment, a group with Britannia above its apex, and a couchant lion at each end.) Respondent pilasters were omitted from the wall face within the portico in order to accommodate Flaxman's twin bas-reliefs salvaged from Smirke's theatre. These have been combined in a long panel extending above the five large round-arched windows originally lighting the staircase and crush bar, but now largely hidden by the mansard-roofed conservatory filling the lower part of the portico. The window openings form an arcade having plain piers, moulded imposts, and moulded archivolts broken by keystones carved with masks, said to have been derived from Greek originals in the Townley Marbles. In the spandrels between the arches are four roundels containing busts of Shakespeare, Jonson, Aeschylus and Aristophanes, carved in high relief by James Tolmie.[23] The Flaxman bas-relief panel has a plain margin, underlined by a moulded stringcourse which is continued in the outer bays of the front, below smaller panels containing isolated groups from the Flaxman frieze. Above the panels, linking the pilaster capitals and the trusses supporting the transverse beams of the portico ceiling, extends a series of panels. Each end panel is filled with a scrolled trophy of musical instruments, whereas those within the portico are plain and contain small circular windows. Instead of a large arch-headed window, each end bay of the front has a niche set in a plain rectangular frame. These niches contain the statues, by Rossi, salvaged from Smirke's theatre, Melpomene in the south niche, and Thalia in the north. The front is finished, above the crowning entablature, with a high pedestal parapet, the forward breaks above the pilasters being surmounted by tall-necked urns. Now painted cream with white relief, the front was originally finished in Portland cement to match the stonework of the portico, and the effect of the Flaxman bas-reliefs was enhanced by a ground of pale blue-grey.

The pronounced horizontal members of the Bow Street front are continued round the side and back elevations of the building, where the general treatment is bold and simple. The Floral Street elevation, also finished in Portland cement and now painted, has a well ordered scheme with the first-, second- and third-storey windows arranged in pairs and grouped, with panelled aprons, into tall rectangular panels. These are recessed in a series of nine equal bays divided by plain piers that die into a horizontal plain band, equalling in width the Corinthian entablature's architrave which appears above the paired pilasters at each end of the elevation. The south side is generally similar to the north, except that its greater length is divided into ten bays, and the lower part is concealed by the adjoining Floral Hall. The west elevation, finished in stock brick with cement dressings, forms the back wall of the stage and painting-room. Here also the windows are grouped into pairs and recessed in four bays, between boldly projecting buttresses round which the cement-faced stringcourses and crowning entablature are returned. Each buttress is finished above the entablature with a tall inverted scroll-console, supporting the lofty attic stage. Unfortunately, the powerful Baroque effect of this elevation has been impaired by the addition, in 1933–4, of a commonplace and small-scaled range of six low storeys containing dressing-rooms, etc. This is faced with red brick above a cement-finished ground storey, and is finished with a steep slated mansard.

The Entrance Hall, Grand Staircase and Crush Bar

The building is now entered from Bow Street by the three doorways formed in the front face of the carriage-way, which has been altered to provide an extension of the original entrance hall. As designed by Barry, this last was an oblong apartment, 60 feet wide and 25 feet deep, simply decorated with a Doric order of plain pilasters and antae dividing each long wall into four bays, and each end wall into two. The four bays of the east wall contained doorways into the carriage-way, and a doorway at each end of the west wall led, through a lobby, to the lower (pit) corridor. The east bay of the north wall contained a door to the impresario's office, and the two bays at the south end were open, the east giving access to a space before the box-office, and the west opening to the grand staircase. The width of the entrance hall has now been reduced by one bay at the north end, to make way for a kiosk and an ante to the men's cloakroom; the doors in the east (entrance) wall have been removed; and there are three doorways in the west wall, serving the stalls and stalls circle. The decorative scheme is simple; the pilasters have bronzed bases and caps, and the Siena-marbled shafts carry branch-lights; the plain ceiling, divided by cross beams into corniced compartments, is ivory-white; and the woodwork, generally, is of polished mahogany.

The grand staircase is 12 feet wide, the first flight of twenty-two risers ascending south to a spacious half-landing, where the second flight of eleven risers returns north to stop at the first-floor landing gallery (Plate 67a). Here a wide and tall glazed double door opens to the crush bar, a French window opens east to the conservatory in the portico, and a small doorway in the west wall gives access to the grand tier and to the staircase linking the various tiers. The first flight of the staircase rises between walls, but the second is furnished with a handsome railing of gilt ironwork resembling an openwork Vitruvian scroll enriched with acanthus leaves. Rising from a plinth of veined white marble, the railing begins with a newel composed of twisted baluster-bars surrounding a scale-patterned column; it is returned with a quadrant curve and continued across the landing gallery, and it is capped with a broad mahogany handrail. The walls of the oblong compartment are simply decorated with panels formed by plain raised mouldings. In the large rectangular panels on the south, east and west walls are festooned garlands, placed over gilt-framed still-life paintings in rich golden tones. On the north wall, flanking the glazed doorway to the crush bar, are two Baroque figure paintings, placed below horizontal panels containing floral festoons. A moulded architrave finishes the walls, and a high segmental panelled cove rises to the flat ceiling. This is quartered by mouldings to form four panels surrounding a central boss from which hangs a fine crystal chandelier. The general colour scheme is restrained, in two tones of French blue relieved with white.

The handsome crush bar (Plate 67c) is 25 feet wide and 26 feet 6 inches high, but its original length of 81 feet 6 inches has been reduced to 69 feet by the construction of an exit staircase at the north end of the front range. Ionic plain-shafted pilasters divide the long walls into four wide bays and a narrow one at the north end, and each end wall into three, wide between narrow. Formerly there was a recess for a buffet at the north end, screened by two columns. The four wide east side bays contain large round-arched windows, originally opening to the portico but now leading to the conservatory-bar. An unbroken architrave serves to finish the walls, and the flat ceiling is divided by cross beams into oblong compartments, each quartered by mouldings forming four panels round a central boss. The original appearance of this room has been substantially changed by the addition of a staircase which rises in twin flights against the west wall, to meet at a landing in front of a door leading to the balcony-stalls tier. This staircase is simply detailed, with cut strings and a mahogany handrail supported by straight and wavy bar-balusters. The spandrel spaces below the flights are open, but the landing is supported by two small Ionic columns on tall pedestals, flanking the entrance to the grand tier. On the west wall, the bays flanking the staircase landing are decorated with raised mouldings, forming large panels enriched with festooned garlands above gilt-framed paintings of Baroque figure compositions by a Dutch artist, Augustyn Terwesten (1645–1711).[24] The room is illuminated by a crystal chandelier, hanging from the ceiling in front of the staircase landing, and by bronzed metal branches on the pilaster-shafts. The former

colour-scheme of white and gold, with Siena-marbled pilasters, was changed in 1967. Now the pilasters have white shafts, and the walls are coloured blackberry relieved with pale blue.

The royal suite, entered from Floral Street, comprises a lobby and a spacious staircase, a foyer or smoking-room in the basement, and a handsome ante-room on the first floor, adjoining the royal box in the grand tier. The foyer appears to have been redecorated in the Edwardian–Adam taste, with plenty of Lincrusta ornament, but the ante-room reflects the style of the auditorium, with arabesque-panelled pilasters supporting an enriched architrave, below a trellis-patterned cove and a guilloche-bordered flat ceiling (Plate 67b). In a shallow recess are double doors opening to the box, where one wall is furnished with a large mirror affording a reflected view of the stage for any attendants sitting at the back of the box.

The Auditorium

Although the prime function of the building was to provide the appropriate setting for seasonal presentations of grand opera to an audience largely composed of box-subscribers, the auditorium (Plates 64–6) was to be adaptable for use as a winter playhouse, as a ballroom, and as a hall for exhibitions and public functions. Fulfilling these requirements, Barry's auditorium seems to present a successful fusion of two theatre forms, the Italianate opera house and the deep-tiered playhouse. If contemporary buildings influenced the design, it might seem that the three horseshoe tiers of boxes derived from Novosielski's Haymarket Opera House of 1790, while Nash's Haymarket Theatre Royal of 1821 could have suggested the general form of the spacious and lofty upper part which, rising above the front part of the deep amphitheatre tier, is square in plan and ceiled with a shallow saucer-dome and pendentives, resting on shallow elliptical arches, 60 feet wide, springing from square piers which appear to be structural, but are in fact decorative features.

The west arch frames a decorated tympanum of parabolic section, designed to serve as a sounding-board above the stage apron which originally projected with a shallow elliptical curve into the orchestra pit. The north and south side arches have wide soffits extending above the amphitheatre slips, and are open to the upper slips, while the east arch spans the front part of the amphitheatre, the rear part of which has a high flat ceiling.

The well of the auditorium is 80 feet deep from the proscenium, and the horseshoe plan of the tiers is based on a semi-circle of 63 feet diameter, its curvature continuing for 3 feet at either end to merge with the straight sides which are canted towards the proscenium, reducing the width to 50 feet. Each tier has an average depth of 13 feet 6 inches which increases on either side towards the proscenium wall, and it was originally furnished with removable partitions of mahogany, forming a series of boxes, generally 8 feet deep and about 5 feet 6 inches wide, entered directly from a corridor some 5 feet 6 inches wide. The first (stalls) tier, with 8 feet 6 inches clear headroom, contained thirty-four boxes and two entrances into the stalls; the second (grand) tier, with 10 feet headroom, contained thirty-three boxes in addition to the wide royal box and the Bedford box, on the north side next to the proscenium; the third (upper box) tier, with 9 feet headroom, contained thirty-six boxes. The generous headroom provided in these three tiers permitted the conversion from level-floored boxes to stepped rows of seating. Originally an additional eight boxes were provided on either side of the amphitheatre tier. Now, the only boxes remaining are those at the sides of the grand and balcony tiers.

Each box tier was finished with a boarded floor within the auditorium and York stone paving in the corridor, the former laid on wood joists and the latter on iron joists, all framed into a series of wrought-iron girders projecting horizontally and at right-angles to the straight or curved walls where they are seated. The girders in the canted sides of the horseshoe vary in length, but those in the semi-circular sweep have a projection of 13 feet 6 inches, of which 6 feet is cantilevered in front of the supporting cast-iron columns. These columns are spaced mostly at 12 feet centres and linked by cross girders to form a horseshoe sequence of nineteen bays, concentric with the tier fronts. Including those in the present stalls corridor, there are four tiers of columns, respectively 9, 8, 7 and 6 inches in diameter, each column being strongly tenoned into the one above it, thus ensuring a rigid framework for all the tiers. The tier fronts of Desachy's patent canvas-reinforced plaster were made in sections moulded to a serpentine profile, except those for the first (stalls) tier which were made vertically straight for easy removal.

The stalls floor was framed on a series of transverse wooden trusses, 2 feet 3 inches deep, each truss being slotted into the deeply bifurcated heads of a series of cast-iron columns. By using wedges it was possible to alter the rake of the floor, or bring it level with the first tier and forestage. As the floor was not dished, the seats were necessarily arranged in straight rows. Originally there were ten widely-spaced and unbroken rows of stalls, with side gangways reached by steps descending, between the boxes, from the stalls tier corridor. Behind the stalls was a shallow pit with eight rows of decreasing length, flanked by gangways reached by a branching stair at the back, ascending from the lower corridor. The pit has long been abolished, and there are now twenty-two rows of stalls seats, arranged in three blocks with two gangways which are reached from the lower corridor by open stairs ascending on either side, in front of the orchestra pit, and centrally at the back of the horseshoe.

Until it was reconstructed in 1964, the fourth tier contained an amphitheatre with seven rows of seats (Plate 66b), separated by a raised barrier from a gallery with nine rows of benches. Both parts were served separately by staircases entered from Floral Street, although the amphitheatre stair was originally approached through a lobby from the lower (pit) corridor. Redesigned by Peter Moro and Partners, the amphitheatre is a comfortable and well-arranged tier with twenty-one generously-spaced rows of seats in three blocks, served by two gangways and entered by two vomitories with steps rising from a spacious new crush bar (Plate 66c).

E. M. Barry claimed that when used for opera the theatre could accommodate 2,300 spectators, and when used for other purposes there was space for 3,000 or more. But according to figures published in *The Builder* in May 1858, the seating capacity during the opera season totalled 1,897, made up of 487 in the stalls and pit, 490 in 121 boxes generally seating four persons, 320 in the amphitheatre stalls, and 600 in the gallery and slips. By removing the box divisions and substituting seats, it was possible to increase the capacity by 600.[25] The present capacity of the opera house is 2,158, made up as follows: stalls 565 seats, stalls circle 305 seats, grand tier 149 seats, balcony 181 seats, amphitheatre 616 seats, lower slips 56 seats, upper slips 143 seats, 15 grand tier boxes with 60 seats, 10 balcony tier boxes with 40 seats, standing passes 43.

Few would dissent from the generally-held view that the Royal Opera House has the most beautiful auditorium in Great Britain. Nevertheless, this distinction is due to the suavity of its general form, its elegant proportions, and the warm yet brilliant colouring set off by the attractive lighting, rather than to the applied ornamentation which is generally uninspired and often coarse in detail. Although the basic form and general proportions are due to Barry, his ideas for the decorations were considerably modified by the impresario, Frederick Gye.

The focal point of the scheme is the proscenium opening, 50 feet wide and 43 feet high (Plate 66a). As there are no proscenium boxes, the opening is dressed with a rich frame of gilt plasterwork, its straight head of coved section ending in quadrant curves to stop on brackets at the top of each jamb. The cove of the head is decorated with large acanthus leaves set in flutes, and there are small stars on the outer fillet. The jambs have two faces, forming a re-entrant angle, and are decorated with three tall and slender colonnets having twisted shafts. An outer moulding enriched with ball ornament finishes the frame. The spandrel spaces flanking the head of the proscenium are simply decorated, above the ceiling line of the former amphitheatre boxes, with plaster panels of diagonal trellis. Similar panels decorate the side walls and piers that rise above the amphitheatre and are finished, like the proscenium wall, with an enriched moulded architrave. This provides a springing for the four great elliptical arches framing the pendentives and saucer-dome of the ceiling, and for the tympanum of parabolic section extending above the proscenium wall. This tympanum, constructed of Desachy's patent plaster, was modelled in bas-relief by Raffaelle Monti with life-size figure subjects in white on a gold ground, the left-hand group representing Music, with Orpheus, and the right-hand group Poetry, with Ossian. Although these groups were generally approved, the central medallion with a profile portrait of Queen Victoria, with figures on either side supporting a corona, was generally condemned as an unsuitable interpolation.[23]

The soffits of the four elliptical arches are decorated alike with a band of double guilloche ornament, gilt and framed in a long panel. Each pendentive is modelled with raised mouldings to form a circular panel and three spandrels, the latter containing gilt trellis, and the former richly moulded and filled with flutes radiating round a wreathed lyre. Within a heavily enriched moulded frame, the saucer-dome begins with a wide border interspaced with large paterae, these impinging on the outer frame and an inner ring of twelve panels filled with scale-patterned trellis. The mouldings dividing these panels are prolonged to divide the main area of the ceiling into twelve sectors, surrounding the enriched frame of the central oculus. Each sector is lightly divided into five triangular shapes by cable-mouldings, resembling the ropework supporting a velarium but here serving to cover the joints in the fibrous plaster slabs. Except for the outer border which is white, the entire ceiling is coloured a greenish-blue, all the mouldings and ornaments being heavily gilt.

The elliptical arches on the north and south sides open to the gallery or upper slips, where the ceiling follows the same curvature as the arch and is simply decorated with large quadrangular panels. In each slip the two rows of benches are placed behind an open railing of gilt ironwork formed in a pattern of interlacing circles. The railing extends between the angle piers, above a projecting cove decorated with gilt trellis.

The tier fronts make a very considerable contribution to the general decorative effect, although the straight vertical front of the first tier is simply treated with fluting ranged between small panels of ornament. The pulvinated or serpentine fronts of the three upper tiers are much more elaborate and basically similar, although differing in minor details. Above a narrow fascia, vertically reeded, the lower part of the swelling pulvino is covered with a band of trellis, over which leaf and flower ornament is heavily modelled to create a scalloped line against the plain upper face. Each front is divided into eighteen bays, being the width of two boxes, by trusses surmounted by terminal figures of female genii with outspread wings, those of the top tier blowing gilt trumpets. Originally, the tier fronts were linked vertically by gilt colonnets with slender twisted shafts, rising above the terminal figures and providing a decorative finish to the box partitions. The royal box on the north side of the grand tier still retains these colonnets, the other remaining boxes now being divided by partitions shaped to give better sighting, some of them finished with a gilt cable moulding.

Except for the greenish-blue ground of the saucer-domed ceiling, the architectural plaster-work is generally finished in white to provide a ground for the heavily gilt mouldings and orna-ments. Otherwise red prevails, in the different tones of the seating, the draperies, the carpets and the vertically-striped paper lining the box in-teriors and the walls behind the tiers. The various reds are united in the stage draperies, the prosce-nium pelmet being composed of dark drapery festooned against a pale ground embroidered in full colours with the royal arms, while the rich red tableau curtains are bordered and appliqued with the Queen's cipher in gold.

When the opera house was first opened, it was illuminated by a large and splendid gas-lit lustre, composed of strings of crystals in three tiers with a tall tent-shaped top (Plate 64a). This was sus-pended from a winch and lowered through the oculus of the domed ceiling, which then formed the principal source of ventilation. Supplemen-tary lighting was provided by candle-branches projecting from the front of the upper-box tier. Now the chandelier has gone, but all three tier fronts carry a splendid array of three- or five-light branches fitted with red-shaded electric candles.

The Stage

The stage is 85 feet wide and 85 feet deep. For a depth of 55 feet from the curtain line the original height was about 70 feet, but the back part below the painting room is only 30 feet high. Below the floor is a basement, with a mezzanine. Much of the original equipment was designed by Barry in close collaboration with the resident scenic artist, William Beverley, and the stage carpenter, H. Sloman. The inner column and return face of each proscenium jamb was made to slide aside to widen the opening. On the stage, the customary grooves were omitted, the back scenes being lowered from the flies, while the side wings were fixed to laterally movable wing ladders, behind which were fixed the gas-lighting battens. Scene recesses, 18 feet wide and 12 feet deep, were pro-vided on each side of the stage, two on the north side and two on the south where they flanked a similar recess containing a large organ. Other sound effects were fixed to the ceiling below the painting room. There were fly-galleries, 8 feet wide, at two levels on each side.[26]

The scene-storage space in the main building evidently proved to be inadequate, for shortly after 1860 a wing containing two large scene docks was built on the site of Nos. 3, 4 and 5 Hart (now Floral) Street, adjoining the north-west angle of the opera house.

Alterations

Although improvements were made to the building from time to time, they were insignifi-cant when compared with the extensive altera-tions carried out during 1899, 1900 and 1901, for the Grand Opera Syndicate. Under the direc-tion of Edwin O. Sachs, a specialist in theatre design, the stage was almost completely gutted, its cellar deepened and its roof raised some 20 feet. A new gridiron and grid galleries were erected, and a Brandt counterweight system for flying scenery was installed. The original raked floor was replaced by a flat one, 80 feet wide and 40 feet deep. This was divided into six sections arranged parallel with the curtain line, all equipped with 40 feet wide movable bridges ex-cept the front section, which was fitted with a series of traps. Electrically controlled, these bridges can be raised or lowered from the normal stage level, the front two 6 feet above or 8 feet below, and the back three 9 feet above or 8 feet below. Between the bridges are drop flaps for ground rows and rising scenes, and at the sides are wing ladders. New stage lighting was installed, the proscenium was fitted with a fireproof cur-tain, and by removing the elliptically-curved apron the orchestra pit was considerably enlarged. The scene docks flanking the stage were re-modelled, and a large new property store was built above the Floral Street wing, where the front scene dock was converted to provide three storeys of rehearsal rooms.

Improvements to the public parts of the build-ing included the provision of two new doorways in the front face of the carriage-way, and new doors from the entrance hall into the lower corri-dor, now serving the stalls. From here new en-trances to the auditorium were formed by providing short staircases ascending at the back of the stalls and on either side of the orchestra pit.[27] In 1892 electricity had replaced gas for lighting the branches on the tier fronts, and it was now installed throughout the house. The great gas chandelier was removed and replaced by two rings of electrical pendants, greatly improving

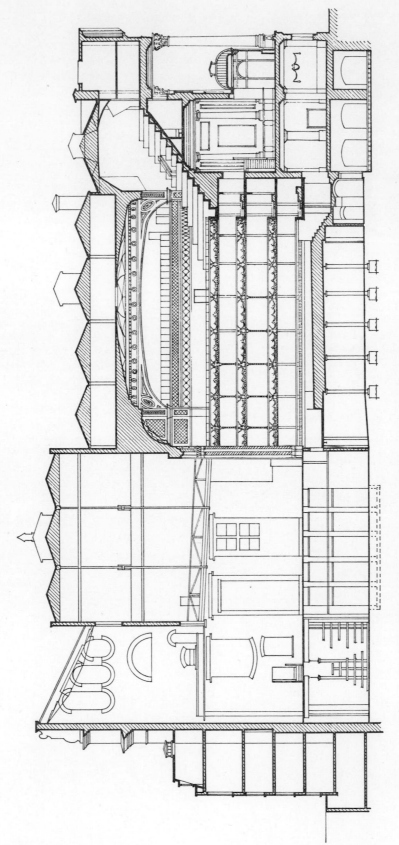

Fig. 14. Section, existing state. Redrawn from plans in the possession of the Greater London Council

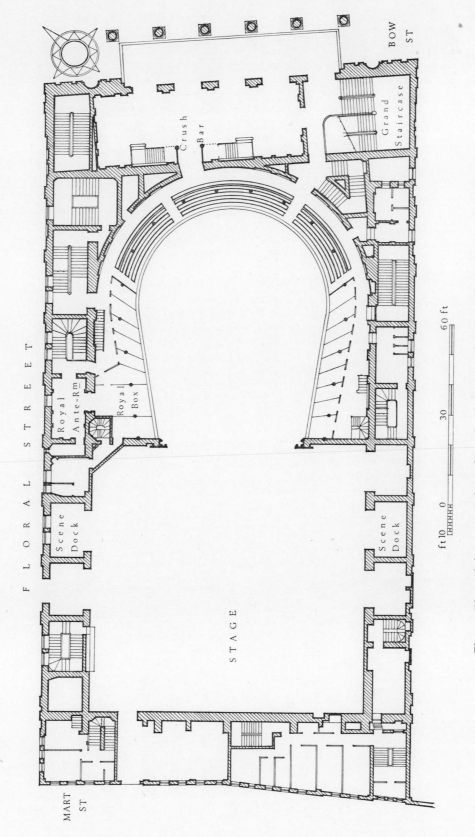

FLORAL STREET

Scene Dock

Royal Ante-Rm

Royal Box

STAGE

MART ST

Crush Bar

Grand Staircase

BOW ST

Scene Dock

ft 10   0   30   60 ft

Fig. 15. Plan, existing state. Redrawn from plans in the possession of the Greater London Council

the view of the stage from the gallery. The saloon, or crush bar, was redecorated at this time, and improved by the addition of some large pictures, presumably the paintings by Terwesten.[28]

In preparation for the Coronation season of 1911, further changes were made to the stage, including laying a new floor of oak to meet the requirements of the Russian ballet. A steam curtain was installed behind the footlights, and new tableau curtains bearing the royal monogram were provided. In 1933 plans were prepared for further alterations and additions to the building, largely to meet the requirements of the London County Council and the Lord Chamberlain's Department. A new range of dressing-rooms, etc., was built against the west wall of the stage, replacing the old north-west wing demolished to form Mart Street. New stage-lighting equipment and a cyclorama were installed on the stage.[29] The elaborate stage-lighting installation completed in 1964 by the Strand Electric and Engineering Company, was designed by William Bundy, stage director to the Royal Opera House, assisted by M. Carr and W. McGee.

THE FLORAL HALL

Enthusiastically greeted at its opening in 1860 as a successful attempt to overcome the architectural disadvantages which seemed to contemporary critics to mar construction in glass and iron, the Floral Hall (Plate 68) has about it still an air of lightness and elegance that the loss by fire in 1956 of the lofty glass vaults and dome with which it was originally crowned has not altogether destroyed. The building is L-shaped, with entrances from Bow Street at the end of the longer arm, and from the Piazza at the end of the shorter arm. The two fronts are constructed wholly of iron castings and glass, and are treated in a similar though not identical manner: panelled pilasters, linked by arches and capped by a decorative frieze and cornice, divide both into bays, five in the Bow Street front and three in the Piazza front, the centre bay in each being a double one. Decorative interest was imparted to the design by a plentiful use of perforated ornament and panelling. In both fronts, the wide central bay was treated as an arch-headed recess, its radial fanlight being concentric with the semi-circular gable ending the roof. Both the recess and the gable were framed by an enriched band of the same width as the flanking pilasters, and forming a continuation of them. Without the barrel vaults of the roof, the two fronts have lost much of their meaning, and the weak parapet with which they are now surmounted has done little to repair the loss. The front facing on to Covent Garden Market incorporates an open arcade in the ground storey, designed to provide a continuation of the public footway round the Piazza.

The interior of the long arm of the L comprises a broad nave, the width of the three centre bays of the Bow Street front, flanked by narrow aisles and divided from them by arcades of circular cast-iron columns. The short arm is un-aisled, and is the same width as the centre nave of the long arm. The aisles, originally open, are now divided horizontally by galleries, with solid walls separating them from the nave and filling the upper half of the arcades. The arcade columns, which have elaborate bases and perforated Corinthian capitals, are hollow, and were intended to communicate with the basement storey, to provide it with ventilation. The castings forming the lateral arches of the arcade, the arches supporting the aisle roofs, and the cantilever brackets which originally supported the roof vaults, meet above each column, and are bolted to the tops of the capitals. Both arms of the L were originally covered with semi-circular vaulted roofs, spanning the width of the nave, the aisles having lean-to roofs. Above the intersection of the two arms rose a hemi-spherical dome, capped by a lantern. The construction of vaults and dome was of thin curved iron ribs and glass, supported on light semi-circular latticed arches. At the intersection, the triangular spaces between the ends of the vaults and the base of the dome were treated as pendentives of glass and iron. Vaults, dome and pendentives were replaced after the fire of 1956 by simple flat roofs and a large triangular-shaped lantern light.

APPENDIX

Names of persons to whom Benjamin Hoare, Christopher Cock and John Rich assigned one fiftieth share in Covent Garden Theatre

Name of assignee	Address	Style	Signatory of Rich's 'Proposals'	Paid into Hoare's Bank £	Date of assignment of $\frac{1}{50}$th share	M.L.R. reference	Remarks
Francis Bedwell	St. Clement Danes	ironmonger	yes	300	1 March 1732/3	1732/5/683	Signed for one share: later bought another (see below).
Sir Thomas Brand	Surbiton, Surrey	knight	yes	300	do.	1733/2/209	
James, Duke of Chandos	—	—	yes	300	do.	1733/1/421	
Brigadier Hon. Charles Churchill	St. George, Hanover Sq.	esquire	yes	300	do.	1733/1/435	
Jane Fellowes	Red Lyon Square	widow	yes	300	do.	1732/5/681	Proposals signed by Rupert Clarke for Martin Fellowes. Assignment to his widow, Jane.
Hon. Henry Finch	St. George, Hanover Sq.	esquire	yes	300	do.	1733/4/172	
William Genew	Ham, Surrey	esquire	yes	300	do.	1734/1/291 cited in	
Walter Greenwood	St. George, Bloomsbury	esquire	yes	200	do.	1735/5/253	Signed for two shares, but also bought a third (see below).
Philip Hubert	St. Martin in the Fields	esquire	yes	300	do.	1732/5/682	
Thomas Moore	Kensington	gentleman	yes	300	do.	1732/5/684	
Edward, 9th Duke of Norfolk	—	—	yes	300	do.	1733/1/359	Thomas, 8th Duke, signed the proposals and died 23 Nov. 1732. Assignment to 9th Duke.
Richard Powell	St. James, Westminster	joiner	no	100	do.	1733/3/107	Also had two other shares (see below).
Sir William Saunderson	East Greenwich, Kent	baronet	yes	300	do.	1732/5/680	Signed for two shares (see below).
William Sharpe	Warwick St., St. James	esquire	yes	300	do.	1733/1/422	
Edward Shepherd	St. George, Hanover Sq.	esquire	yes	300	do.	1741/2/287 cited in	
Henry Talbot	St. George, Hanover Sq.	esquire	yes	300	do.	1732/5/744	
Edward Wilson	Millbank	esquire	no	100	do.	1732/5/745	

Name of assignee	Address	Style	Signatory of Rich's 'Proposals'	Paid into Hoare's Bank £	Date of Assignment of $\frac{1}{50}$th share	M.L.R. reference	Remarks
Richard Powell	St. James, Westminster	joiner	no	see above	1 May 1733	cited in 1735/4/481	Also had two other shares (see above and below).
Rupert Clarke	Lyons Inn	esquire	yes	nil	15 June 1733	1733/2/61	With Christopher Rich bought 17 shares in Lincoln's Inn Fields Theatre.
do.	do.	do.	yes	nil	do.	1733/2/62	
Samuel Clarke	Inner Temple	gentleman	yes	nil	do.	1733/2/63	
William Ann de Grave	St. James, Westminster	esquire	yes	nil	do.	1733/2/157	
John Howard	Hampstead	gentleman	yes	nil	do.	1733/2/156	Proposals signed by Christopher Cock for Howard.
Walter Greenwood	St. George, Bloomsbury	esquire	yes	nil	9 July 1733	1733/2/384	Signed for two shares (see above).
do.	do.	do.	no	nil	10 July 1733	1733/2/385	His third share, unsigned for.
George Campbell	St. Martin in the Fields	goldsmith	yes	nil	1 August 1733	1733/3/100	
James de la Creuze	St. Martin in the Fields	gentleman	yes	nil	do.	1733/3/102	
Edward Ravenell	St. Martin in the Fields	esquire	yes	nil	do.	1733/3/101	
Philip Mercier	Bury Street, St. James	esquire	no	nil	13 August 1733	1733/3/103	
Charles Fleetwood	St. Marylebone	esquire	no	nil	6 September 1733	1733/3/108	
Christian Frederick Zincke	St. Paul, Covent Garden	gentleman	yes	nil	21 September 1733	1733/3/218	
Sir William Saunderson	East Greenwich, Kent	baronet	yes	nil	21 April 1734	1734/1/319	Signed for two shares (see above).
Thomas Holt	Rochford Hall, Suffolk	esquire	no	nil	1 May 1734	not found	Assignment in Bedford Office.
Jane Wakefield	St. James, Westminster	widow	yes	nil	28 May 1734	1734/1/466	
do.	do.	do.	yes	nil	do.	1734/1/467	
Francis Bedwell	St. Clement Danes	ironmonger	no	nil	8 June 1734	1734/2/75	Also signed for another share (see above).
Richard Powell	St. James, Westminster	carpenter (sic)	no	nil	do.	1734/2/52	Also had two other shares (see above).
Thomas Wood	Little Britain, London	stationer	yes	nil	4 September 1734	1734/4/274	
Henry Collins	St. James, Westminster	esquire	yes	nil	– September 1734	cited in 1746/1/543	Also owned three shares in Lincoln's Inn Fields Theatre.
do.	do.	do.	yes	nil	– September 1734	cited in 1746/1/544	

Name of assignee	Address	Style	Signatory of Rich's 'Proposals'	Paid into Hoare's Bank £	Date of Assignment of $\frac{1}{50}$th share	M.L.R. reference	Remarks
Hon. John Cope	St. George, Hanover Sq.	esquire	no	nil	26 September 1734	1734/4/293	Signed for two shares, but probably bought only one. Also owned one share in Lincoln's Inn Fields Theatre.
Charles Hale	St. George the Martyr	esquire	yes	nil	do.	1737/4/108	
Charles, Duke of Richmond and Lennox	—	—	yes	nil	do.	1735/3/465	Also owned two shares in Lincoln's Inn Fields Theatre.
William Samber	Lyons Inn	gentleman	no	nil	do.	1737/4/374	
John Paul Yvonnett	St. Anne, Westminster	esquire	yes	nil	do.	1734/5/63 cited in 1747/1/9	Signed proposals, and owned a share 1744.
William Workman	St. Andrew, Holborn	gentleman	yes	300	not known		
Stephen de la Creuze	St. Martin's Lane	gentleman	no	nil	26 January 1737/8	1737/5/396	Edward Shepherd was a consenting party to this assignment.
Robert Knight	Barnells, Warwickshire	esquire	yes	400	not known	not found	Signed for one share, but in 1744 owned two.
do.	do.	do.					

References

ABBREVIATIONS

B.M.   British Museum.
B.O.L.   Bedford Office, 29A Montague Street, London, w.c.1, records in the possession of the Trustees of the Bedford Settled Estates.
Colvin   H. M. Colvin, *A Biographical Dictionary of English Architects, 1660–1840, 1954.*
D.N.B.   *Dictionary of National Biography.*
E/BER   Records in the possession of the Trustees of the Bedford Settled Estates, now deposited in Greater London Record Office, County Hall, s.e.1.
Enthoven   Enthoven Theatre Collection in Victoria and Albert Museum.
G.E.C.   *The Complete Peerage*, ed. G.E.C., 1910–1959.

G.L.C.   Greater London Council.
H.M.C.   Historical Manuscripts Commission.
L.C.C.   London County Council.
M.L.R.   Middlesex Land Register in Greater London Record Office, County Hall, s.e.1.
P.C.C.   Prerogative Court of Canterbury, records at Somerset House.
P.P.   *Parliamentary Papers.*
P.R.O.   Public Record Office, Chancery Lane.
R.I.B.A.   Royal Institute of British Architects, Portland Place, w.1.
W.P.L.   Westminster Public Library, Buckingham Palace Road.

CHAPTER I (pp. 1–8)

The Killigrew and Davenant Patents

1. P.R.O., C66/3013, no. 20.
2. *Ibid.*, C66/3009, no. 3.
3. Company House, file 52738.
4. Harold Rosenthal, *Two Centuries of Opera at Covent Garden*, 1958, p. 675.
5. 6 and 7 Vict. c. 68, public general.
6. Leslie Hotson, *The Commonwealth and Restoration Stage*, 1928, p. 124.
7. John Freehafer, 'The Formation of the London Patent Companies in 1660' in *Theatre Notebook*, vol. xx, 1965, p. 13.
8. *The Diary of Samuel Pepys*, 24 May 1660.
9. A. Harbage, *Thomas Killigrew: Cavalier Dramatist 1612–1683*, 1930, p. 116.
10. P.R.O., SP44/5, p. 158.
11. *Ibid.*, SP29/8, no. 1.
12. B.M., Add. MS. 19256, ff. 47–8.
13. P.R.O., SP29/10, no. 108.
14. Freehafer, *op. cit.*, p. 29.
15. *The London Stage 1660–1800, Part 1, 1660–1700,* ed. William Van Lennep, 1965, p. xxxv.
16. B.M., Add. MS. 12,201, ff. 130–5.
17. P.R.O., C7/194/57.
18. *Ibid.*, C7/194/47.
19. P.C.C., 36 Drax.
20. P.R.O., C7/194/47; C7/194/51.
21. B.M., Add. MS. 12,201, f. 142.

22. *Ibid.*, Add. Ch. 9320; P.C.C., 13 Romney.
23. Hotson, *op. cit.*, pp. 226–9, 232, 238.
24. Percy Fitzgerald, *A New History of the English Stage*, vol. i, 1882, pp. 154–8.
25. P.R.O., LC7/3, ff. 119–20.
26. *Ibid.*, C8/348/95, confirmed by B.M., Add. Ch. 9299.
27. B.M., Add. Ch. 9299.
28. Fulwar Skipwith, *A Brief Account of the Skipwiths of Newbold, Metheringham and Prestwould*, 1867, pp. 29–30.
29. P.R.O., C5/284/40; B.M., Add. Ch. 9302.
30. Hotson, *op. cit.*, p. 293.
31. P.R.O., C5/284/40.
32. *Ibid.*, C8/481/66.
33. P.C.C., 444 Cheslyn.
34. P.R.O., C10/261/51.
35. *Ibid.*, LC7/3, ff. 8–9.
36. Van Lennep, *op. cit.*, p. 445.
37. P.R.O., LC5/154, p. 35.
38. Fitzgerald, *op. cit.*, vol. i, pp. 252–7.
39. *An Apology for the Life of Mr. Colley Cibber Written by Himself*, ed. R. W. Lowe, vol. ii, 1889, p. 59.
40. P.R.O., C12/1728/34.
41. *Ibid.*, LC5/154, ff. 224, 437.
42. *Ibid.*, LC7/3, f. 40.
43. *Ibid.*, LC5/155, pp. 44, 157, 261; LC5/156, p. 31; LC5/157, p. 282.
44. *Ibid.*, LC7/3, f. 40; LC5/155, pp. 157, 261.
45. John Loftis, *Steele at Drury Lane*, 1952, pp. 35–6.
46. P.R.O., LC5/156, p. 31.
47. *Ibid.*, C66/3501, no. 13.

48. *Ibid.*, C66/3586, no. 5; C66/3621, no. 15; C66/3682, no. 45; C66/3806, no. 4; C66/4124, no. 4.
49. B.M., Add. Ch. 9303; *The London Stage 1660–1800, Part 2, 1700–1729*, ed. Emmett L. Avery, 1960, p. xxxii.
50. *Modern Language Notes*, vol. LXIV, Baltimore, 1949, pp. 19–21.
51. Avery, *op. cit.*, p. 334.
52. P.C.C., 228 Aston.
53. P.R.O., C12/1728/34.
54. B.M., Collection of Memoranda . . . relating to Drury Lane Theatre arranged by James Winston, vol. v (B.M. pressmark C 120 h 1). See also MS. note in the theatre collection now in the possession of Mr. Robert Eddison.
55. B.M., Add. Ch. 9320.
56. P.C.C., 13 Romney.
57. M.L.R. 1730/1/190.
58. B.M., Add. Ch. 9320; Add. MS. 12201, ff. 4–12.
59. *Ibid.*, Add. Ch. 9311.
60. M.L.R. 1767/6/50–1.
61. *Ibid.*, 1767/6/245–6; 1767/7/307–8.
62. *Ibid.*, 1768/6/187–8.
63. P.R.O., C54/6378, no. 11.
64. M.L.R. 1774/5/331–4.
65. *Ibid.*, 1784/3/279.
66. *Ibid.*, 1786/3/477.
67. *Ibid.*, 1801/3/380–2.
68. *D.N.B.*
69. M.L.R. 1780/2/498.
70. *Ibid.*, 1782/4/271, confirmed by 1796/1/470.
71. *Ibid.*, 1792/5/718; 1806/4/621.
72. *Ibid.*, 1792/5/718; Orlo Cyprian Williams, *The Clerical Organization of the House of Commons, 1660–1850*, 1954, p. 77; *D.N.B.*
73. *The Letters of Richard Brinsley Sheridan*, ed. Cecil Price, vol. 1, 1966, pp. 116–21.
74. Ian Donaldson, 'New Papers of Henry Holland and R. B. Sheridan', in *Theatre Notebook*, vol. XVI, 1962, pp. 117–25.
75. *Survey of London*, vol. XXIX, 1960, pp. 233–6; vol. XXXI, 1963, pp. 276–8.
76. The full text is printed in Fitzgerald, *op. cit.*, vol. II, pp. 334–8 and in *P.P.*, *Report of the Select Committee of the House of Commons to inquire into the Laws affecting Dramatic Literature*, 1831–2, vol. VII, appendix 4, pp. 241–3.
77. *Sheridan Letters*, vol. 1, pp. 229–32; *The London Chronicle*, 28–31 July 1792.
78. *Sheridan Letters*, vol. 1, p. 268n.
79. *The London Chronicle*, 28–31 July 1792.
80. *Ibid.*, *loc. cit.*; P.R.O., C12/1728/34.
81. *Sheridan Letters*, vol. 1, p. 256.
82. *Ibid.*, vol. 1, p. 248n.; Enthoven, Drury Lane legal documents.
83. Enthoven, Drury Lane legal documents; B.M., Add. MS. 42720, f. 22.
84. M.L.R. 1806/4/525; Enthoven, Drury Lane legal documents.
85. P.R.O., C66/4124, no. 4.
86. 50 Geo. III, c. 214, local and personal.
87. Enthoven, Drury Lane legal documents.
88. *Ibid.*, *loc. cit.*; *The Gentleman's Magazine*, vol. 84, 1814, p. 96; Williams, *op. cit.*, p. 77.
89. Alfred Bunn, *The Stage: both before and behind the Curtain*, vol. II, 1840, pp. 280–1.
90. E/BER, lease of 11 July 1812 to the Company of Proprietors of Drury Lane Theatre.
91. *Ibid.*, Drury Lane Theatre papers.
92. B.O.L., London Reports, vol. II, p. 429.
93. E/BER, surrender of 14 July 1897.
94. *Ibid.*, Solicitors' Papers, no. 61.
95. M.L.R. 1803/5/461; P.R.O., C54/7757 no. 7.
96. M.L.R. 1806/4/620–1.
97. *The Law Journal*, vol. v, 1827, Easter Term, pp. 131–9 (B.M. pressmark PP1345).
98. Williams, *op. cit.*, p. 77.
99. P.C.C., 45 Bridport.
100. P.R.O., C13/2587, Const *v.* Kemble; E. R. Brayley, *Accounts of London Theatres*, 1826, pp. 13–20.
101. P.C.C., 90 Henschell.
102. P.R.O., C13/2587, Const *v.* Kemble; *P.P.*, *Report of Commons Committee on Laws affecting Dramatic Literature*, 1831–2, vol. VII, p. 98.
103. P.C.C., 692 Vaughan.
104. *Ibid.*, 1855/50; *D.N.B.*
105. *The Times*, 18 March 1856.
106. P.R.O., KB 122/1418, f. 31.
107. M.L.R. 1858/9/606.
108. *Ibid.*, 1916/7/969.
109. *The Times*, 4 July 1928.

CHAPTER II (pp. 9–29)

The Theatre Royal, Drury Lane: the Management

1. B.M., Add. MS. 19,256, f. 47.
2. *The London Stage 1660–1800, Part 1, 1660–1700*, ed. William Van Lennep, 1965, pp. xxxiv–xxxv.
3. E/BER, Muniment of Title, Middlesex, D, bundle 5, no. 6; E/BER, lease of 26 Feb. 1654/5 to William Outing.
4. B.M., Add. MS. 20,726, no. 1; P.R.O., C7/194/57.

5. B.M., Add. MS. 20,726, no. 1; Leslie Hotson, *The Commonwealth and Restoration Stage*, 1928, p. 243.
6. B.M., Add. MS. 10, 117, p. 321.
7. *The Diary of Samuel Pepys*, 6 Feb. 1662/3, 8 May 1663.
8. P.R.O., C7/317/57.
9. *Ibid.*, LC5/138, p. 417.
10. *Pepys*, 19 March 1665/6.
11. H.M.C., *Earl of Mount Edgcumbe MSS.*, 1871, p. 22.
12. *Ibid.*, *Lyttelton Annesley MSS.*, 1893, p. 270.
13. *Ibid.*, *Earl of Mount Edgcumbe MSS.*, 1871, p. 22; Cornelius Walford, *The Insurance Cyclopedia*, 1876, vol. IV, p. 43.
14. P.R.O., SP29/183, no. 72.
15. Hotson, *op. cit.*, p. 254.
16. B.M., Add. MS. 20,726, no. 1.
17. Hotson, *op. cit.*, p. 255.
18. Lennep, *op. cit.*, p. 214.
19. P.R.O., C6/221/48.
20. Allardyce Nicoll, *A History of English Drama 1660–1900, vol. 1, Restoration Drama 1660–1700*, 1952 ed., pp. 323–30.
21. Percy Fitzgerald, *A New History of the English Stage*, 1882, vol. I, pp. 154–8; Hotson, *op. cit.*, p. 271.
22. Hotson, *op. cit.*, p. 273.
23. B.M., Add. Ch. 9298.
24. Hotson, *op. cit.*, p. 293.
25. E/BER, lease of 29 June 1695 to C. Killigrew and others.
26. B.O.L., Estate Papers, 'The Case of the Building Proprietors', N.D.
27. *Ibid.*, *loc. cit.*; P.R.O., C10/261/51; C10/299/33.
28. P.R.O., LC5/154, ff. 224, 298–300, 417.
29. *Ibid.*, LC5/154, f. 437.
30. *Ibid.*, LC7/3, f. 40.
31. *An Apology for the Life of Mr. Colley Cibber Written by Himself*, ed. R. W. Lowe, 1889, vol. II, p. 92.
32. B.M., Add. MS. 20,726, no. 5.
33. *The London Stage 1660–1800, Part 2, 1700–1729*, ed. Emmett L. Avery, 1960, p. 202.
34. B.M., Add. MS. 20,726, no. 5; P.R.O., C11/1175/59.
35. E/BER, lease of 16 March 1710/11 to C. Killigrew and others.
36. P.R.O., C11/1175/59.
37. *Ibid.*, LC7/3, f. 40; LC5/155, pp. 157, 261.
38. *Ibid.*, LC5/156, p. 31.
39. R. H. Barker, *Mr. Cibber of Drury Lane*, 1939, p. 102; John Loftis, *Steele at Drury Lane*, 1952, pp. 39–40.
40. Avery, *op. cit.*, p. 329.
41. Loftis, *op. cit.*, p. 42.
42. P.R.O., C66/3501, no. 13.
43. Loftis, *op. cit.*, pp. 47–8.
44. Barker, *op. cit.*, p. 96.
45. Loftis, *op. cit.*, pp. 121–7.
46. P.R.O., LC5/157, pp. 265, 279–80, 282.
47. Loftis, *op. cit.*, pp. 139, 155.
48. P.R.O., LC5/157, pp. 415–16.
49. Loftis, *op. cit.*, p. 229.
50. P.R.O., C66/3586, no. 5.
51. Barker, *op. cit.*, pp. 167, 170.
52. *The London Stage 1660–1800, Part 3, 1729–1747*, ed. Arthur H. Scouten, 1961, pp. lxxxix–xc.
53. P.R.O., C11/778/28.
54. E/BER, lease of 21 March 1731/2 to C. Killigrew and others.
55. Scouten, *op. cit.*, p. 321.
56. *Ibid.*, pp. xcii–xciii; P.R.O., C11/778/28.
57. Scouten, *op. cit.*, pp. xciii–xcvi.
58. *The Letters of David Garrick*, ed. David M. Little and George M. Kahrl, 1963, vol. I, p. 47.
59. *Ibid.*, vol. III, p. 1349.
60. *Ibid.*, vol. III, p. 1348; M.L.R. 1745/3/246.
61. *Letters of David Garrick*, vol. I, p. 47; vol. III, p. 1345.
62. *Ibid.*, vol. I, p. 74.
63. *Ibid.*, vol. III, pp. 1344–8.
64. P.R.O., C66/3621, no. 15.
65. M.L.R. 1747/2/345.
66. *The London Stage 1660–1800, Part 4, 1747–1776*, 1962, ed. George Winchester Stone, p. 7.
67. *Ibid.*, p. 56.
68. *Ibid.*, p. 121.
69. E/BER, lease of 24 Aug. 1748 to J. Lacy and D. Garrick.
70. M.L.R. 1753/3/441.
71. *Ibid.*, 1753/3/442.
72. Dorset Record Office, D86.
73. P.R.O., C66/3682, no. 45.
74. E/BER, lease of 24 March 1762 to J. Lacy and D. Garrick.
75. H. W. Pedicord, *The Theatrical Public in the Time of Garrick*, 1954, pp. 5–6.
76. *Letters of David Garrick*, vol. III, p. 922.
77. M.L.R. 1776/1/26; Dorset Record Office, D 54/T203.
78. *Letters of David Garrick*, vol. III, pp. 1066–7.
79. M.L.R. 1776/6/496–501.
80. *Ibid.*, 1777/4/385–6, 409.
81. B.M., Add. MS. 38,607, ff. 134–59; *The Letters of Richard Brinsley Sheridan*, ed. Cecil Price, 1966, vol. I, pp. 169–70.
82. M.L.R. 1780/3/554–66; 1785/4/447, and 1780–90 *passim*.
83. *Ibid.*, 1789/5/97; B.M., Add. MS. 42,720, ff. 132–5.

84. M.L.R. 1789/5/98.
85. P.R.O., C66/3806, no. 4.
86. E/BER, agreement of 30 July 1791 with Sheridan and Linley.
87. *Sheridan Letters*, vol. II, p. 20n.
88. P.C.C., 195 Harris.
89. *Sheridan Letters*, vol. I, p. 260n.
90. Enthoven, Drury Lane legal documents.
91. M.L.R. 1798/4/52; B.M., Add. MS. 42,720, ff. 132–5.
92. *Sheridan Letters*, vol. III, p. 325, 325n.
93. *Ibid.*, vol. II, pp. 19n., 59n.
94. *Ibid.*, vol. II, p. 166n.
95. *Ibid.*, vol. II, p. 116.
96. *Ibid.*, vol. II, p. 199n.
97. Enthoven, Drury Lane legal documents; P.C.C., 568 Marriott.
98. M.L.R. 1806/4/525.
99. *Sheridan Letters*, vol. III, pp. 316–21.
100. M.L.R. 1797/1/734; 1797/2/176.
101. MSS. and drawings in the possession of Mr. Robert Eddison.
102. B.M., Collection of Memoranda . . . relating to Drury Lane Theatre arranged by James Winston, vol. VI (B.M. pressmark C 120 h 1).
103. *Ibid.*, vol. VII.
104. *Biographica Dramatica*, 1812, vol. I, p. xlix.
105. *Sheridan Letters*, vol. I, p. 218.
106. *The Morning Chronicle*, 24 Dec. 1801; *Sheridan Letters*, vol. I, p. 218.
107. M.L.R. 1798/1/617; 1798/2/192–205; MSS. and drawings in the possession of Mr. Robert Eddison.
108. M.L.R. 1797/2/177–88.
109. *Ibid.*, 1798/2/439; 1798/4/52.
110. B.M., Add. MS. 42,720, ff. 14–42; for examples of sales, see M.L.R. 1797/1/171–4, 364–8, 487; 1797/4/907–9; 1798/4/470; 1799/2/97–106; 1800/2/107.
111. B.M., Add. MS. 42,723, ff. 6–7; *Sheridan Letters*, vol. II, p. 164n.
112. Enthoven, report of lecture by Professor Cecil Price on 'Richard Brinsley Sheridan and the Finances of Drury Lane Theatre'.
113. B.M., Add. MS. 42,720, ff. 14–42.
114. *Ibid.*, collection of newspaper cuttings (pressmark 11795 K 22); *Authentic Account of the Fire*, 1809 (pressmark 1430 a 22).
115. *Parliamentary Debates, First Series*, vol. XII, pp. 1105–6.
116. Thomas Moore, *Memoirs of the Life of Richard Brinsley Sheridan*, 1825, vol. II, pp. 368–9.
117. B.M., collection of newspaper cuttings (pressmark 11795 K 22); Ian Donaldson, 'New Papers of Henry Holland and R. B. Sheridan' in *Theatre Notebook*, vol. XVI, 1962, pp. 90–6.
118. *Sheridan Letters*, vol. III, p. 60.
119. Roger Fulford, *Samuel Whitbread, 1764–1815. A Study in Opposition*, 1967, p. 278.
120. *Sheridan Letters*, vol. III, pp. 59–61.
121. *Ibid.*, vol. III, p. 84, 84n.
122. *Ibid.*, vol. III, p. 131n.
123. 50 Geo. III, c. 214, local and personal.
124. *Sheridan Letters*, vol. III, p. 77n.; *D.N.B.*
125. B.M., Add. MS. 42,721, f. 71; Benjamin Dean Wyatt, *Observations on the Design for the Theatre Royal, Drury Lane*, 1813, p. viii.
126. Enthoven, Drury Lane legal documents, Reports to the Second, Fourth and Fifth General Assemblies of the Theatre Royal Drury Lane Company of Proprietors.
127. Samuel Arnold, *A Letter to All the Proprietors of Drury-Lane Theatre*, 1818, p. 28.
128. Enthoven, Drury Lane legal documents, Report to First General Assembly of Proprietors.
129. J. Britton and A. Pugin, *Illustrations of the Public Buildings of London*, 1825, vol. I, p. 241n.
130. Enthoven, Drury Lane legal documents, Reports to First and Second General Assemblies.
131. 52 Geo. III, c. 19, local and personal.
132. Alfred Bunn, *The Stage: both before and behind the Curtain*, 1840, vol. II, p. 79.
133. *Proceedings of the General Assembly of Proprietors*, 1836, p. 20 (B.M. pressmark 11799 e 32(2)).
134. B.M., Add. MS. 42,721, f. 71.
135. *Ibid.*, Collection of Memoranda . . . relating to Drury Lane Theatre arranged by James Winston, vol. XII (pressmark C 120 h 1).
136. Wyatt, *op. cit.*, p. ix.
137. Enthoven, Drury Lane legal documents, Report to Second General Assembly of Proprietors.
138. B.M., Collection of Memoranda . . ., vol. XIII (pressmark C 120 h 1).
139. Wyatt, *op. cit.*, p. 10.
140. *Ibid.*, p. 50.
141. P.R.O., C66/4124, no. 4.
142. E/BER, lease of 11 July 1812 to Theatre Royal Drury Lane Company of Proprietors.
143. Fulford, *op. cit.*, p. 290.
144. Arnold, *op. cit.*, pp. 14, 27; B.O.L., Misc. theatre letters.
145. B.M., Collection of Memoranda . . ., vols. XV–XVII (pressmark C 120 h 1).
146. Archives of Coutts and Company, L 695.
147. B.M., Collection of Memoranda . . ., vol. XVIII (pressmark C 120 h 1).
148. *Ibid.*, Add. MS. 27,831, ff. 110–12.
149. George Raymond, *Memoirs of Robert William Elliston*, 1845, vol. II, pp. 200–1.
150. *Ibid.*, vol. II, p. 220; B.M., Collection of Memoranda . . ., vol. XVII (pressmark C 120 h 1).
151. Sir John Summerson, *Georgian London*, 1962 ed., p. 255.

152. Raymond, *op. cit.*, vol. II, p. 475n.
153. B.M., Collection of Memoranda . . ., vol. XIX (pressmark C 120 h 1).
154. Colvin.
155. Raymond, *op. cit.*, vol. II, pp. 315, 451, 474, 476.
156. B.M., Collection of Memoranda . . ., vol, XXIII (pressmark C 120 h 1); Add. MS. 27,831, ff. 110–12.
157. *Ibid.*, Add. MS. 27,831, ff. 110–12.
158. Bedfordshire Record Office, X297/93.
159. B.M., Add. MS. 27,831, ff. 110–12; James Robinson Planché, *Recollections and Reflections*, 1872, vol. I, p. 178.
160. Henry Saxe Wyndham, *The Annals of Covent Garden Theatre*, 1906, vol. II, p. 81.
161. Bunn, *op. cit.*, vol. III, p. 289.
162. Bedfordshire Record Office, GA2777.
163. W.P.L., H. 839, pp. 268, 299, 304.
164. Bedfordshire Record Office, GA 2778.
165. *Proceedings of the Sub Committee of the Theatre Royal, Drury Lane*, 1835, p. 24 (B.M. pressmark 11799 e 32(3)).
166. Bunn, *op. cit.*, vol. II, pp. 74–6.
167. Enthoven, Drury Lane box for 1836.
168. E/BER, misc. papers, Drury Lane Theatre.
169. W.P.L., H.841, pp. 272–4, 285–7.
170. H. Barton Baker, *The London Stage*, 1889, vol. I, p. 109.
171. Enthoven, Drury Lane box for 1839.
172. B.M., Add. MS. 27,831, ff. 110–12; Bunn, *op. cit.*, vol. III, pp. 256, 259, 273.
173. *The Annual Register*, 1839.
174. Barton Baker, *op. cit.*, vol. I, p. 110; Bunn, *op. cit.*, vol. III, p. 270.
175. *The Diaries of William Charles Macready 1833–1851*, ed. William Toynbee, 1912, vol. II, pp. 118, 121, 130; *The Illustrated London News*, 17 June 1843, p. 421.
176. *Macready Diaries*, vol. II, pp. 182, 213; William Archer, *William Charles Macready*, 1890, pp. 139, 143.
177. *Macready Diaries*, vol. II, p. 216.
178. 6 and 7 Vict., c. 68, public general.
179. Enthoven, Drury Lane boxes for 1843–9.
180. Barton Baker, *op. cit.*, vol. I, pp. 113–14; *The Era*, 13 April 1851, p. 1; 10 Aug. 1851, p. 11.
181. *The Era*, 21 Dec. 1851, p. 10; Jan–May 1852, *passim*.
182. *Ibid.*, 1 Aug. 1852, p. 10.
183. Planché, *op. cit.*, vol. II, p. 200.
184. *The Era*, 25 July 1852, p. 10; 1 Aug. 1852, p. 10.
185. *Ibid.*, 10 Oct. 1852, p. 1; 17 Oct. 1852, p. 11.
186. E/BER, Misc. Papers, Drury Lane Theatre; Edward Stirling, *Old Drury Lane*, 1881, vol. I, pp. 249–50; *The Illustrated London News*, 3 Feb. 1855, p. 103.
187. B.O.L., Annual Report, 1852, p. 5.
188. *Ibid.*, Annual Report, 1853, p. 3.
189. Barton Baker, *op. cit.*, vol. I, p. 114.
190. *Ibid.*, vol. I, p. 115.
191. *Ibid.*, *loc. cit.*; Enthoven, Drury Lane Theatre box for 1862.
192. Barton Baker, *op. cit.*, vol. I, p. 116.
193. C. L. Kenney, *Poets and Profits at Drury Lane Theatre*, 1875, p. 11.
194. Barton Baker, *op. cit.*, vol. I, p. 116; Stirling, *op. cit.*, vol. I, p. 274.
195. Kenney, *op. cit.*, pp. 18–58; *The Era*, 13 April 1873, p. 11.
196. Stirling, *op. cit.*, p. 274; *The Builder*, 15 June 1878, p. 624.
197. Barton Baker, *op. cit.*, vol. I, p. 117.
198. B.O.L., Annual Report, 1893, p. 108.
199. Raymond Mander and Joe Mitchenson, *The Theatres of London*, 1963 ed., p. 69.
200. B.O.L., Letter Book, 1891, p. 171.
201. *Ibid.*, Annual Report, 1893, pp. 107–8.
202. *Ibid.*, London Reports, vol. II, p. 348.
203. *The Builder*, 14 July 1906, p. 39.
204. E/BER, agreement of 17 May 1894 with Sir A. Harris.
205. *Ibid.*, Solicitors' Papers, no. 61, Drury Lane Theatre.
206. Company House, file 52,738.
207. *The Builder*, 11 July 1906, p. 39.
208. E/BER, agreement of 29 March 1897 with A. Collins; B.O.L., London Reports, vol. III, pp. 51, 60.
209. E/BER, surrender of 14 July 1897 by Sir A. Harris's executors; agreement of 29 March 1897 with A. Collins.
210. Company House, file 52,738A, vol. I.
211. *Ibid.*, file 52,738; *The Times*, 17 Sept. 1897.
212. E/BER, lease of 31 Dec. 1900 to Theatre Royal Drury Lane Ltd.
213. *The Times*, 19 Jan. 1920.
214. *Ibid.*, 19, 22 Jan., 6 March 1920; Company House, file 165,835.
215. *The Times*, 26 Feb. 1919 and *passim* to April 1919.
216. Mander and Mitchenson, *op. cit.*, p. 70.
217. *Ibid.*, p. 71.
218. Federation of Theatre Unions, *Theatre Ownership in Britain*, 1953, p. 58.
219. *The Times*, 6 March 1958.

CHAPTER III (pp. 30–9)

The Theatre Royal, Drury Lane: the Site

1. E/BER, Drury Lane, lease of 16 March 1615/16 to Sir Edward Cecil; rental, 1618.
2. *Ibid.*, survey, 1635.

3. P.R.O., LC5/134, f. 51; Joseph Quincy Adams, *Shakespearean Playhouses*, N.D. (1921), pp. 422–3.

4. E/BER, rental, 1661/2; P.R.O., C7/194/47.

5. B.M., Add. MS. 20,726, no. 1.

6. E/BER, Drury Lane Theatre, leases of 29 June 1695 and 16 March 1710/11 to C. Killigrew and others and lease of 21 March 1731/2 to C. Killigrew jun. and others.

7. B.M., Map Room 3495 (130); *ibid.*, Dept. of Prints and Drawings, Crowle's *Pennant*, vol. 6, p. 33.

8. Cited in lease of 1703, E/BER, Drury Lane, lease of 20 Sept. 1703 to C. Rich.

9. E/BER, account of J. Clendon for year ending 29 Sept. 1664.

10. P.R.O., C10/82/82.

11. *Ibid.*, C10/360/16.

12. E/BER, Drury Lane, lease of 20 Sept. 1703 to C. Rich.

13. *Ibid.*, lease of 6 July 1710 to C. Rich.

14. *Ibid.*, lease of 12 May 1739 to J. Bassan.

15. W.P.L., ratebooks of St. Martin in the Fields.

16. *The London Stage 1660–1800, Part 4, 1747–1776*, ed. George Winchester Stone, 1964, p. 122.

17. Leslie Hotson, *The Commonwealth and Restoration Stage*, 1928, p. 256.

18. E/BER, Muniment of Title, Middlesex, D, bundle 3, no. 1.

19. B.O.L., Muniment Register 111, p. 11, bundle 6, no. 5.

20. P.R.O., C8/309/5.

21. *Ibid.*, C11/1175/59.

22. E/BER, Drury Lane Theatre, lease of 4 Aug. 1748 to D. Garrick and J. Lacy.

23. *Ibid.*, Solicitors' Papers, Covent Garden Theatre.

24. *Ibid.*, Russell Street, lease of 20 Sept. 1749 to D. Garrick and J. Lacy.

25. *The General Advertiser*, 21 Nov. 1752.

26. E/BER, Brydges Street, lease of 22 June 1753 to D. Garrick and J. Lacy.

27. *Ibid.*, Drury Lane Theatre, lease of 24 March 1762 to D. Garrick and J. Lacy.

28. *Ibid.*, Muniment of Title, Middlesex, A, bundle 10, no. 10.

29. *Ibid.*, Drury Lane Theatre, lease of 10 July 1766 to D. Garrick and J. Lacy.

30. *Ibid.*, plan file 2/46.

31. M.L.R. 1778/3/305.

32. *Ibid.*, 1775/3/282.

33. B.M., Add. MS. 38,607, ff. 145–6; E/BER, Solicitors' Papers, Ben Jonson's Head.

34. B.O.L., Muniment Register v, p. 76, bundle 13, nos. 16–17.

35. E/BER, Drury Lane Theatre, lease of 3 May 1776 to D. Garrick and J. Lacy; Solicitors' Papers, Macnamara *v.* Duke of Bedford.

36. *Ibid.*, Solicitors' Papers, Macnamara *v.* Duke of Bedford.

37. B.M., Add. MS. 38,607, ff. 148–9.

38. M.L.R. 1778/3/576; B.O.L., Muniment Register 111, p. 20, bundle 6A, no. 64.

39. *The Letters of Richard Brinsley Sheridan*, ed. Cecil Price, 1966, vol. 1, pp. 215–19; E/BER, Drury Lane Theatre, agreement of 30 July 1791 to T. Linley and R. B. Sheridan.

40. B.O.L., Muniment Register 111, p. 33, bundle 11, nos. 33–4.

41. E/BER, Drury Lane Theatre, agreement of 30 July 1791 to Linley and Sheridan.

42. *Ibid.*, lease of 6 Aug. 1791 to Linley and Sheridan.

43. B.O.L., Muniment Register 111, p. 25, bundle 8, nos. 22, 24–5.

44. E/BER, Drury Lane Theatre, agreement of 30 July 1791 to Linley and Sheridan; MSS. and drawings in the possession of Mr. Robert Eddison.

45. E/BER, Solicitors' Papers, Macnamara *v.* Duke of Bedford; agreement of 30 July 1791, to Linley and Sheridan.

46. E/BER, Solicitors' Papers, Macnamara *v.* Duke of Bedford; B.O.L., Annual Report, 1815.

47. E/BER, Drury Lane Theatre, lease of 11 July 1812 to the Theatre Royal Drury Lane Company of Proprietors.

48. *Ibid.*, Drury Lane Theatre, lease of 31 Dec. 1900 to Theatre Royal Drury Lane Company Limited.

49. *Ibid.*, Covent Garden estate sale documents.

50. Information kindly supplied by the Bedford Settled Estates.

51. E/BER, Drury Lane Theatre, lease of 1 July 1814 to the Theatre Royal Drury Lane Company of Proprietors.

52. *Ibid.*, lease of 7 Jan. 1813 to the Theatre Royal Drury Lane Company of Proprietors.

53. J. Britton and A. Pugin, *Illustrations of the Public Buildings of London*, 1825, vol. 1, p. 258; *Report of the General Assembly of Proprietors*, 3 Sept. 1814 (B.M. pressmark C 120 h 1, vol. xiv).

54. Britton and Pugin, *op. cit.*, vol. 1, p. 248.

55. E/BER, Drury Lane Theatre, misc. papers.

56. *Ibid.*, Drury Lane Theatre, lease of 29 March 1897 to A. Collins.

57. *Ibid.*, licence for assignment 10 June 1897 from Collins to Theatre Royal Drury Lane Company Limited.

58. *Ibid.*, lease of 31 Dec. 1900 to Theatre Royal Drury Lane Company Limited.

59. *Ibid.*, Drury Lane, lease of 31 Dec. 1900 to Theatre Royal Drury Lane Company Limited.

60. L.C.C. Minutes, 21 March 1899, p. 405.

61. M.L.R. 1918/11/515; *The Times*, 19 Jan. 1920.

CHAPTER IV (pp. 40–70)

The Theatre Royal, Drury Lane: the Buildings

1. Balthasar De Monconys, *Journal des Voyages de Monsieur De Monconys*, Lyons, 1666, part 2, pp. 25–6.
2. *The Diary of Samuel Pepys*, 1 June 1664.
3. Lorenzo Magalotti, *Travels of Cosmo the Third, Grand Duke of Tuscany, through England*, 1821, pp. 190–1.
4. Edward A. Langhans, 'Pictorial Material on the Bridges Street and Drury Lane Theatres', in *Theatre Survey*, vol. VII, 1966, pp. 80–100 (publication of the American Society for Theatre Research, copy in B.M., pressmark PP 8001 ni).
5. Hamilton Bell, 'Contributions to the History of the English Playhouse', in *The Architectural Record*, New York, vol. XXXIII, 1913, pp. 359–68.
6. Eleanore Boswell, *The Restoration Court Stage 1660–1702*, 1932, pp. 10–21, 27, 29.
7. *The London Stage 1660–1800, Part 1, 1660–1700*, ed. William Van Lennep, 1965, p. 234.
8. Boswell, *op. cit.*, p. 208.
9. Leslie Hotson, *The Commonwealth and Restoration Stage*, 1928, p. 253.
10. Henri Misson, *Memoirs and Observations in his Travels over England*, trans. John Ozell, 1719, pp. 219–20.
11. T. D'Urfey, *Collin's Walk through London and Westminster*, 1690, canto IV, p. 149.
12. *An Apology for the Life of Mr. Colley Cibber Written by Himself*, ed. R. W. Lowe, 1889, vol. II, pp. 81–5.
13. Illustrated in Allardyce Nicoll, *The Development of the Theatre*, 1966 ed., pp. 160–1.
14. Richard Leacroft, 'Wren's Drury Lane', in *The Architectural Review*, vol. CX, 1951, pp. 43–6.
15. Edward A. Langhans, 'Wren's Restoration Playhouse', in *Theatre Notebook*, vol. XVIII, 1964, pp. 91–100.
16. Donald Mullin and Bruce Koenig, 'Christopher Wren's Theatre Royal', in *Theatre Notebook*, vol. XXI, 1967, pp. 180–7.
17. *The London Stage 1660–1800, Part 4, 1747–1776*, ed. George Winchester Stone, 1962, p. 125.
18. *The General Advertiser*, 21 Nov. 1752.
19. Stone, *op. cit.*, pp. xl, xli.
20. Thomas Davies, *Memoirs of the Life of David Garrick Esq.*, 1780, vol. I, pp. 332–3.
21. *The Public Advertiser*, 30 Sept. 1775.
22. Sir John Soane's Museum, Adam drawings, vol. 14, no. 16.
23. *Ibid.*, Adam drawings, vol. 27, no. 85.
24. MSS. and drawings in the possession of Mr. Robert Eddison.
25. Ralph, *A Critical Review of the Public Buildings . . . in and about London and Westminster*, 1783 ed., p. 76.
26. Richard Southern, *The Georgian Playhouse*, 1948, p. 25.
27. B.M., Collection of Memoranda . . . relating to Drury Lane Theatre arranged by James Winston, vol. V (B.M. pressmark C 120 h 1).
28. MS. in the possession of Mr. Robert Eddison.
29. *Journals of the House of Commons*, vol. XLIX, p. 291.
30. Two of these drawings are in the Victoria and Albert Museum, Dept. of Prints and Drawings, no. 7075; the other three are in Sir John Soane's Museum, drawer 61/34–6.
31. Plans in the possession of Mr. Robert Eddison.
32. One in the possession of Mr. Robert Eddison: the other in Sir John Soane's Museum, drawer 61/33.
33. Copy in B.M., Dept. of Prints and Drawings, Crace Views Portfolio XVIII, sheet 68, no. 134.
34. B.M., Dept. of Prints and Drawings, Crace Views Portfolio XVIII, sheet 67, no. 133.
35. Copy in Raymond Mander and Joe Mitchenson Theatre Collection.
36. Victoria and Albert Museum, Dept. of Prints and Drawings, no. 7075/1–2.
37. E. W. Brayley, *Accounts of the London Theatres*, 1826, p. 5.
38. Rand Carter, 'The Drury Lane Theatres of Henry Holland and Benjamin Dean Wyatt', in *Journal of the Society of Architectural Historians* [of America], vol. XXVI, 1967, pp. 200–16.
39. MS. in the possession of Mr. Robert Eddison; *Survey of London*, vol. XXIX, 1960, p. 238.
40. E.g., W. J. Macqueen Pope, *Theatre Royal, Drury Lane*, N.D., p. 58, and Rand Carter, *op. cit.*
41. B.M., Collection of Memoranda . . . relating to Drury Lane Theatre, vol. VII (pressmark C 120 h 1).
42. *The Picture of London for 1806*, pp. 263–9.
43. Rupert Gunnis, *Dictionary of British Sculptors 1660–1851*, N.D., p. 120.
44. B.M., Collection of newspaper cuttings relating to Drury Lane Theatre (pressmark 11795 k 22).
45. Robert Wilkinson, *Theatrum Illustrata*, 1825, p. 152.

46. Benjamin Dean Wyatt, *Observations on the Design for the Theatre Royal, Drury Lane,* 1813, pp. ix, xi.
47. Sir John Soane's Museum, drawer 61.
48. Wyatt, *op. cit.*, p. 1.
49. *Ibid.*, p. 10.
50. *Ibid.*, p. 8.
51. *Ibid.*, p. 3.
52. *Ibid.*, p. 2.
53. *Ibid.*, p. 21.
54. *Ibid.*, p. 38.
55. *Ibid.*, pp. 42–3.
56. James Elmes, *Metropolitan Improvements,* 1827, p. 136.
57. Wyatt's drawings in R.I.B.A. library.
58. *The Picture of London for 1816,* pp. 217–19.
59. *The London Theatre 1811–1816. Selections from the diary of Henry Crabb Robinson,* ed. Eluned Brown, 1966, p. 48.
60. B.M., Collection of Memoranda . . . relating to Drury Lane Theatre, vol. xiv (pressmark C 120 h 1).
61. *The Picture of London for 1818,* pp. 286–8.
62. B.M., Collection of Memoranda . . . relating to Drury Lane Theatre, vol. xvii (pressmark C 120 h 1).
63. *Leigh's New Picture of London,* 1819, pp. 433–4.
64. George Raymond, *Memoirs of Robert William Elliston,* 1845, vol. ii, p. 315; J. Britton and A. Pugin, *Illustrations of the Public Buildings of London,* 1825, vol. i, p. 247.
65. Britton and Pugin, *op. cit.*, vol. i, pp. 252–3.
66. *Ibid.*, vol. i, p. 254.
67. *Ibid.*, vol. i, p. 255.
68. *Leigh's New Picture of London,* 1822, pp. 413–14.
69. Raymond, *op. cit.*, vol. ii, p. 475n.
70. Alfred Bunn, *The Stage: both before and behind the Curtain,* 1840, vol. ii, pp. 125–7.
71. *The Builder,* 20 Oct. 1847, pp. 465, 471.
72. *The Era,* 21 Dec. 1851, p. 10.
73. *The Builder,* 2 April 1870, p. 270.
74. *Ibid.*, 22 April 1871, p. 304.
75. See *Survey of London,* vol. xxxiv, 1966, p. 355 and Plate 40.
76. *The Builder,* 14 April 1922, p. 558.

CHAPTER V (pp. 71–85)

Covent Garden Theatre and the Royal Opera House: the Management

1. *The London Stage 1660–1800, Part 2, 1700–1729,* ed. Emmett L. Avery, 1960, p. xxxii.
2. E/BER, four leases of 16 March 1730/1 to John Rich; see also B.O.L., Contract Book for Covent Garden and Bloomsbury from Dec. 1730, nos. 4–7, pp. 5–22.
3. *The Daily Courant,* 12 Jan. 1730/1.
4. *The London Stage 1660–1800, Part 3, 1729–1747,* ed. Arthur H. Scouten, 1961, pp. xxvii–xxviii.
5. *The British Journal,* 20 Feb. 1730/1.
6. *The Daily Advertiser,* 29 April 1731.
7. P.R.O., C11/2662/1.
8. Basil Francis, 'John Rich's Proposals', in *Theatre Notebook,* vol. xii, 1957, pp. 17–19.
9. Scouten, *op. cit.*, pp. xxviii–xxx.
10. B.M., Add. MS. 32, 428.
11. P.R.O., C11/2662/1; C11/2732/81.
12. Scouten, *op. cit.*, pp. lxxvi–lxxvii.
13. For examples of shares sold at a premium see M.L.R. 1735/1/224; 1735/3/414; 1735/5/406; 1738/5/473; 1749/1/313; 1774/7/425.
14. Hoare's Bank records, ledgers 33/123, 34/123, John Rich.
15. E.g., Basil Francis in *The Bankers' Magazine,* vol. clxxiii, 1952, pp. 565–9, and in *Theatre Notebook,* vol. xii, 1957, pp. 17–19; also Scouten, *op. cit.*, p. xxviii.
16. B.M., Add. Ch. 9319.
17. *Survey of London,* vol. xxxi, 1963, p. 270.
18. M.L.R. 1738/5/473.
19. This point is explicitly made in P.R.O., C11/2662/1.
20. P.R.O., C11/2732/81.
21. Scouten, *op. cit.*, pp. xxxii, lxxiv.
22. B.M., Add. Ch. 9312, and Add. MS. 12201, ff. 30–3; M.L.R. 1735/4/322.
23. M.L.R. 1743/1/493–6; 1743/2/273.
24. Recited in B.M., Add. MS. 12201, ff. 30–3.
25. P.C.C., 444 Cheslyn.
26. B.O.L., lease of 2 Dec. 1765 to Priscilla Rich.
27. M.L.R. 1767/6/50–1.
28. *The New Complete Guide,* 1774, p. 229.
29. *Baldwin's New Complete Guide,* 1770, p. 164.
30. B.M., Add. MS. 33,218; Eugene R. Page, *George Colman the Elder,* 1935, *passim.*
31. B.M., Add. MS. 33,218.
32. M.L.R. 1768/6/187–8; *Baldwin's New Complete Guide,* 1770, p. 139.
33. P.R.O., C12/1024/36.
34. Page, *op. cit.*, pp. 177–83.
35. *Ibid.*, pp. 190–1, 198, 202, 203n.
36. P.R.O., C54/6378, no. 11.
37. *The Letters of Richard Brinsley Sheridan,* ed. Cecil Price, 1966, vol. i, p. 85.
38. *Ibid.*, vol. i, pp. 116–21, 171.
39. See, for instance, M.L.R. 1784/3/279; 1785/2/605; 1785/3/40.
40. See, for instance, *ibid.*, 1781/3/466; 1782/2/538.

41. George Saunders, *A Treatise on Theatres*, 1790, pp. 83–4; *The Morning Chronicle*, 24 Sept. 1782.
42. B.O.L., Estate Letters, 21 Feb., 5 March 1785.
43. *Sheridan Letters*, vol. I, 1966, p. 213.
44. E/BER, agreement for a lease to Thomas Harris, 7 April 1792.
45. *The Gentleman's Magazine*, vol. 62, 1792, p. 862.
46. *The Public Advertiser*, 15 Sept. 1792.
47. *Ibid.*, 18 Sept. 1792.
48. *Ibid.*, 2 Oct. 1792.
49. *Ibid.*, 17 Sept. 1793; Dorothy Stroud, *Henry Holland. His Life and Architecture*, 1966, p. 125.
50. E/BER, lease of 13 June 1793 to Thomas Harris.
51. *The Gazetteer*, 16 Sept. 1794; Stroud, *loc. cit.*
52. P.R.O., C54/7757, no. 7; M.L.R. 1803/5/461.
53. Herschel Baker, *John Philip Kemble, The Actor in His Theatre*, 1942, p. 274.
54. James Boaden, *Memoirs of the Life of John Philip Kemble*, 1825, vol. II, pp. 372–4.
55. *Mr. G. White's Letter to Mr. Harris, June 5 1804, with Mr. Harris's Answer, June 17 1804* (B.M. pressmark, 11795 K 31 no. 24).
56. M.L.R. 1806/4/620–1.
57. *Ibid.*, 1806/4/622.
58. *The Gentleman's Magazine*, vol. 78, 1808, pp. 846–7, 1038; Westminster Abbey Muniments, Inquisitions and Depositions for 1808, nos. 54–65
59. E/BER, leases of 4 March 1806 to Thomas Harris and of 1 May 1818 to Thomas and Henry Harris and J. P. Kemble; Covent Garden Theatre Papers, notes on conversation of 29 Sept. 1808 between Messrs. Harris, Kemble and Adam.
60. *The Gentleman's Magazine*, vol. 78, 1808, p. 1033.
61. *P.P.*, *Report of the Select Committee of the House of Commons to inquire into the Laws affecting Dramatic Literature*, 1831–2, vol. VII, p. 102.
62. *The Gentleman's Magazine*, vol. 79, 1809, p. 81.
63. B.M., Add. MS. 31,977.
64. *Ibid.*, Covent Garden Theatre playbills (pressmark, play bills 92).
65. *The Illustrated London News*, 12 Dec. 1846, p. 373.
66. *P.P.*, *Report of Commons Committee on Laws affecting Dramatic Literature*, 1831–2, vol. VII, p. 206.
67. *The Law Journal*, vol. v, 1827, Easter Term, pp. 131–9 (B.M. pressmark, PP 1345).
68. B.O.L., Estate Letters, 10 June 1817.
69. Baker, *op. cit.*, pp. 345–6.
70. P.R.O., C13/2587, Const *v.* Kemble; *The Law Journal*, *loc. cit.*
71. *The Law Journal*, vol. VII, 1829, Hilary Term, pp. 79–84 (B.M. pressmark, PP 1345); Richard Bligh, *New Reports of Cases heard in the House of Lords in 1831*, vol. v, 1834, pp. 730–54 (B.M. pressmark, 708 c 8).
72. *P.P.*, *Report of Commons Committee on Laws affecting Dramatic Literature*, 1831–2, vol. VII, p. 100.
73. Henry Saxe Wyndham, *The Annals of Covent Garden Theatre from 1732 to 1897*, 1906, vol. II, pp. 55–8.
74. *P.P.*, *Report of Commons Committee on Laws affecting Dramatic Literature*, 1831–2, vol. VII, pp. 43, 49, 52, 115, 250.
75. Saxe Wyndham, *op. cit.*, vol. II, *passim*.
76. *Ibid.*, vol. II, pp. 172, 177.
77. *The Times*, 18 March 1856.
78. E/BER, Covent Garden Theatre Papers, Adam to Haedy, 21 July 1832.
79. *Ibid.*, Haedy to Adam, 28 April 1837.
80. Saxe Wyndham, *op. cit.*, vol. II, pp. 181–2.
81. *The Illustrated London News*, 6 Dec. 1856, pp. 562–4.
82. *Ibid.*, *loc cit*; *The Builder*, 10 April 1847, pp. 165–6.
83. *The Illustrated London News*, 10 April 1847, pp. 225, 233–4; *The Builder*, 10 April 1847, pp. 165–6.
84. Saxe Wyndham, *op. cit.*, vol. II, p. 187.
85. *The Builder*, 19 Feb. 1848, p. 88; II, 18 March 1848, pp. 125, 135.
86. Harold Rosenthal, *Two Centuries of Opera at Covent Garden*, 1958, p. 87.
87. Royal Opera House archives, agreement of 24 Sept. 1849.
88. Rosenthal, *op. cit.*, pp. 93–4.
89. *Survey of London*, vol. XXIX, 1960, p. 243.
90. Saxe Wyndham, *op. cit.*, vol. II, p. 200.
91. *The Illustrated London News*, 8 March 1856, p. 243.
92. E/BER, Covent Garden Theatre Papers, Haedy to the Duke, 10 March 1856.
93. *The Illustrated London News*, 9 Jan. 1858, p. 38.
94. E/BER, Covent Garden Theatre Papers, H. Surman to Haedy, 17 March 1856; *The Times*, 18 March 1856.
95. P.R.O., KB122/1418, f. 31.
96. B.O.L., Annual Report, 1856, pp. 2–4.
97. *The Builder*, 15 Dec. 1855, pp. 603–4.
98. E/BER, Covent Garden Theatre Papers, Parker to proprietors of Piazza Hotel, 16 Jan. 1857.
99. M.L.R. 1857/12/259.
100. B.O.L., Annual Report, 1894, p. 200.
101. M.L.R. 1857/12/379.
102. B.O.L., deed of compromise between F. Gye and the contributors to the building fund, 29 June 1873.
103. *The Builder*, 18 Feb. 1860, pp. 102–3.

104. *Ibid.*, 22 May 1858, pp. 345–7; *The Illustrated London News*, 10 July 1858, p. 34.
105. *The Builder*, 11 Feb. 1860, pp. 85–7.
106. B.O.L., Annual Report, 1858, pp. 3–4.
107. *The Illustrated London News*, 22 May 1858, p. 507.
108. Saxe Wyndham, *op. cit.*, vol. II, p. 224.
109. M.L.R. 1858/9/606.
110. *The Illustrated London News*, 10 April 1858, p. 367.
111. M.L.R. 1858/10/41.
112. *The Builder*, 2 April 1859, pp. 235–6.
113. *Ibid.*, 11 Feb. 1860, p. 88.
114. *The Times*, 8 March 1860.
115. B.O.L., Annual Report, 1861, p. 7.
116. *Ibid.*, Annual Report, 1882, vol. 2, p. 6.
117. *Ibid.*, Annual Report, 1862, pp. 8–9.
118. *Ibid.*, Annual Report, 1871, p. 126.
119. *The Illustrated London News*, 13 May 1865, p. 465.
120. B.O.L., Annual Report, 1872, p. 218.
121. *Ibid.*, Annual Report, 1882, vol. 2, p. 6.
122. *Ibid.*, Annual Report, 1887, p. 174.
123. *The Times*, 7 April 1956.
124. P.C.C., 1879/442.
125. M.L.R. 1875/19/621; *The Annual Register*, 1895, p. 208.
126. P.C.C., 1879/442; Saxe Wyndham, *op. cit.*, vol. II, p. 270.
127. Felix Remo, *Music in the Land of Fogs*, English ed., 1886, p. 177.
128. M.L.R. 1883/25/679; 1885/9/833.
129. Rosenthal, *op. cit.*, p. 198.
130. Saxe Wyndham, *op. cit.*, vol. II, pp. 283, 290.
131. P.C.C., 1895/135b; *The Annual Register*, 1895, p. 208.
132. M.L.R. 1916/7/969; *The Times*, 4 July 1928.
133. *The Times*, 2, 5 Feb. 1931.
134. M.L.R. 1916/7/969.
135. *Ibid.*, 1916/7/970.
136. Rosenthal, *op. cit.*, pp. 279–80, 359.
137. *The Times*, 6 Nov. 1925.
138. M.L.R. 1917/1/814.
139. *The Times*, 4 July 1928; Rosenthal, *op. cit.*, pp. 391–2.
140. M.L.R. 1929/8/70; *The Times*, 16 Nov. 1928.
141. *The Times*, 3, 5, 8, 31 July 1930.
142. *The Annual Register*, 1930, part I, p. 94.
143. *The Times*, 6 Dec. 1930.
144. *The Annual Register*, 1932, part I, p. 96.
145. *Ibid.*, 1932, part II, p. 48.
146. *The Times*, 14, 17 Dec. 1932.
147. *Ibid.*, 6 July 1933.
148. *Ibid.*, 15 July 1933.
149. Rosenthal, *op. cit.*, p. 393.
150. *The Times*, 8 Dec. 1933; 19 Jan. 1934; 20 July 1939.
151. Rosenthal, *op. cit.*, pp. 394–5.

152. *The Times*, 20 July 1939.
153. Rosenthal, *op. cit.*, p. 553.
154. *Ibid.*, p. 581; *The Times*, 10 July 1944.
155. *The Times*, 20 July 1944.
156. *Ibid.*, 26 Oct. 1945.
157. *Ibid.*, 21 Feb. 1946.
158. *Fourth Annual Report of the Arts Council of Great Britain 1948–9*, pp. 20–1.

CHAPTER VI (pp. 86–108)

Covent Garden Theatre and the Royal Opera House: the Buildings

1. P.R.O., C11/2662/1.
2. *The Gentleman's Magazine*, vol. 33, 1763, p. 97.
3. *Walpole Society*, vol. 22, 1934 (George Vertue Note Book III), p. 62.
4. Robert Seymour, *A Survey of the Cities of London and Westminster*, vol. II, 1735, p. 670.
5. Chatsworth MSS., box 143, 'Pope-Burlington Correspondence and Kent Letters'.
6. *The Town and Country Magazine*, 1775, p. 488.
7. *The Morning Chronicle*, 24 Sept. 1782.
8. George Saunders, *A Treatise on Theatres*, 1790, pp. 81–7.
9. B.M., Crace Maps, portfolio XIII, sheet 47.
10. *The Public Advertiser*, 2 Oct. 1792.
11. *Ibid.*, 17 Sept. 1793.
12. *The Gazetteer*, 16 Sept. 1794.
13. *The Times*, 13 Sept. 1796.
14. *Ibid.*, 13 Sept. 1803.
15. J. Britton and A. Pugin, *Illustrations of the Public Buildings of London*, 1825, vol. I, p. 216.
16. *Ibid.*, vol. I, p. 217.
17. *Ibid.*, vol. I, pp. 216–19; *The Gentleman's Magazine*, vol. 79, 1809, p. 880.
18. Britton and Pugin, *op. cit.*, vol. I, p. 212.
19. *The Gentleman's Magazine*, vol. 79, 1809, p. 880.
20. Britton and Pugin, *op. cit.*, vol. I, pp. 220–1.
21. *Ibid.*, vol. I, p. 222.
22. *The Illustrated London News*, 6 Dec. 1856, pp. 562–4.
23. *Ibid.*, 10 July 1858, pp. 33–4.
24. *Country Life*, 25 June 1948, p. 1281.
25. *The Builder*, 22 May 1858, pp. 345–7; *Transactions of the Royal Institute of British Architects, First Series*, vol. X, 1859–60, p. 64.
26. *The Builder*, 11, 18 Feb. 1860, pp. 85–7, 102–3.
27. *Ibid.*, 4 May, 1 June 1901, pp. 440, 537–40.
28. *Ibid.*, 24 May 1902, p. 521.
29. Rosenthal, *op. cit.*, pp. 359, 485.

Index

NOTE

Symbols in the left-hand margin denote:

PLATES

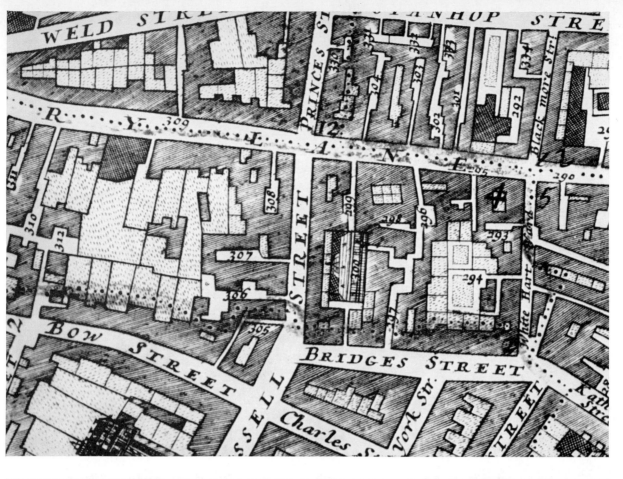

b. Extract from Ogilby and Morgan's map of 1681–2 showing
Drury Lane Theatre

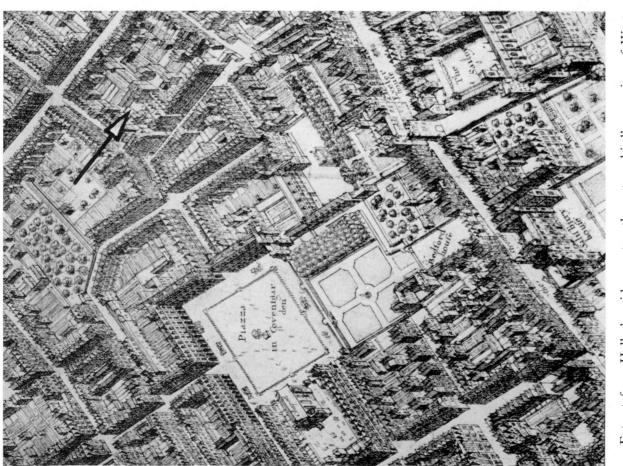

a. Extract from Hollar's mid seventeenth-century bird's-eye view of West
London. Arrow points to the Riding Yard

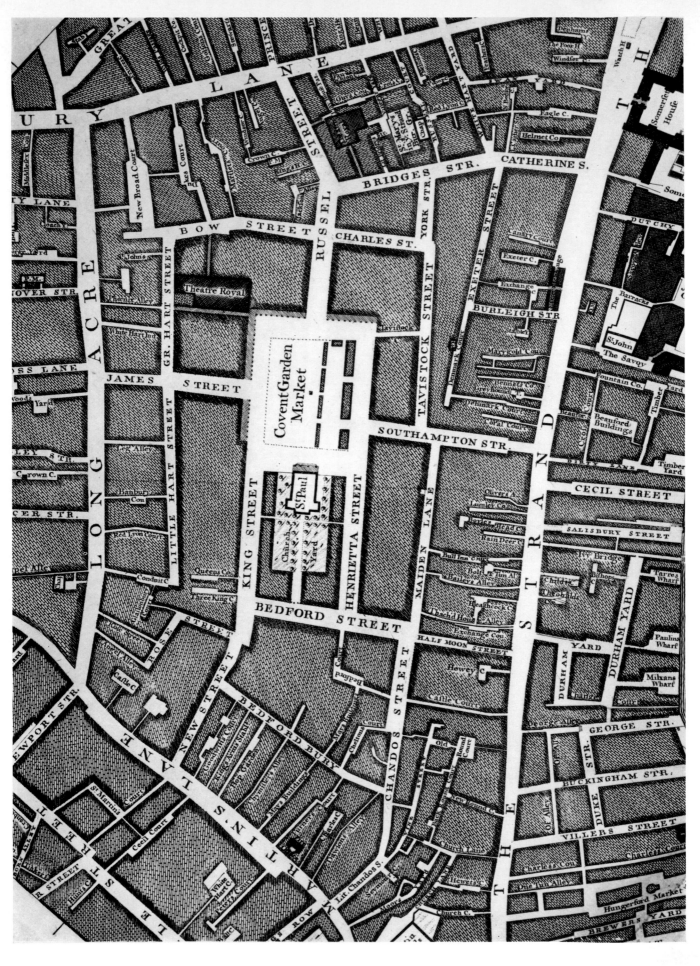

Extract from Rocque's map of 1746

3

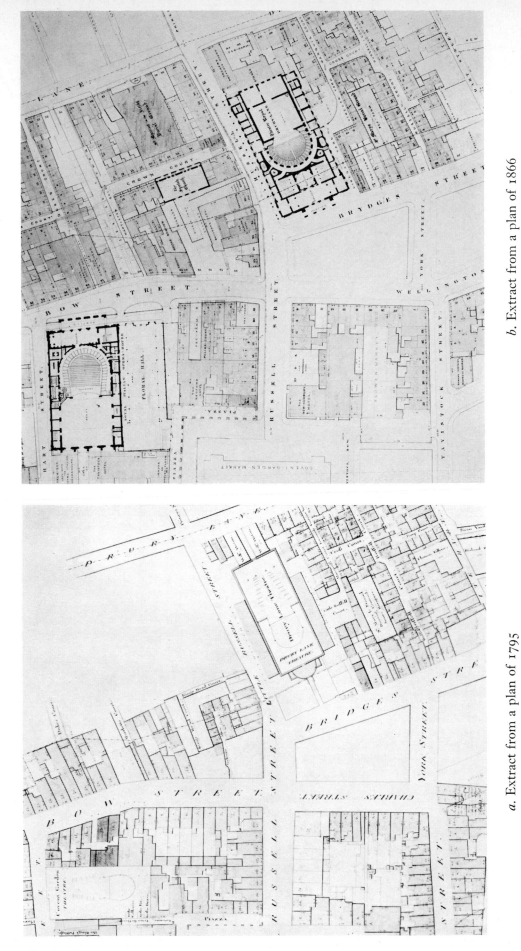

b. Extract from a plan of 1866

a. Extract from a plan of 1795

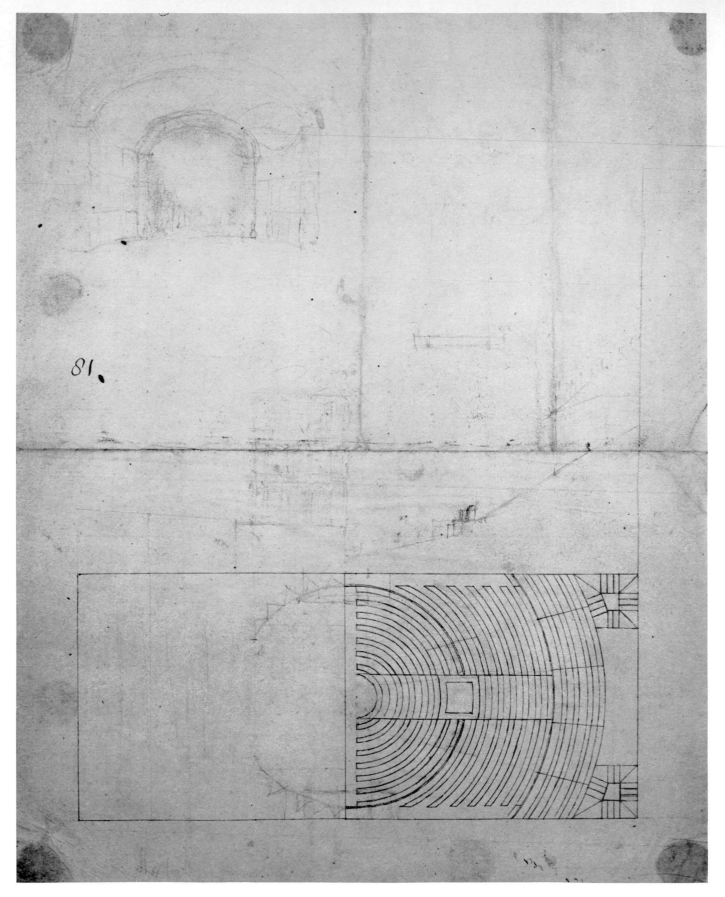

Design among the Wren drawings at All Souls for a playhouse
on the antique Roman model (p. 40)

5

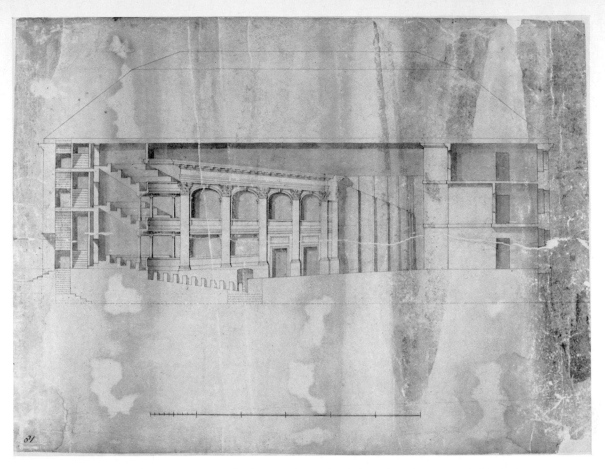

a. Longitudinal section for a playhouse, from the Wren drawings at All Souls (p. 43)

b. Engraving from *Ariadne,* an opera performed at Drury Lane
in 1674 (p. 44)

6

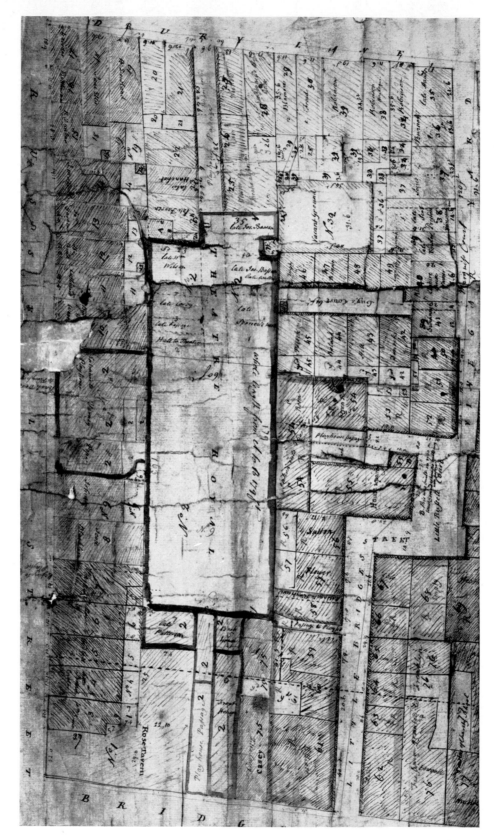

THE THEATRE ROYAL, DRURY LANE, OF 1672–4: site plan in c. 1748

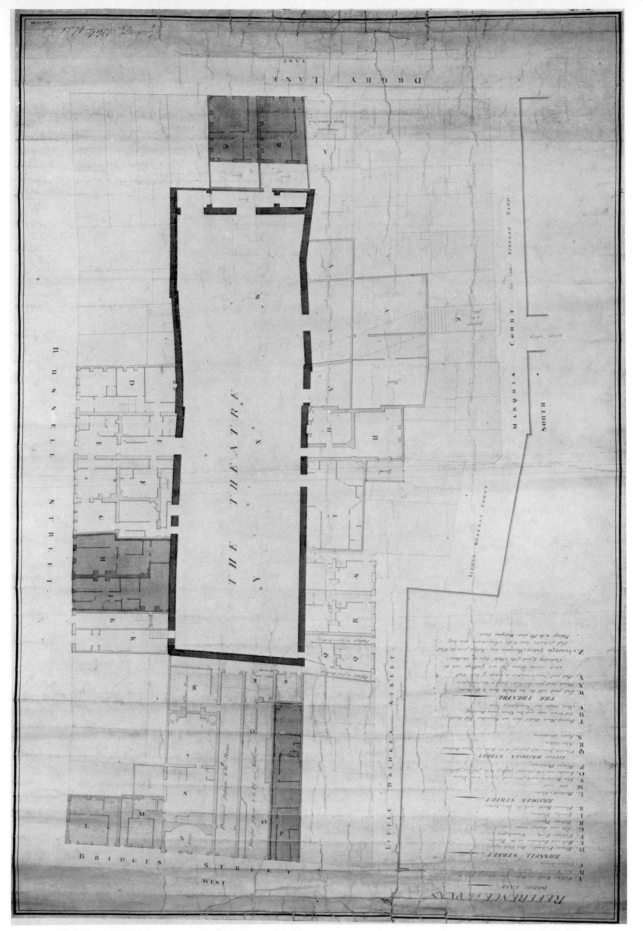

The Theatre Royal, Drury Lane, of 1672–4: site plan in 1778 after reconstruction by Robert Adam. This plan is redrawn in fig. 3 on page 34

8

THE THEATRE ROYAL, DRURY LANE, OF 1672–4: Brydges Street front, 1775.
Robert Adam, architect

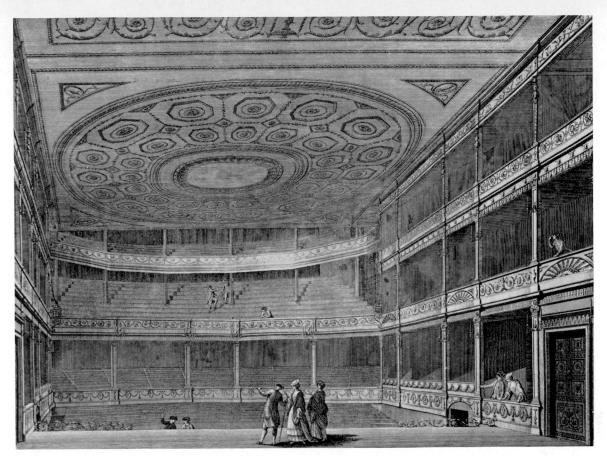

a. Auditorium

b. Proscenium in 1778

THE THEATRE ROYAL, DRURY LANE, OF 1672–4 after reconstruction by
Robert Adam in 1775

a. Design executed in 1775

b. Unexecuted design, 1776

THE THEATRE ROYAL, DRURY LANE, OF 1672–4: ceiling designs
by Robert Adam

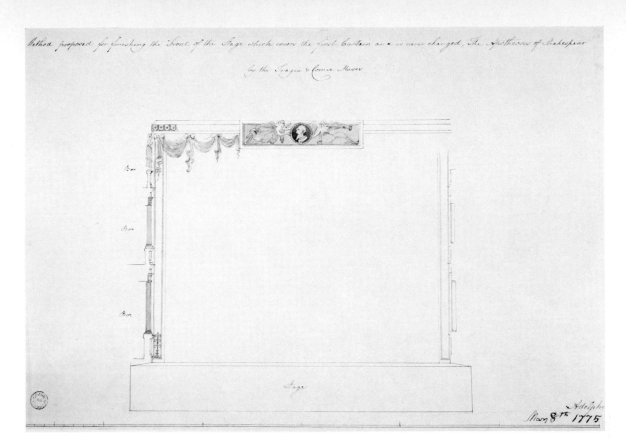

a. Design for proscenium, 1775

b. Auditorium after redecoration by T. Greenwood and W. Capon in 1783

THE THEATRE ROYAL, DRURY LANE, OF 1672–4 as reconstructed by Robert Adam

12

a. Cross section

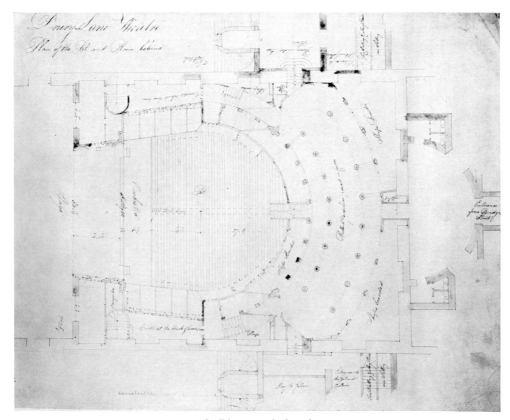

b. Plan at pit level

THE THEATRE ROYAL, DRURY LANE, OF 1791–4.
Henry Holland, architect: first designs, 1792

a. Cross section

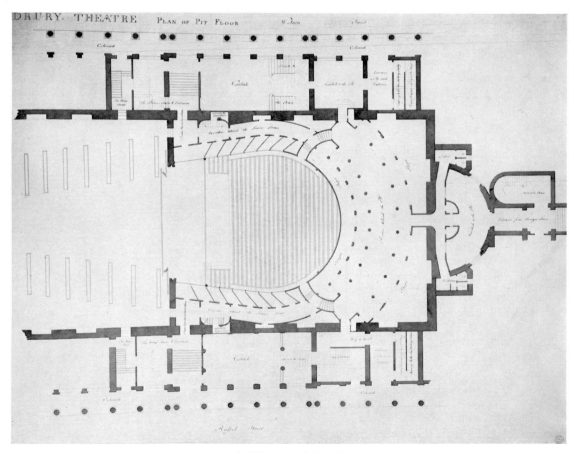

b. Plan at pit level

THE THEATRE ROYAL, DRURY LANE, OF 1791–4. Henry Holland, architect: executed designs, 1793

14

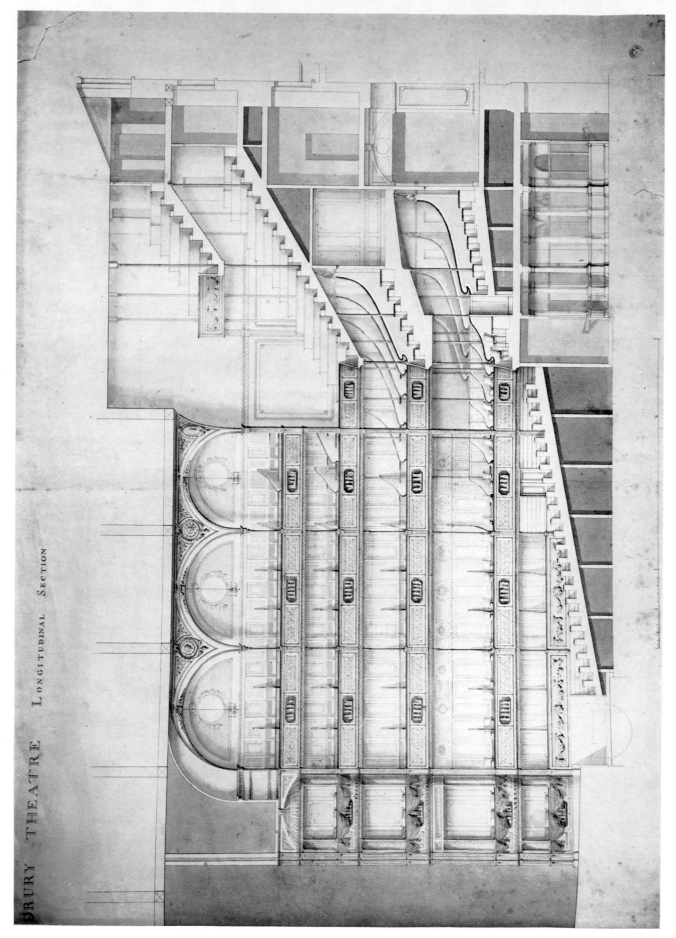

DRURY THEATRE   LONGITUDINAL SECTION

The Theatre Royal, Drury Lane, of 1791–4. Henry Holland, architect: executed design, 1793, longitudinal section

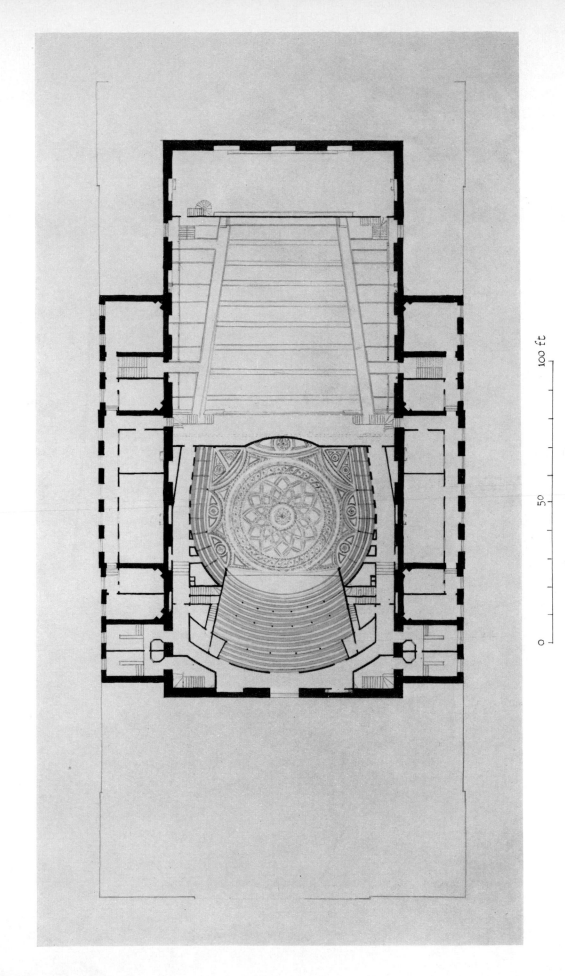

The Theatre Royal, Drury Lane, of 1791–4. Henry Holland, architect: plan at fourth-tier level showing ceiling as executed

0   50   100 ft

16

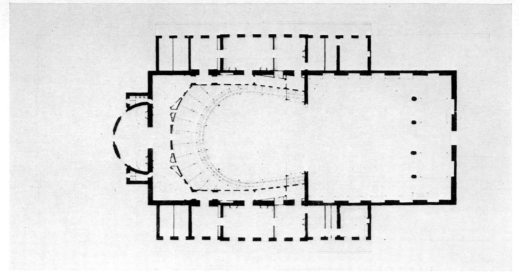

a. First-tier
level

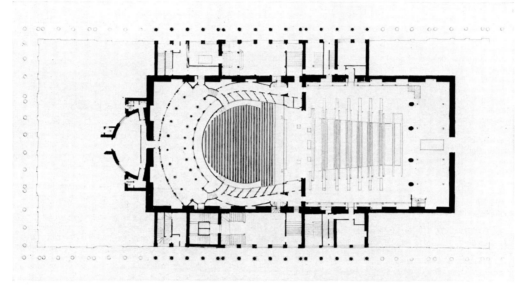

b. Pit level

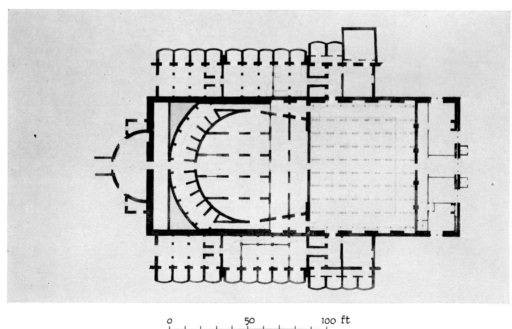

c. Basement
level

0   50   100 ft

THE THEATRE ROYAL, DRURY LANE, OF 1791–4. Henry Holland,
architect: plans, generally as executed

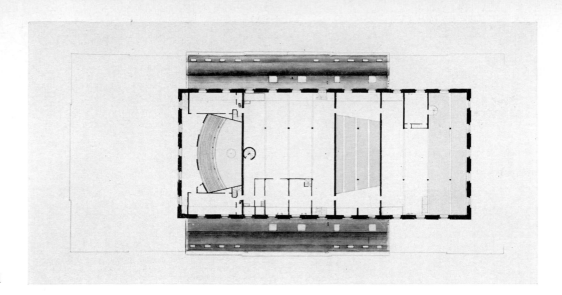

a. Upper-gallery level

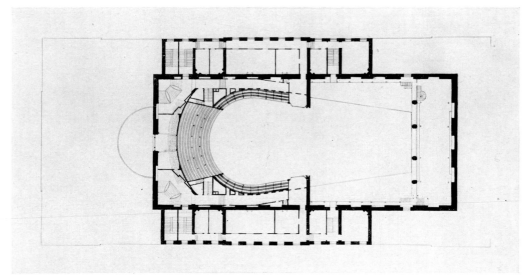

b. Third-tier level

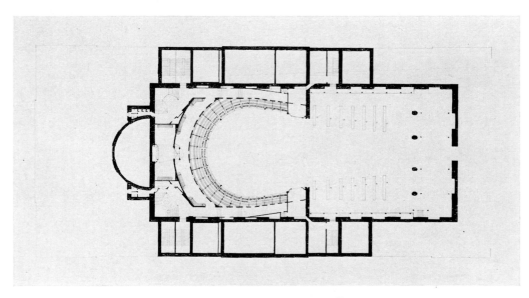

c. Second-tier level

THE THEATRE ROYAL, DRURY LANE, OF 1791–4. Henry Holland,
architect: plans, generally as executed

a

b

THE THEATRE ROYAL, DRURY LANE, OF 1791–4: auditorium
after alterations of 1797. Henry Holland, architect

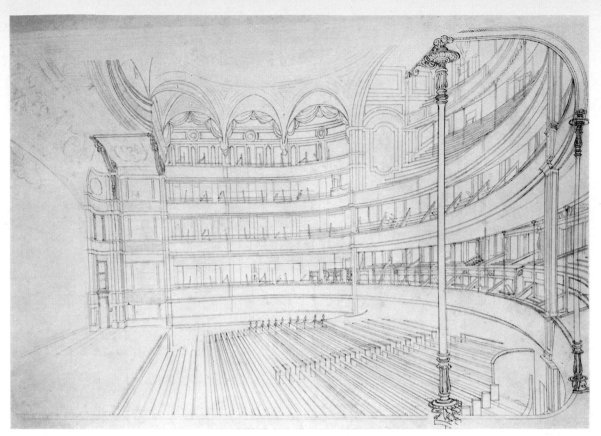

a. Auditorium in 1805

b. Auditorium after alterations of 1806

THE THEATRE ROYAL, DRURY LANE, OF 1791–4. Henry Holland, architect

a. First, arcaded, design, *c.* 1792

b. First, arcaded, design, with theatre shell omitted

c. Final, colonnaded, design, 1793

THE THEATRE ROYAL, DRURY LANE, OF 1791–4,
exterior designs. Henry Holland, architect

a. Russell Street front looking west

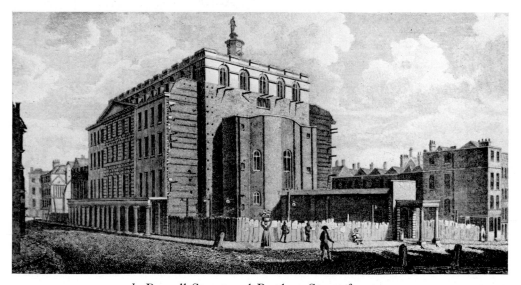

b. Russell Street and Brydges Street fronts

c. Brydges Street front after the fire of 1809

THE THEATRE ROYAL, DRURY LANE, OF 1791–4,
exterior as built. Henry Holland, architect

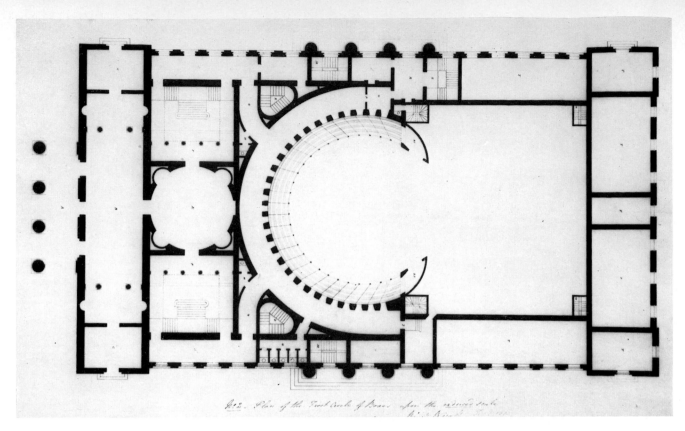

a. Plan at first-tier level

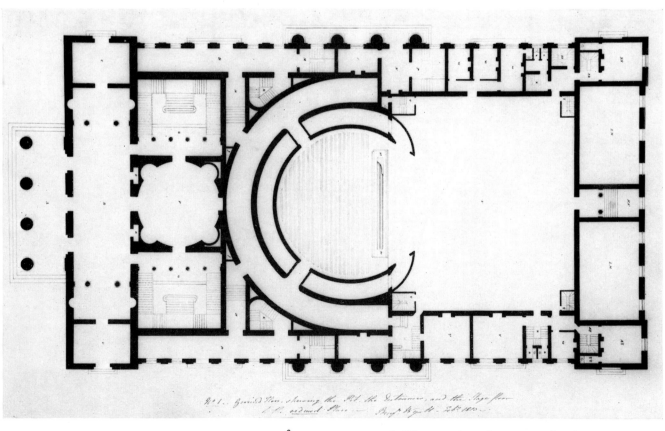

0   50   100 ft   *b.* Plan at pit and entrance level

THE THEATRE ROYAL, DRURY LANE, OF 1810–11, preliminary designs, 1810.
Benjamin Dean Wyatt, architect

0   50   100 ft   *a.* Front elevation

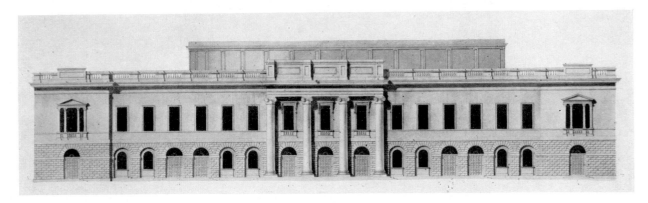

b. Side elevation

c. Proscenium

THE THEATRE ROYAL, DRURY LANE, OF 1810–11, preliminary designs, 1810.
Benjamin Dean Wyatt, architect

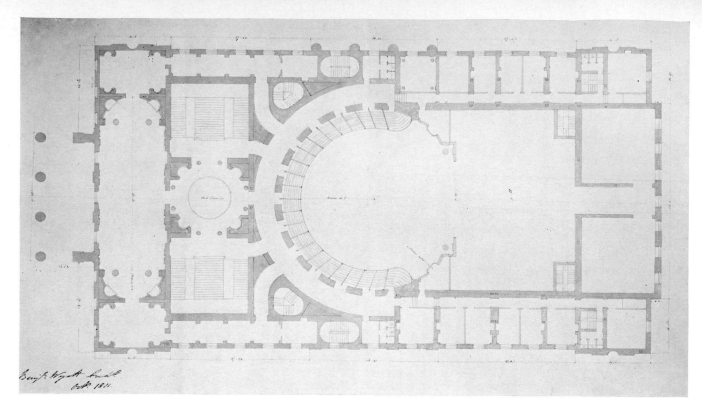

a. Plan at first-tier level

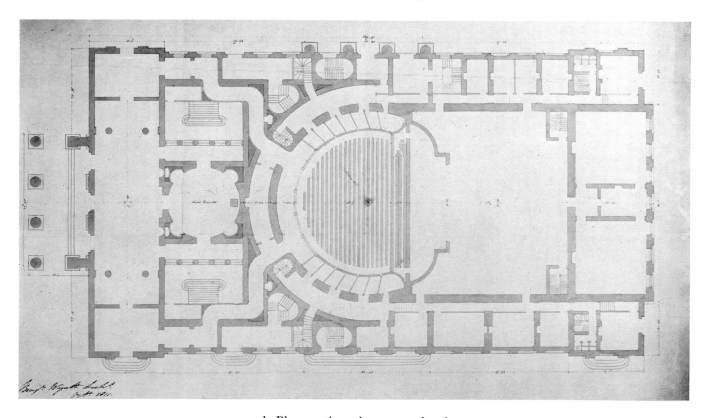

b. Plan at pit and entrance level

0   50   100 ft

THE THEATRE ROYAL, DRURY LANE, OF 1810–11, revised designs, 1811.
Benjamin Dean Wyatt, architect

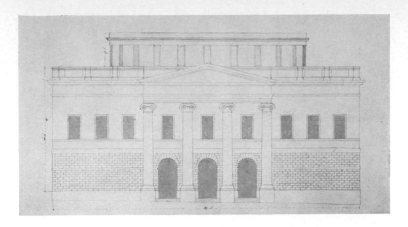

a. Front elevation

b. Side elevation

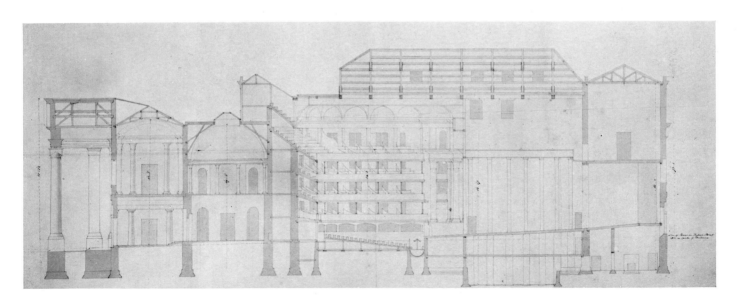

c. Longitudinal section

0   50   100 ft

THE THEATRE ROYAL, DRURY LANE, OF 1810–11, revised designs, 1811.
Benjamin Dean Wyatt, architect

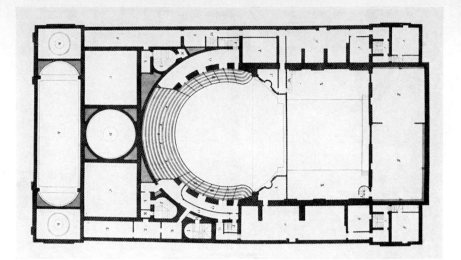

a. Plan at
fourth-tier level

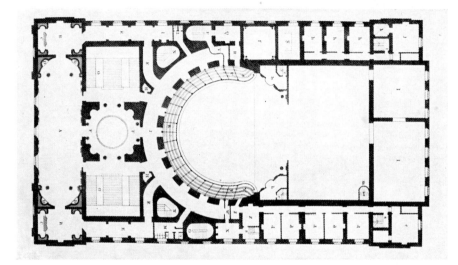

b. Plan at
first-tier level

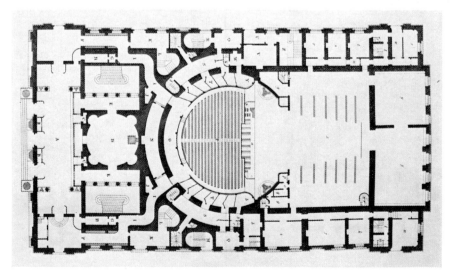

c. Plan at pit
and entrance level

0   50   100 ft

THE THEATRE ROYAL, DRURY LANE, OF 1810–11,
executed designs. Benjamin Dean Wyatt, architect

a. Proscenium

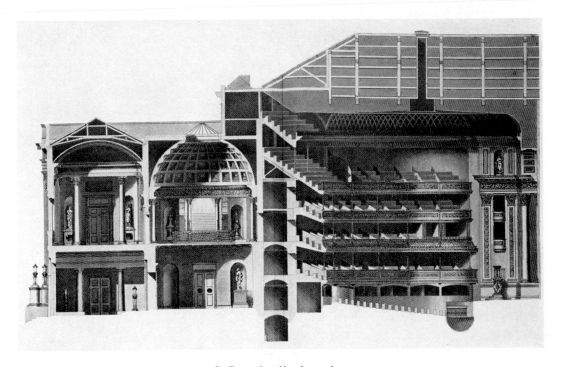

b. Longitudinal section

THE THEATRE ROYAL, DRURY LANE, OF 1810–11, executed designs.
Benjamin Dean Wyatt, architect

a. Section through the entrance hall and saloon

b. Section through the rotunda and staircases

THE THEATRE ROYAL, DRURY LANE, OF 1810–11, executed designs.
Benjamin Dean Wyatt, architect

a. Penultimate design for the Brydges Street front

b. North and west fronts as built

THE THEATRE ROYAL, DRURY LANE, OF 1810–11. Benjamin Dean Wyatt, architect

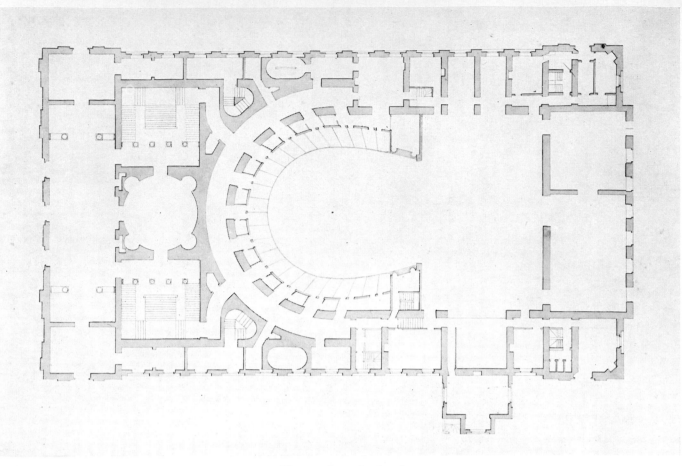

a. Plan at first-tier level

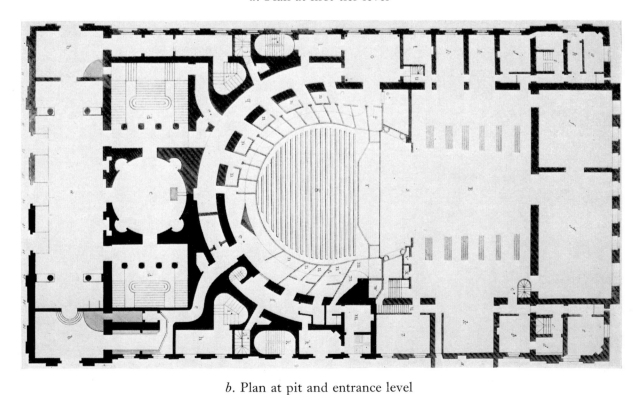

b. Plan at pit and entrance level

0   50   100 ft

THE THEATRE ROYAL, DRURY LANE, OF 1810–11 after reconstruction by
Samuel Beazley in 1822

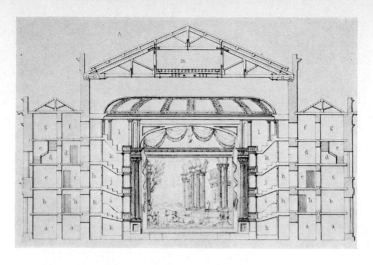

a. Cross section

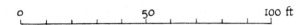

0   50   100 ft

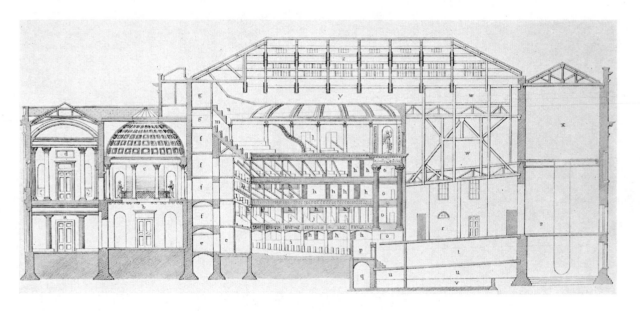

b. Longitudinal section

THE THEATRE ROYAL, DRURY LANE, OF 1810–11 after reconstruction by
Samuel Beazley in 1822

31

a. Auditorium in 1813

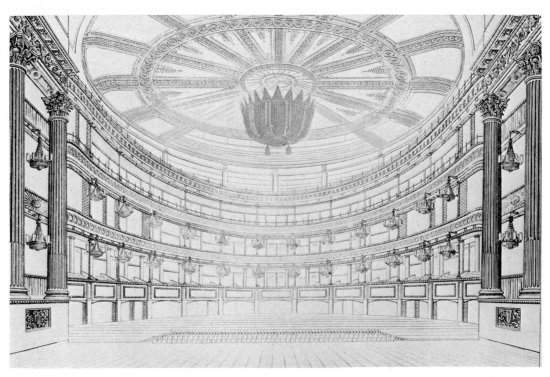

b. Auditorium after Beazley's alterations of 1822

THE THEATRE ROYAL, DRURY LANE, OF 1810–11. Benjamin
Dean Wyatt, architect

a. Auditorium, in use for a public meeting, 1842

b. Auditorium, in use for a grand dinner, 1841

THE THEATRE ROYAL, DRURY LANE, OF 1810–11 after redecoration by Crace in 1836–7

34

a

b

THE THEATRE ROYAL, DRURY LANE, OF 1810–11: auditorium in 1897–8

a. Auditorium in 1921 showing alterations made by Philip Pilditch in 1901

b. Auditorium in 1922 after reconstruction by J. Emblin Walker and associates

THE THEATRE ROYAL, DRURY LANE, OF 1810–11

36

b. Staircase (Prince's side) in 1965

a. The rotunda in 1965

THE THEATRE ROYAL, DRURY LANE, OF 1810–11.
Benjamin Dean Wyatt, architect

a. Saloon in 1965

b. The Royal retiring room in 1965

THE THEATRE ROYAL, DRURY LANE, OF 1810–11.
Benjamin Dean Wyatt, architect

38

b. Russell Street colonnade in 1965: S. Beazley, architect, 1831

a. Catherine Street front in 1965: portico by (?) J. Spiller, architect, 1820

THE THEATRE ROYAL, DRURY LANE, OF 1810–11. Benjamin Dean Wyatt, architect

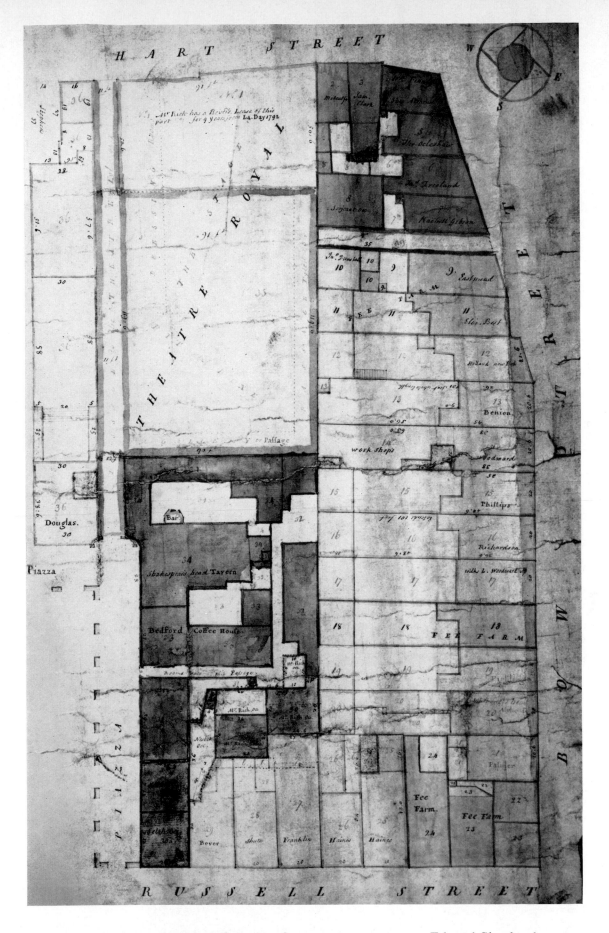

THE THEATRE ROYAL, COVENT GARDEN, OF 1731–2. Edward Shepherd,
architect: site plan in *c.* 1760

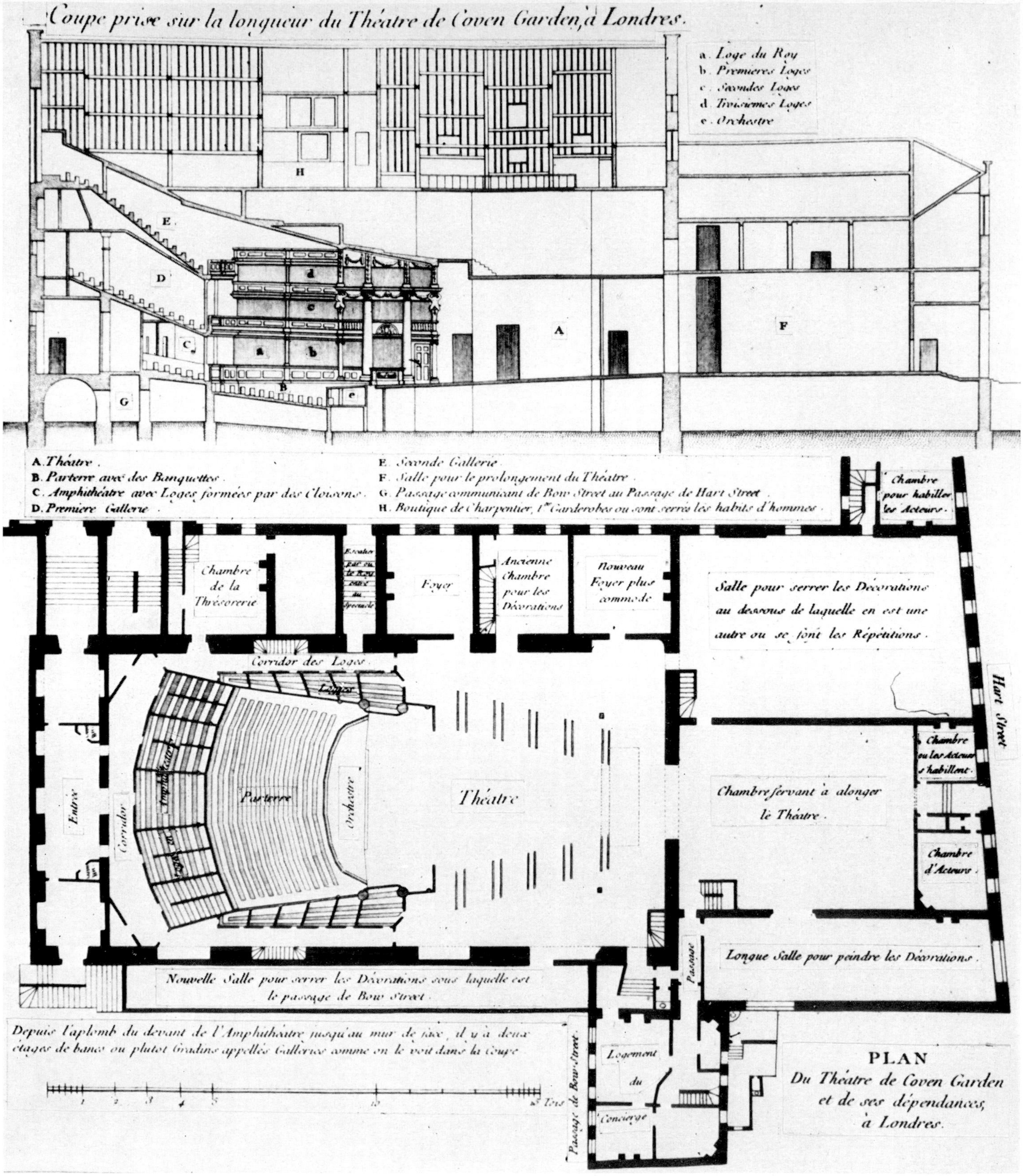

Coupe prise sur la longueur du Théatre de Coven Garden, à Londres.

a. *Loge du Roy*
b. *Premieres Loges*
c. *Secondes Loges*
d. *Troisiemes Loges*
e. *Orchestre*

A. *Théatre.*
B. *Parterre avec des Banquettes.*
C. *Amphithéatre avec Loges formées par des Cloisons.*
D. *Premiere Gallerie.*
E. *Seconde Gallerie.*
F. *Salle pour le prolongement du Théatre.*
G. *Passage communicant de Bow Street au Passage de Hart Street.*
H. *Boutique de Charpentier, l'e Garderobes ou sont serrés les habits d'hommes.*

Chambre de la Thrésorerie

Escalier ... au Spectacle

Foyer

Ancienne Chambre pour les Décorations

Nouveau Foyer plus commode

Salle pour serrer les Décorations au dessous de laquelle en est une autre ou se font les Répétitions.

Chambre pour habiller les Acteurs.

Corridor des Loges

Loges

Entrée

Corridor

Loges d'Amphithéatre

Parterre

Orchestre

Théatre

Chambre servant à alonger le Théatre.

Chambre ou les Acteurs s'habillent.

Chambre d'Acteurs.

Hart Street

Nouvelle Salle pour serrer les Décorations sous laquelle est le passage de Bow Street.

Longue Salle pour peindre les Décorations.

Depuis l'aplomb du devant de l'Amphithéatre jusqu'au mur de face, il y a deux étages de bancs ou plutot Gradins appellés Galleries comme on le voit dans la Coupe.

Passage de Bow Street.

Logement du Concierge

Passage

PLAN
Du Théatre de Coven Garden et de ses dépendances, à Londres.

THE THEATRE ROYAL, COVENT GARDEN, OF 1731–2. Edward Shepherd,
architect: plan and section, engraved *c.* 1774

a. Entrance from the Piazza   *b.* Proscenium in *c.* 1759

c. Stage and auditorium during the riots of 1763

THE THEATRE ROYAL, COVENT GARDEN, OF 1731–2. Edward Shepherd, architect

a. Auditorium

b. Auditorium in 1786

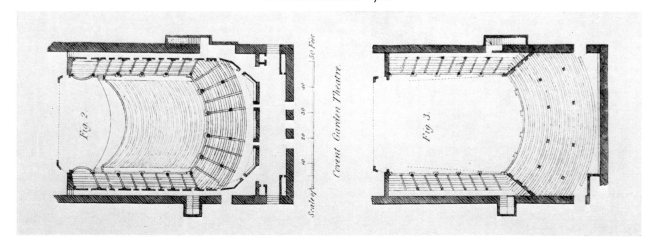

c. Plans at pit and first-gallery levels in 1790

THE THEATRE ROYAL, COVENT GARDEN, OF 1731–2 after remodelling
by John Inigo Richards in 1782

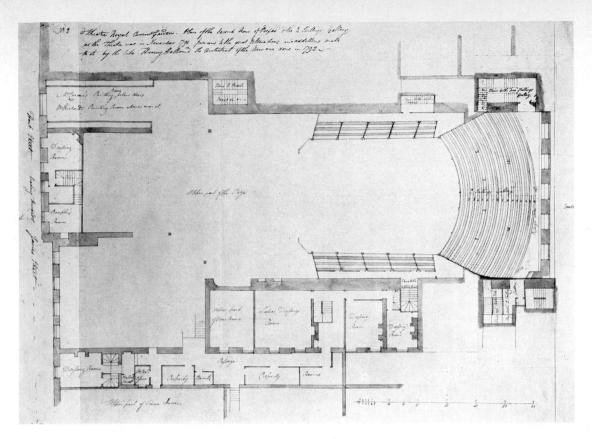

a. Plan at first-gallery level, 1791

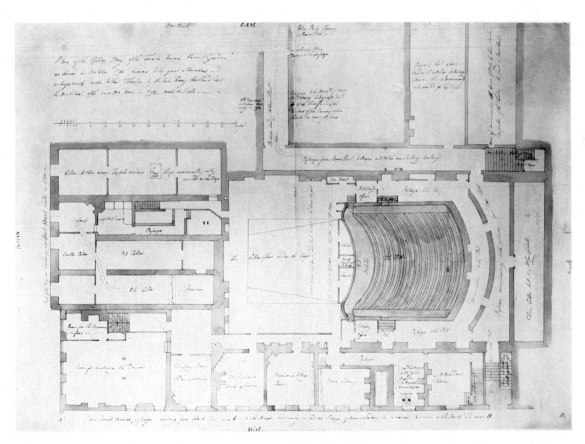

b. Plan at pit level, 1791

THE THEATRE ROYAL, COVENT GARDEN, OF 1731–2 after
remodelling by John Inigo Richards in 1782

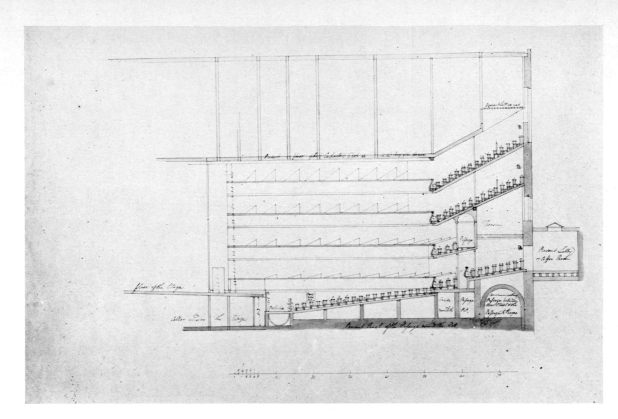

a. Longitudinal section

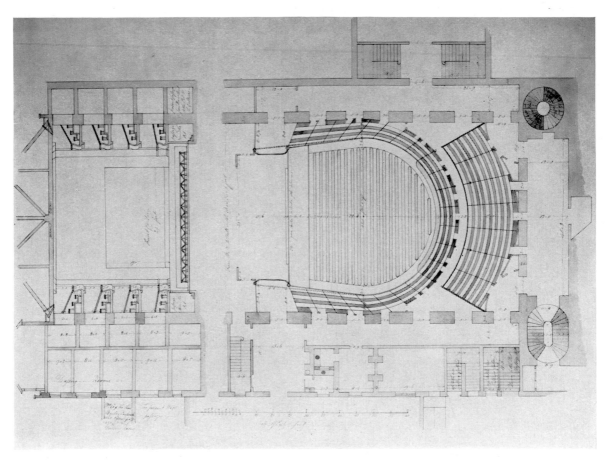

b. Plan at first-tier level showing pit, and cross section

THE THEATRE ROYAL, COVENT GARDEN, OF 1731–2: Henry Holland's
first proposals for remodelling, 1791

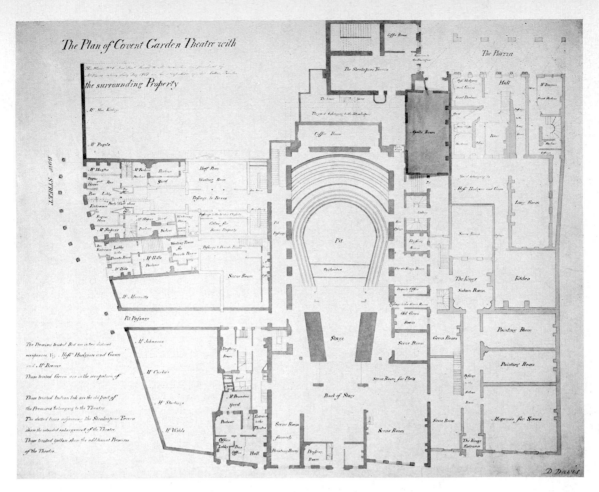

a. Plan of theatre and adjacent buildings in *c.* 1808

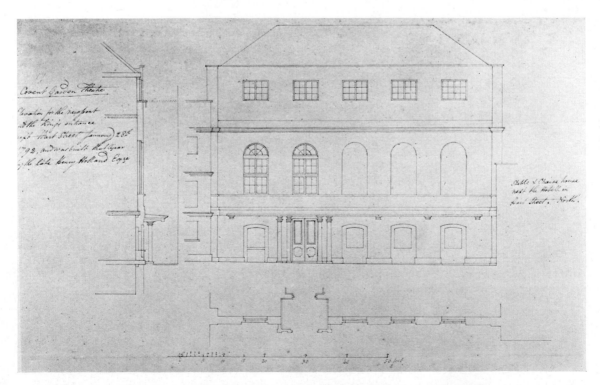

b. Elevation of new scene rooms and Royal entrance in Hart Street

THE THEATRE ROYAL, COVENT GARDEN, OF 1731–2 after reconstruction
by Henry Holland in 1792

a

b

THE THEATRE ROYAL, COVENT GARDEN, OF 1731–2: auditorium after
reconstruction by Henry Holland in 1792

a. Stage and auditorium

b. Stage and auditorium in 1808 showing alterations made by Creswell and Philips in 1803

THE THEATRE ROYAL, COVENT GARDEN, OF 1731–2 after reconstruction by
Henry Holland in 1792

THE THEATRE ROYAL, COVENT GARDEN, OF 1731–2 after reconstruction by Henry
Holland in 1792: Bow Street (*left*) and Hart Street (*right*) fronts

a. Bow Street and Hart Street fronts

b. Bow Street front looking north

THE THEATRE ROYAL, COVENT GARDEN, OF 1808–9. (Sir) Robert Smirke, architect

Elevation of the New Theatre Covent Garden.

a. Bow Street front

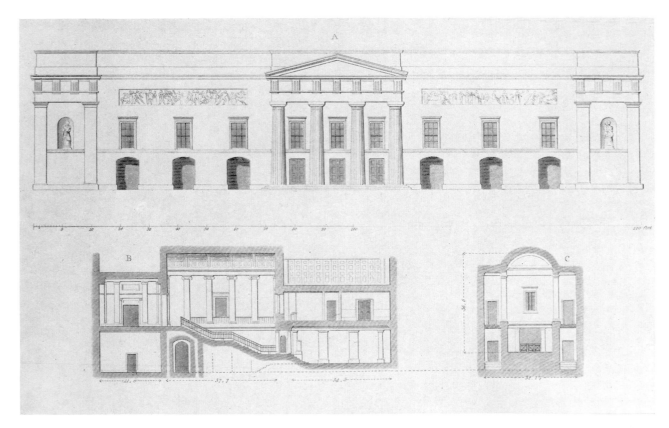

b. Bow Street front and sections through principal staircase

THE THEATRE ROYAL, COVENT GARDEN, OF 1808–9. (Sir) Robert Smirke, architect

a. Statues on the Bow Street front by J. C. Rossi

b. Frieze on the Bow Street front, carved by Rossi from models by John Flaxman

c. North and west elevations from Hart Street

THE THEATRE ROYAL, COVENT GARDEN, OF 1808–9. (Sir) Robert Smirke, architect

52

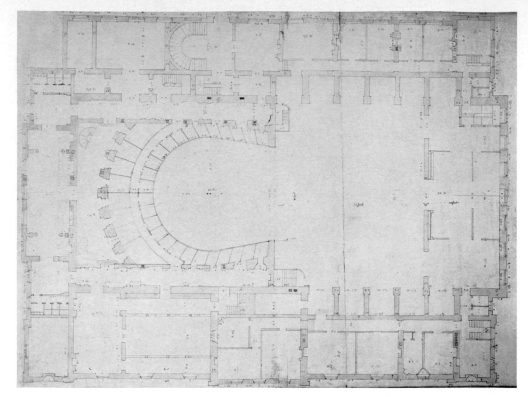

a. Plan at first-tier level, probably as built

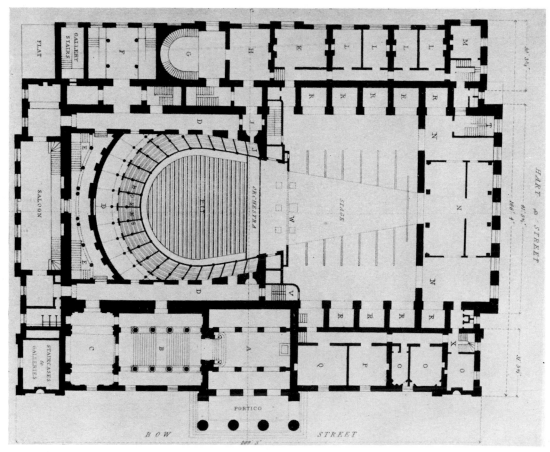

b. Plan at first-tier level showing pit in 1824

THE THEATRE ROYAL, COVENT GARDEN, OF 1808–9. (Sir) Robert
Smirke, architect

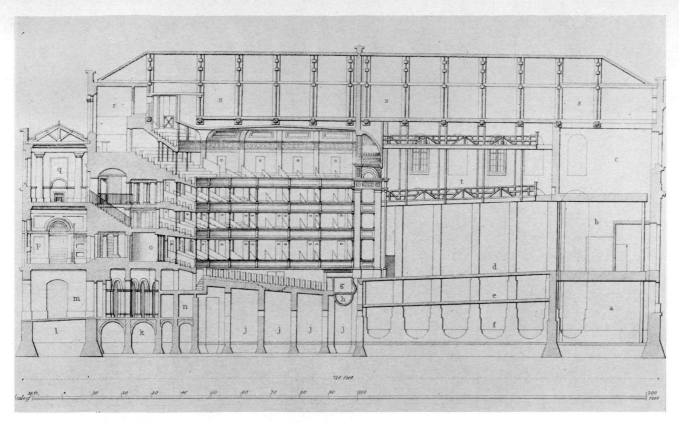

a. Longitudinal section in 1824

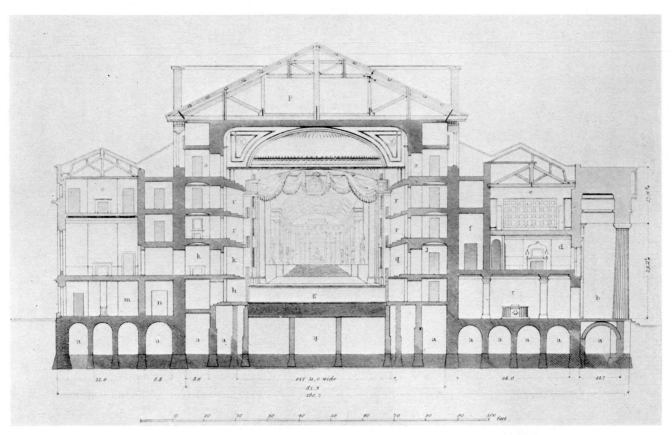

b. Cross section in 1824

THE THEATRE ROYAL, COVENT GARDEN, OF 1808–9. (Sir) Robert Smirke, architect

a

b

THE THEATRE ROYAL, COVENT GARDEN, OF 1808–9: auditorium
in 1810. (Sir) Robert Smirke, architect

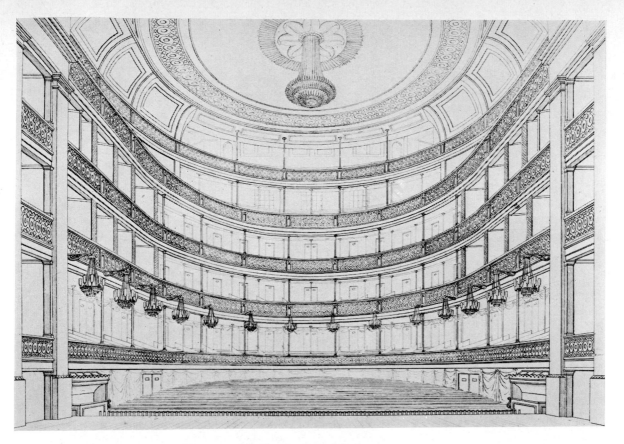

a. Auditorium in 1825

b. Auditorium in 1833

THE THEATRE ROYAL, COVENT GARDEN, OF 1808–9 after the alterations
of 1812 and 1813. (Sir) Robert Smirke, architect

56

a. Principal staircase in 1810

b. Principal staircase in 1824

c. Saloon in 1810

THE THEATRE ROYAL, COVENT GARDEN, OF 1808–9.
(Sir) Robert Smirke, architect

a. Ceiling

b. Auditorium

THE THEATRE ROYAL, COVENT GARDEN, OF 1808–9 as reconstructed by
Benedict Albano in 1846–7 and renamed THE ROYAL ITALIAN OPERA HOUSE

a. Stage looking north

b. Looking south from the stage into the auditorium

THE ROYAL ITALIAN OPERA HOUSE after destruction by fire in 1856

THE ROYAL (ITALIAN) OPERA HOUSE, COVENT GARDEN, OF 1856–8:
Bow Street front in 1965. E. M. Barry, architect

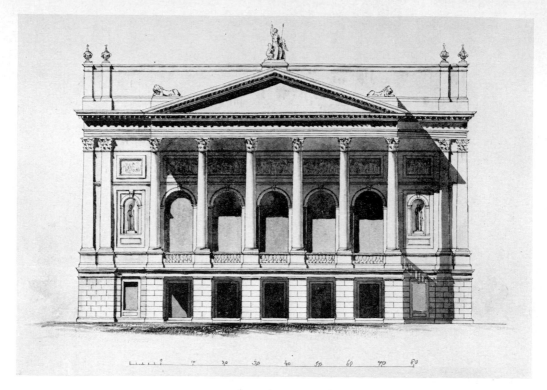

a. Bow Street elevation

b. Hart Street elevation

THE ROYAL (ITALIAN) OPERA HOUSE, COVENT GARDEN, OF 1856–8.
E. M. Barry, architect, executed designs of 1857

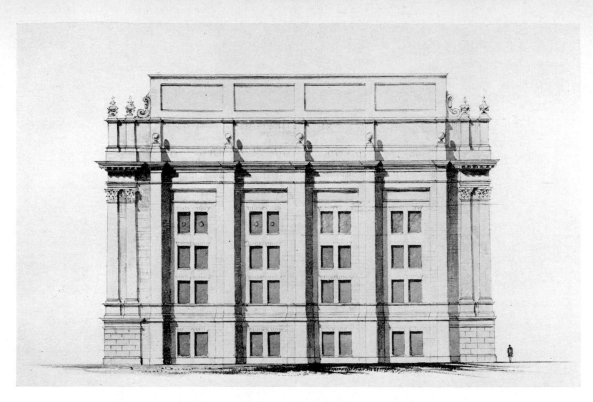

a. West elevation, executed design of 1857

b. Bow Street and Floral (formerly Hart) Street fronts in 1968

THE ROYAL (ITALIAN) OPERA HOUSE, COVENT GARDEN, OF 1856–8.
E. M. Barry, architect

62

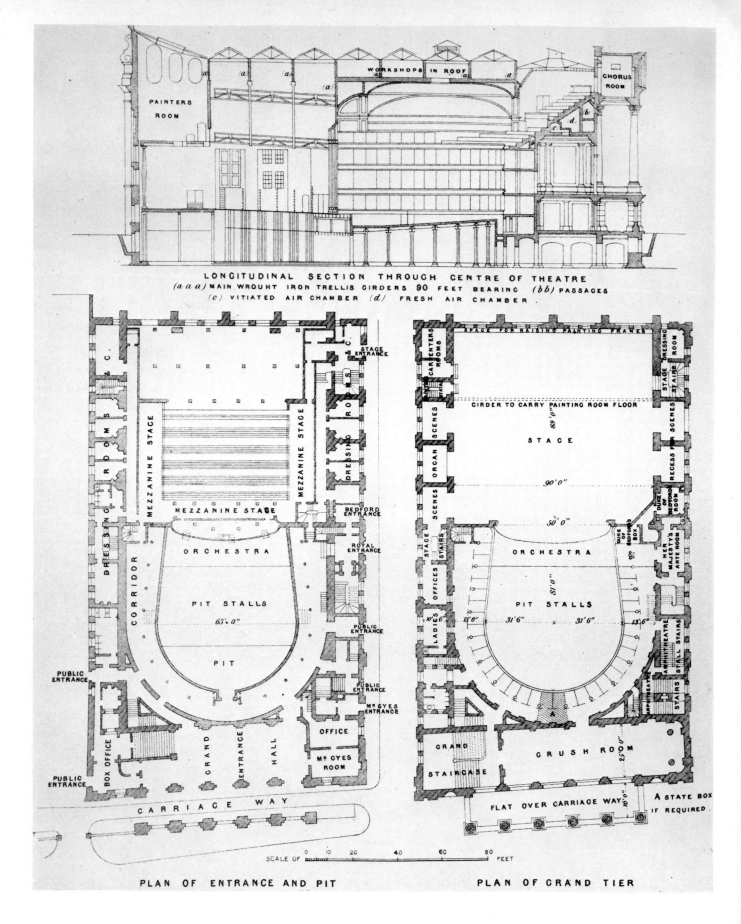

LONGITUDINAL SECTION THROUGH CENTRE OF THEATRE
(a a a) MAIN WROUHT IRON TRELLIS GIRDERS 90 FEET BEARING (bb) PASSAGES
(c) VITIATED AIR CHAMBER (d) FRESH AIR CHAMBER.

PLAN OF ENTRANCE AND PIT   PLAN OF GRAND TIER

THE ROYAL (ITALIAN) OPERA HOUSE, COVENT GARDEN, OF 1856-8.
E. M. Barry, architect: plans and section, 1859-60

63

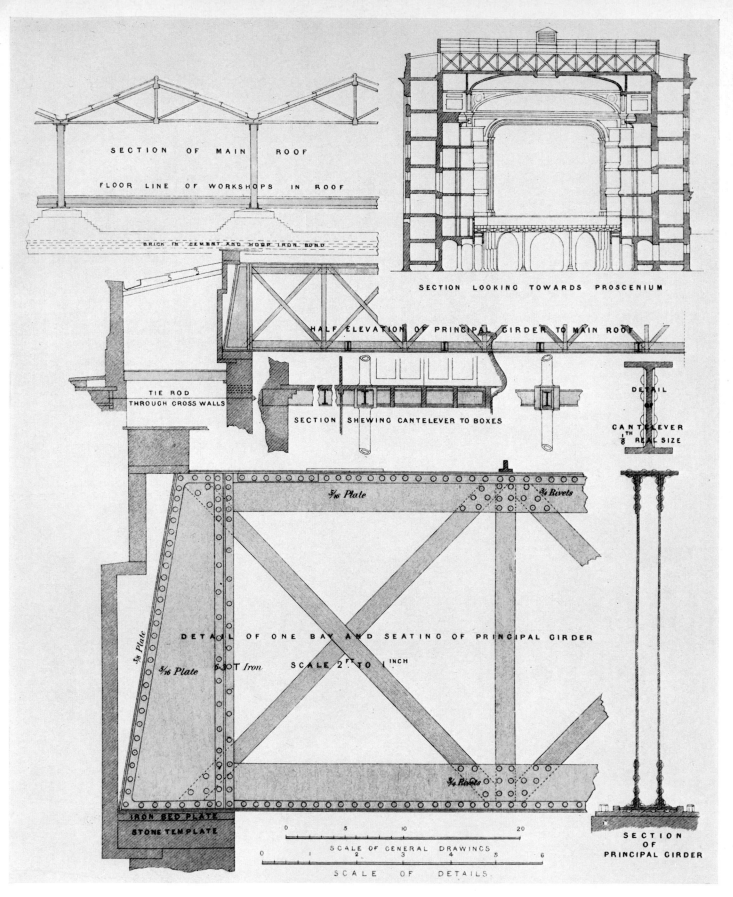

SECTION OF MAIN ROOF

FLOOR LINE OF WORKSHOPS IN ROOF

BRICK IN CEMENT AND HOOP IRON BOND

SECTION LOOKING TOWARDS PROSCENIUM

HALF ELEVATION OF PRINCIPAL GIRDER TO MAIN ROOF

TIE ROD THROUGH CROSS WALLS

SECTION SHEWING CANTELEVER TO BOXES

DETAIL CANTELEVER 1/8 REAL SIZE

5/16 Plate   3/4 Rivets

DETAIL OF ONE BAY AND SEATING OF PRINCIPAL GIRDER
SCALE 2 FT TO 1 INCH

3/8 Plate   5/16 Plate   6 x 3 T Iron   3/4 Rivets

IRON BED PLATE
STONE TEMPLATE

SECTION OF PRINCIPAL GIRDER

SCALE OF GENERAL DRAWINGS
SCALE OF DETAILS.

THE ROYAL (ITALIAN) OPERA HOUSE, COVENT GARDEN, OF 1856–8.
E. M. Barry, architect: section and constructional details, 1859–60

a. Auditorium in 1858

b. Auditorium in 1897–8

THE ROYAL (ITALIAN) OPERA HOUSE, COVENT GARDEN, OF 1856–8.
E. M. Barry, architect

THE ROYAL (ITALIAN) OPERA HOUSE, COVENT GARDEN, OF 1856–8.
E. M. Barry, architect: auditorium in 1965

a

b

a, b. Auditorium in 1948

c. Auditorium in 1965, showing amphitheatre as reconstructed in 1964

THE ROYAL (ITALIAN) OPERA HOUSE, COVENT GARDEN, OF 1856–8.
E. M. Barry, architect

a. Grand staircase

b. Royal ante-room

c. Crush bar

THE ROYAL (ITALIAN) OPERA HOUSE, COVENT GARDEN, OF 1856–8 in 1948.
E. M. Barry, architect.

a. Bow Street front

b. Piazza front and plan

c. The Volunteers' Ball, March 1860

THE FLORAL HALL, 1858–60. E. M. Barry, architect